DATE DUE

GAYLORD			PRINTED IN U S A

MUNICIPAL WATER SYSTEMS

MUNICIPAL WATER SYSTEMS

The Challenge for
Urban Resource Management

Edited by
David Holtz and Scott Sebastian
Holcomb Research Institute

Indiana University Press
Bloomington and London

Manufactured in the United States of America

Library of Congress Cataloging in Publication Data
Main entry under title:

Municipal water systems.

   Includes papers presented at a conference held in
French Lick, Ind. Oct. 10–14, 1976.
   Includes index.
   1. Municipal water supply—Congresses.   I. Holtz,
David.   II. Sebastian, Scott.
TD201.M86   1977   363.6'1   77-74425
ISBN 0-253-33938-3   1 2 3 4 5 82 81 80 79 78

CONTENTS

This book attempts a comprehensive review of the most important problems in the management of municipal water systems. To our knowledge, such a work does not exist at the present time. The field has evolved rapidly in recent years, and many people have confirmed our belief that a state-of-the-art review is needed.

There are a number of ways to go about preparing such a review. In this case, we first chose to hold a national conference on the subject. After careful discussion of the relative importance of various issues, the conference program was designed with a view toward a balanced presentation of opposing viewpoints. Speakers were invited to represent utilities management, regulatory agencies, and academic research.

In order to focus the discussion and to present a framework for debate, a background monograph was prepared by Duane Baumann and Daniel Dworkin of Southern Illinois University, in collaboration with the staff of the Holcomb Research Institute. This monograph presents a brief overview of the field and forms the first section of this two-part book.

The conference was held in French Lick, Indiana, from October 10 to 14, 1976. The papers presented at the conference have been carefully edited and organized into chapters. These form the second and larger section of the book.

We hope that the product of this effort is a broad, interdisciplinary summary of the most important problems in the management of municipal water supply and wastewater treatment. Our intent has been to make the text accessible to as wide a readership as could reasonably be expected to take an interest in the subject. This readership includes not only water managers and students of the subject but also those citizens who are becoming more aware of our many water-related problems.

Inevitably, such a book will be biased. We have, at least, tried to make our biases explicit. We have also tried to present opposing viewpoints on controversial issues. We hope this book will become a useful step in unifying a complex and important field.

David Holtz
Scott Sebastian
Holcomb Research Institute
Butler University
Indianapolis, Indiana

ACKNOWLEDGMENTS

The initial impetus for this project came from Dr. Thomas F. Malone, Director of the Holcomb Research Institute. We are grateful to Dr. Malone for the continuous support which has made this book possible.

Special thanks are due to Barbara Andrews of the Holcomb Institute staff for her assistance in organizing the conference and in the preparation and evaluation of many portions of this book. Thanks are also proffered to James N. Rogers, whose editorial acumen has contributed greatly to a consistency of style and format. Barbara Whitcraft ably handled most of the administrative and secretarial duties connected with the project.

In planning the conference at which the papers of this volume were presented, the staff of the Holcomb Institute was fortunate in having the able services of the following persons, who agreed to serve as a conference planning committee. They provided much valuable time in the development of the conference program and were generous with their advice and direct assistance over a period of many months.

Duane Baumann, Department of Geography,
Southern Illinois University

Lawrence K. Cecil, AIChE,
Consulting Chemical Engineer

Daniel Dworkin, Department of Geography,
Southern Illinois University

J. Ernest Flack, Department of Civil and Environmental Engineering,
University of Colorado

Maurice C. Stout, Senior Vice-President,
Indianapolis Water Company

Victor Wagner, President,
Water Pollution Control Federation

Daniel Wiersma, Director, Water Resources Research Center,
Purdue University

Finally, we would like to express our appreciation to the Technology Transfer Program of the U.S. Environmental Protection Agency which provided partial funding for the conference.

PART ONE
An Overview

THE NEED FOR PLANNING

The need for effective planning of the nation's urban water systems is greater today than at any time in history. In the past, water was not considered to be an economic good, subject to the laws of supply and demand, but rather a physical substance required by a particular community. Issues of waste disposal and water quality were rarely of much interest to those concerned with water supply. Typically, in response to either a burgeoning demand or a prolonged drought, communities sought to increase their available supply, often through the construction of a new reservoir. Other alternatives seldom were considered; the emphasis was clearly on a narrow range of choice through the reliance on what some refer to as the "technological fix."

The contemporary scene is dramatically different. Higher living standards and urbanization have resulted in ever-increasing demands for water for relatively small areas. New reservoir sites are scarce, and in many areas of the country, groundwater is generally available only as a supplemental source. Resistance to interbasin transfer has become more intense. Energy costs for pumping have been translated into increased water costs. Higher interest rates are now a serious consideration in planning multimillion-dollar water resource projects.

At the same time we perceive the natural limits to traditional sources of supply, we realize that water has a limited capacity to absorb our wastes. The critical role of water in waste disposal has in the past not been widely appreciated. Nonetheless, growing concern with environmental degradation and public health have led to national legislation setting stringent standards for the quality of water returned to the environment. Thus, planning is no longer simply a matter of good management, but in many cases is now mandated under federal statute.

The response to these considerations has been a growing recognition among water resource planners of the need to evaluate the full range of choices available for the intelligent management of water systems. The effectiveness of many alternatives is still relatively untested, and other potential solutions require further research. Moreover, appropriate methodologies must be developed in order to identify the economic, social, and environmental benefits and costs of various combinations of potential adjustments.

The following sections survey the range of alternatives that have been proposed for the planning of urban water systems, and make some pre-

3

liminary assessments of the practicability of these adjustments. An attempt has been made to identify the areas of needed research, and to stress that the problems will require complex solutions, generally involving a balance among several components. Such solutions demand, by their very nature, a considerably more sophisticated level of planning than has generally been evident in the past.

CALCULATING SUPPLY AND DEMAND

To assure the orderly development of the capacity of municipal water systems, water planners and engineers have relied on forecasting of both future water demands and the yields from any sources that might be tapped to satisfy those demands. Some forecasts are short-term and involve the development and utilization of local water sources. However, long-term forecasts become necessary as additional sources of local supply become scarce and as alternative sources become more costly. Thus, long-term forecasting of both demand and supply has become an integral element in municipal water system planning.

PROJECTING URBAN DEMAND FOR WATER

Forecasting water demand is a complex procedure which in recent years has involved a growing number of legal, economic, environmental, and engineering considerations. For some systems, forecasting is required for water demands 25 to 50 years into the future. Table 1, on pages 6 and 7, illustrates a number of U.S. cities which made projections of this type during the 1950s and 1960s. The outcome of an earlier long-term projection made by the city of Detroit is shown in figure 1 on page 8.

Demand forecasts can be prepared by projecting water use from the past or by estimating the changes in the components which make up demand. The most common elements in component projections are population and per capita use. Other forecasts, however, estimate changes in economic activity, expansions of the system to serve additional areas, reduction of leakage, fluctuations in price, additional industrial use, or changes in technology or lifestyle to predict future demands for water. For example, one set of projections prepared in 1937 for the Indianapolis Water Company considered the effect of the Depression on population growth and per capita water use. The projections indicated that while population growth was not affected by the Depression, per capita use had decreased and would grow again only with the return of "good business conditions" (Alvord, Burdick, and Howson 1937).

In addition to consideration of individual variables which affect demand, the use of water by residential, industrial, and commercial sectors

5

Table 1

PROJECTIONS OF FUTURE WATER NEEDS — NINE U.S. CITIES†

| City | Date and Time Horizon of Projection | Per Capita Use In Gallons Daily | | Method of Projecting Need* |
		Current	Projected	
New York	1966–2010	154	182	Extrapolate use trends for projected population for each borough.
Chicago	1955–80	234	245	Extrapolate use trends for projected domestic and industrial users separately for each community.
Philadelphia	1946–2000	180	180	For population increase of 20%, estimated that increases in air conditioning and suburban use would be offset by increases in industrial and distributional efficiency.
Philadelphia (including Trenton)	1965–2010	115 maximum	169	Extrapolates increased per capita use for projected population and economic activity.
Detroit (6 counties)	1957–2000	242	350	Extrapolates increased per capita use for projected population for separate communities.
	1959–2000	147	164	Extrapolates to 1980 for separate communities on basis of load, and extrapolates for aggregate thereafter.
	1966–2000	157	159	Using population projections from several sources, estimates slight increases in use.

(continued)

(table 1, continued)

| City | Date and Time Horizon of Projection | Per Capita Use In Gallons Daily | | Method of Projecting Need* |
		Current	Projected	
Baltimore	1962–2010	146 (1960)	203	Separate estimates for domestic, public, commercial, and industrial users.
Houston	circa 1960–2010	aggregate only		
Washington	1946–2000	155 (1940)	161	Applies modest increase in per capita use to estimated increase in population.
Washington (metropolitan area)	1962–2010	160	210	Separate estimates for increased standard of living and for increased industrial activity.
St. Louis	1966–80	259	300	Extrapolate per capita use trends.
Minneapolis– St. Paul	1960–80	aggregate only		Extrapolate per capita use trends for projected population.

*The description of projection methods does not give the details of calculations. Attention is directed at any factors other than linear projection of past trends in population and per capita use.

Sources
1. *Report of the Board of Water Supply of the City of New York on the Third City Tunnel, 1st Stage,* 1966.
2. Alvord, Burdick, and Howson, *Report upon Adequate Water Supply for Chicago Metropolitan Area, 1955–1980.*
3. Bureau of Municipal Research of Philadelphia, *Philadelphia's Water Supply,* 1946.
4. U.S., 87th Congress, 2d Session, *Delaware River Basin,* House Document no. 522, 1960.
5. National Sanitation Foundation, *A Report on the Water Supply for the Six County Metropolitan Area, Southeastern Michigan,* 1957.
6. *Detroit's Water Development Program for the Metropolitan Area.* Report to the City of Detroit Board of Water Commissioners, 1959.
7. *Detroit's Water Development Program for Southeastern Michigan,* 1966.
8. A. F. Broyles, "Planning the Future of a Distribution System," *Journal of American Water Works Association,* 1966, pp. 526–34.
9. Brown and Root, Inc., *The Long Range Plan of Water Supply for the City of Houston, Texas,* n.d.
10. U.S., 79th Congress, 2d Session, *Adequate Future Water Supply for District of Columbia and Metropolitan Area,* House Document no. 480, 1946.
11. U.S., Army Engineer District, *Potomac River Basin,* 1962, V, Appendix E.
12. Personal communications from W. T. Malloy, Director of Public Utilities, and D. C. Guilfoy, Deputy Water Commissioner, St. Louis.
13. Twin Cities Metropolitan Planning Commission, *Metropolitan Plan Report no. 6, Metropolitan Water Study, part III,* 1960.

†Source: White, Gilbert F. 1970, pp. 124–25.

Figure 1

ACTUAL WATER USE & 1924 PROJECTION
FOR DETROIT METROPOLITAN AREA, 1900 – 1960

(WHITE, 1970)

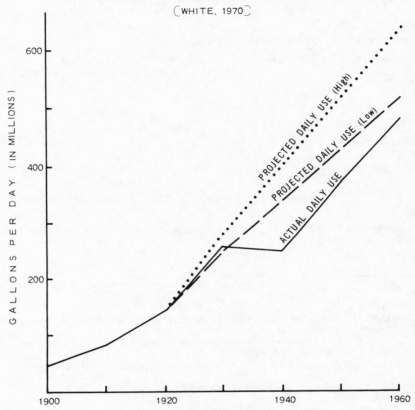

can be projected separately. These projections, which are similar to the projections of aggregate usage, can be based on extrapolations of past trends or on the estimation of future changes in individual variables. Such separate projections are useful for increasing the accuracy of forecasting. Therefore, before reviewing various available methods of projection, the following sections briefly describe the major components or sectors of water demand.

The Components of Demand

Water-using customers are most commonly categorized according to the following sectors of demand: residential, commercial, and industrial. Depending on the composition of a municipality and its geographic location, each sector may represent a varying proportion of total use. Forecasting for each sector must rely on variables which have provided an understanding of water use in the past.

The residential sector. Residential water demand was studied extensively in a program at Johns Hopkins University from 1961–66. The study areas were homogeneous sections of cities in which average and peak water demands were recorded over a two-year period. The average demand for a residential unit was forecast as a function of water price, house value, number of persons per dwelling unit, and evapotranspiration (Linaweaver, Geyer, and Wolff 1966a; Howe and Linaweaver 1967; Howe 1968; Hittman Associates 1969). The American Water Works Association Committee on Water Use has commended the Johns Hopkins study but has reserved judgment on its application until further studies demonstrate the relationship between theoretical and actual use (AWWA Committee on Water Use 1973). In a study of Boulder, Colorado, for example, the elasticity of water demand for sprinkling was found to be 0.35, as compared to 0.70 in the Howe-Linaweaver study (Burns et al. 1975).

A number of other studies have attempted to measure residential water demand according to a variety of parameters. In one such examination in Colorado Springs, Colorado, the variables which accounted for more than 75 percent of residential demand for twelve years of record were season, price, population, departure from mean rainfall, and time. For those interested in a state-of-the-art survey of residential water use, a recent report, *Household Water Use* (McPherson 1976), details the quantity as well as other aspects of this particular sector of demand.

The commercial sector. On a national basis, the commercial sector accounts for approximately 12 percent of total water use, although such an estimate excludes some institutional users such as schools (McPherson 1976). In projecting the total commercial demand for water, analysis should be made of existing water use and projections made of demands of new or enlarged commercial establishments. Price is another factor which must be considered carefully. For example, in Colorado Springs, Colorado, water use declined with increased price in the commercial sector more than in any of the other sectors of demand.

The Johns Hopkins study (Wolff, Linaweaver, and Geyer 1966) is the most extensive investigation of the use of water by the commercial sector. Recording of total water use was made by three-month periods, by day, and by hour, for a number of commercial and institutional users. These records of use were compared with design capacities for annual maximum day and peak hours. In all cases the expected use on the basis of recorded data was less than design capacity; in some cases there was as much as a twofold difference between these two factors (see table 3 on pages 11 and 12).

The industrial sector.   Use of water by industry represents over 25 percent of use of all public water supplies. Some municipal systems have no industrial users, while in others industrial users predominate. In a discussion of industrial supply, Sherwani (1964) states:

> It is extremely difficult to forecast future demand of industrial water. Very few reliable data are available on the costs, pattern of water use and water technology of self-supplied industries. Industries vary greatly in their requirements of water. . . . Technological process changes permitting a reduction in the quantity or quality of water used, changes in production functions eliminating water use altogether, and the changes in industrial water use technology to increase reuse and recycling will have major impacts on net water requirements. It is, therefore, not possible to say that a product requires a specific quantity of water (p. 194).

Sherwani indicates that technological change will be influenced by the increasing costs of water which will decrease the use of water per unit of industrial output. White (1970), on the other hand, finds that industrial managers give only minimal consideration to the costs of water, and are more responsive to the costs of waste treatment.

Whether from increased costs of supply or increased costs of waste treatment mandated by pollution control regulations, the costs of both water intake and discharge will rise. As predicted by Sherwani, these rising costs should then result in the employment of technology to decrease the use of water per unit of production. Such results have also been forecast by Wollman and Bonen (1971), who see increasing rates of recycling for all industrial categories. Their estimates of the increase of recycled water by various industries to the year 2020 are shown in table 2.

Table 2
PERCENT WATER RECYCLED BY INDUSTRY

Industry	1960	2020 (projected)
Food products	52	65
Paper products	68	77
Chemicals	38	68
Petroleum	77	88
Primary metals	35	67

Source: Adapted from Wollman and Bonen 1971.

Table 3

WATER USE BY VARIOUS SECTORS OF DEMAND*

Type of Establishment or Institution	Selected Parameter	Annual Water Use (gpd/unit)		Maximum Day Water Use (gpd/unit)		Peak Hour Water Use (gpd/unit)		Hours of Peak Occurrence
		Expected	Design	Expected	Design	Expected	Design	
Primary and Secondary Schools								
Public Elementary	gpd/student	5.38	8.67	9.68	13.0	49.1	52.4	1 p.m. — 2 p.m.
Public Junior High	gpd/student	5.64	9.75					
Public Senior High	gpd/student	6.63	12.2	19.6	25.2	121	127	4 p.m. — 5 p.m.
Private Elementary	gpd/student	2.27	6.09	3.10	6.92	25.7	29.5	10 a.m. — 11 a.m.
Private Senior High	gpd/student	10.4	18.6	15.7	23.9	38.7	46.9	4 p.m. — 5 p.m.
Combined (grades 1–12)	gpd/student	8.49	18.7	16.8	27.0	51.3	61.5	5 p.m. — 6 p.m.
Colleges								
Students in residence	gpd/student	106	179	114	187	250	323	1 p.m. — 2 p.m.
Non-resident students	gpd/student	15.2		27.0		57.8		8 a.m. — 9 a.m.
Hospitals	gpd/bed	346	559	551	764	912	1120	11 a.m. — 12 noon
Nursing Homes and Institutions	gpd/bed	133	209	146	222	424	500	4 p.m. — 5 p.m.
Apartments								
High Rise	gpd/occupied unit	218	322	426	530	745	849	11 a.m. — 12 noon
Garden Type	gpd/occupied unit	213	315	272	374	671	773	8 a.m. & 6 p.m.
Hotels	gpd/sq. ft.	0.256	0.326	0.294		0.433		6 p.m. — 7 p.m.
Motels	gpd/sq. ft.	0.224		0.461	0.563	1.55	1.65	10 a.m. — 11 a.m.
Office Buildings General offices less than 10 yrs. old	gpd/sq. ft.	0.093	0.164	0.173	0.244	0.521	0.592	12 noon — 1 p.m.

11

(table 3, continued)

General offices more than 10 yrs. old	gpd/sq. ft	0.142	0.273					
Medical offices	gpd/sq. ft.	0.618		1.66		4.97		11 a.m. & 4 p.m.
Department Stores	gpd/sq. ft. of total sales area	0.216	0.483		0.655	0.958	1.23	12 noon — 1 p.m.
Shopping Centers	gpd/sq. ft. of total sales area	0.160		0.232		0.412		2 p.m. — 3 p.m.
Car Washes	gpd/sq. ft.	4.78		10.3		31.5		12 p.m. — 2 p.m.
Service Stations	gpd/sq. ft. of garage and office space	0.251	0.485	0.590	0.824	4.89	5.12	12 a.m. — 1 p.m.
Laundries								
Commercial Laundries & Dry Cleaners	gpd/sq. ft.	0.253	0.639	0.326	0.712	1.57	1.96	2 p.m. — 3 p.m.
Laundromats	gpd/sq. ft.	2.17	6.39					
Restaurants								
Drive-ins (parking only)	gpd/car space	109						
Drive-ins (seating and parking)	gpd/seat	40.6						
Conventional Restaurants	gpd/seat	24.2	55.2	83.4	114	167	198	2 p.m. — 3 p.m.
Clubs								
Golf Clubs	gpd/membership	66.1						
Swimming Clubs	gpd/membership	16.5						
Boating Clubs	gpd/membership	10.5						
Churches	gpd/member	0.138		0.862		4.70		8 p.m. — 9 p.m.
Barber Shops	gpd/chair	54.6	97.5	80.3	123	389	432	2 p.m. — 3 p.m.
Beauty Salons	gpd/station	269	532	328	591	1,070	1,330	2 p.m. — 3 p.m.

*Source: Linaweaver, Geyer, Wolff 1966, table 4-1.

Methods of Projection

In selecting a method for forecasting future water demand, the forecaster may choose from a wide variety of techniques ranging from the simple to the complex. However, sophistication should not be confused with reliability of results. While fifty-year forecasts based on elaborate techniques may appear precise, the history of most long-term forecasts indicates a low probability of accuracy. For example, in the previously cited study of Detroit the actual water use after 16 years was lower than the low projection by as much as 40 percent, and was 75 percent less than the high projection.

The lack of precision notwithstanding, projections are required for long-term planning. The planner should be aware of the limitations in any long-term projection, no matter how sophisticated the technique. Such awareness might result in selecting, to the extent possible, smaller increments of capacity with an ongoing review of projections of future change. Russell, Arey, and Kates (1970) examined the possible losses which would result if such projections failed to accurately reflect growth rates, and concluded that *"Only in relatively unusual circumstances would even a serious underestimate of demand growth imply very large losses, if planners take the reasonable precautions of checking their assumptions"* (p. 162, emphasis in original).

Where there is a relationship between the cost of preparing a projection and its accuracy, the planner should select that methodology for which the cost of providing an accurate projection is equal to the cost imposed by the limitations in accuracy (see figure 2). The relationship between cost and accuracy does not always exist nor does the available input data often provide the basis for elaborate projections. In such cases, simple statistical models or graphic representations are most appropriate.

From the approximately 150 different forecasting techniques available for estimating future water demands, three major categories can be identified (Mitchell et al. 1975). These include time series and projections, models and simulations, and holistic methods. Each of these is considered separately and in some detail in the following sections.

Time series and projections. The class of time series and projections includes those techniques based on the assumptions that forecasts can be extrapolated, patterns of change recognized, or probabilities of events predicted from historical record. Extrapolation, the most common method of forecasting, is applicable to aggregate information such as pumpage rates and data on demand sectors or on an individual component of demand such as population. Extrapolation may be graphic or mathematical; graphic techniques involving plotting the historical data on arithmetic, probability, or logarithmic paper, and extending the plot into

Figure 2

COST OF FORECASTING VERSUS COST OF INACCURACY

(CHAMBER, MULLICK & SMITH, 1971)

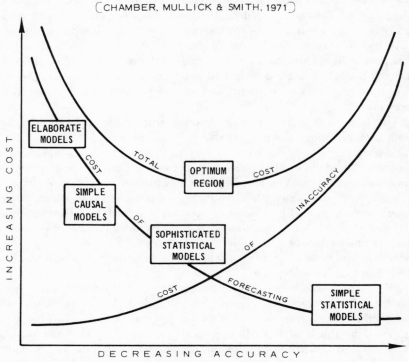

the future. Often all three types of plots are used in an effort to obtain a straight line or a simple curve.

Mathematical techniques can also be used to extrapolate trends. The objective of mathematical analysis is to extract from the data the mathematical equation which will best conform to the historical data. The method most commonly used is simple regression analysis in which historical data are used as the dependent variables and time as the independent variable. More sophisticated mathematical techniques include computer programs which will fit the historical data to a number of different curve types and select the best fit. One interesting curve-fitting method which has gained wide usage is the logarithmic curve first proposed by Verhulst in 1838 and later independently rediscovered by Pearl, based on his observation of the growth of fruit flies in a jar. In using this method, the forecaster is assuming that municipalities go through a period of slow growth in the initial and late stages, which are separated by a period of rapid expansion, and that growth is determined by some unknown "natural" factor.

If the data base for an area is inadequate for extrapolation, projections for a larger area can be used to provide a basis for estimating future population growth in the study area. Known as the "ratio method," this technique relies on the logical assumption—true for most U.S. communities—that areas which have similar underlying conditions affecting growth, and which in the past have exhibited comparable trends in population and employment, are likely to continue to share such trends in the future. Ratios can reflect either a fixed or changing relationship over time.

Figure 3 demonstrates one application of the ratio method. Here, the growth of Indianapolis, the State of Indiana, and the United States, is compared, and the convergence of the growth rate of all three is indicated. The population of Indianapolis is finally projected at a rate which decreases slightly in comparison with that of the United States. In general, however, despite its logical basis, the ratio method should be used with caution since it incorporates all errors inherent in the original forecast, and transfers these errors to the forecast of the study area.

Figure 3

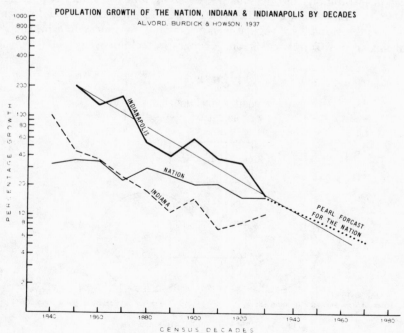

POPULATION GROWTH OF THE NATION, INDIANA & INDIANAPOLIS BY DECADES

ALVORD, BURDICK & HOWSON, 1937

In addition to the problem of inadequate data, the impact of random or external factors on the variable being forecast also complicates the extrapolation process. For example, residential water use during the summer months is dependent on rainfall conditions. Simply stated, when rainfall is low, water is used extensively to irrigate lawns and gardens. However, the relationship is often complex; for example, while there is a negative correlation between rainfall and water use, a more significant factor involves accumulated departure from mean rainfall for the summer season. In another case, industrial use of water is dependent upon fluctuating or unpredictable economic conditions. Unless relationships such as these are identified and considered, forecasts based on elevated usage during drought periods and periods of unusual economic activity will be in error. Sophisticated computer programs can identify these patterns where they are not readily apparent (Mitchell et al. 1975).

Models and simulations.   Models and simulations are useful in forecasting situations in which the state of a system is dependent on the changes and interrelationships between the components of that system. For example, one simple model commonly used in water demand projections is a population-forecasting model in which the three components are births, deaths, and in-and-out migration (shown in figure 4 below). A model developed by Howe (1968) uses lot size, income, sewers, price, evapotranspiration, and persons per dwelling unit to predict residential water use. In another example, Whitford (1972) suggests a model which involves the variables of regulations, pricing policy, education campaigns, housing trends, supply costs, and changes in technology.

Figure 4

POPULATION MODEL
(MITCHELL. ET AL .1975)

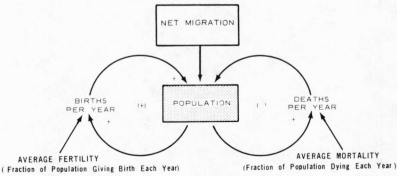

FEEDBACK LOOPS FOR POPULATION GROWTH

In using a model such as Whitford's, the forecaster assigns probabilities to each variable. For example, highest demand would result from a lack of water usage regulations; an unchanging situation in declining block rate pricing; the absence of an education campaign designed to restrain use; the character of the suburban housing pattern; the low cost of water; and a lack of technological changes aimed at reducing water consumption. Whitford explains that this type of model has the advantage of producing "a probability distribution of future water use rather than a single number. This distribution would emphasize the uncertainties of forecasting, facilitate staged development, and permit water systems to be designed for a calculated probability of failure..." (p. 83).

Holistic methods.   Holistic methods of demand projection aim at examining the total system under varying assumptions through the use of scenarios, which are more qualitative than simulations. Scenarios rely on other forms of projection as inputs, and are then formulated on the basis of either a single or alternative assumptions of the future. In discussing the value of scenarios, Mitchell et al. (1975) state:

> In general [holistic methods] are the least developed of the forecasting techniques.... Without doubt, however, they represent the area where the most professional attention is currently being paid. In the opinion of many... holistic forecasting techniques are the leading edge of the art and emerging science of looking ahead.

To date, this potentially important approach has received little significant practical application.

Projecting Future U.S. Demand

Whatever the forecasting techniques used or the uncertainties involved in demand projections, one prediction is sure: the future demand for water in the United States will increase. What is debatable, however, is the actual rate of this increase. As the U.S. National Water Commission (1973) aptly recognized, the basing of planning decisions on a single projection presents problems:

> How much water will be used, where and for what purposes will depend on the policies that are adopted. A range of "alternative futures" is possible, depending upon population levels and distribution, per capita energy consumption, rate of national income growth, technological development, water pricing policies, consumer habits and lifestyles, various governmental policies, and other variables (p. 3).

To assess the consequences of different combinations of the factors affecting demand, the National Water Commission analyzed a range of possible outcomes or alternative futures based on the interaction of variable levels of population, constraints regarding waste-heat disposal, amounts of dissolved oxygen required in fresh waters, and types of sewage treatment. Depending upon the combination of factors, the projected demand for withdrawal use in the year 2020 may be as low as 570 bgd or as high as 2,280 bgd—nearly twice the average annual streamflow. Consumptive use of water is expected to increase from 87 bgd in 1970 to between 150 and 250 bgd by 2020 (U.S. National Water Commission 1973).

In shifting focus from a national perspective, it is evident that several regions of the country are already faced with an imminent threat of shortage, especially in the Rio Grande, Lower Colorado, and Great Basin regions where withdrawals exceed mean annual streamflow (see table 4 on page 19). The Lower Colorado, for example, has a consumptive use of 5 bgd which is twice the mean annual streamflow, with the deficiency made up by groundwater and surface water transfers.

As the process of urbanization continues, large demands for water within relatively small areas will add to the pressure for greater efficiency in water use. Furthermore, such concentrated demands for water will create intense competition for the available supply, such as might occur between the municipal and agricultural sectors. Based upon one set of projections (U.S. Federal Water Resources Council 1968), the relative importance of consumptive municipal use is expected to increase while that of withdrawal uses remains approximately the same. In 1965, United States urban areas consumed 5.2 bgd, representing 7 percent of the total consumptive use; by 2020, this figure is expected to rise to 24.6 bgd, accounting for 16 percent of all consumptive use. Whereas withdrawal use for cities is projected to rise from 27 bgd in 1970 to 74.3 bgd in 2020, the proportion it represents of all withdrawal uses is seen as remaining approximately the same (7 percent) or even possibly declining (5 percent). This is primarily because of expected increased efficiency in water use and a threefold increase in demand for water for cooling in electric power generation.

PROJECTING WATER SUPPLY

Calculations of the potential water supply from sources ranging from small streams to entire river basins can be made. Indeed, with the advent of large-scale computer simulations, these calculations have reached a high degree of sophistication. However, any such calculations are at the mercy

Table 4

STREAMFLOW COMPARED WITH
CURRENT WITHDRAWALS AND CONSUMPTION
(billion gallons per day)

Region	Annual Flow Available[2]					
	Mean Annual Run-Off[2]	50% of the Years	90% of the Years	95% of the Years	Fresh Water Consumptive Use 1970	Withdrawals 1970[1]
North Atlantic	163	163	123	112	1.8	55
South Atlantic-Gulf	197	188	131	116	3.3	35
Great Lakes	63.2	61.4	46.3	42.4	1.2	39
Ohio	125	125	80	67.5	.9	36
Tennessee	41.5	41.5	28.2	24.4	.24	7.9
Upper Mississippi	64.6	64.6	36.4	28.5	.8	16
Lower Mississippi	48.4	48.4	29.7	24.6	3.6	13
Souris-Red Rainy	6.17	5.95	2.6	1.91	.07	.3
Missouri	54.1	53.7	29.9	23.9	12.0	24
Arkansas-White-Red	95.8	93.4	44.3	33.4	6.8	12
Texas-Gulf	39.1	37.5	15.8	11.4	6.2	21
Rio Grande	4.9	4.9	2.6	2.1	3.3	6.3
Upper Colorado	13.45	13.45	8.82	7.50	4.1	8.1
Lower Colorado	3.19	2.51	1.07	0.85	5.0	7.2
Great Basin	5.89	5.82	3.12	2.46	3.2	6.7
Columbia-North Pacific	210	210	154	138	11.0	30
California	65.1	64.1	33.8	25.6	22.0	48
Conterminous United States	1,201				87	365
Total United States	1,794				88	371

[1]Murray, C. Richard, and Reeves, E. Bodette 1972. *Estimated Use of Water in the United States in 1970.* Washington, D.C.: Geological Survey Circular 676. U.S. Geological Survey, p. 17.

[2]U.S. Water Resources Council 1968. *The Nation's Water Resources.* Washington, D.C.: U.S. Government Printing Office, p. 3-2-6.

Source: Modified from National Water Commission 1973.

of our still incomplete understanding of meteorology. As Hirschleifer, DeHaven, and Milliman noted in their study of New York, "Here we have a case where predictions about the social phenomena of use, while off the mark, still proved far more reliable than predictions as to the natural phenomena of supply" (1960, p. 372). Thus, as in the case of demand projections, highly sophisticated predictive models of supply are not necessarily superior to relatively straightforward graphic or mathematical techniques.

In discussions of supply, water resources are generally divided into surface water and groundwater. The distinction is made because the technologies for and the constraints upon the exploitation of each are markedly different. Thus, surface water and groundwater are treated separately herein. However, it must be recognized that the two sources are intimately connected and in balance with each other.

Surface Water Yields

Water diverted from rivers and streams and stored in reservoirs accounts for about 75 percent of the U.S. muncipal water supply. A wide range of techniques is available to determine the amount of storage required to supply a given yield at a given level of assurance, or alternatively, to assess the amount of yield available from a given amount of storage.

Simple methods of yield analysis are available which do not consider the sequential variations in streamflows or demand. The most common of these techniques is the mass curve or Rippl method of yield estimation (Hydrological Engineering Center 1975). With this type of graphic analysis, it is possible to construct a mass curve which will indicate the amount of storage required for any given sequence of inflows and out-flows. Nonsequential techniques provide an analysis of low-flow events and their probable occurrence during the length of record examined. From these data, a family of curves is constructed which represents the probability that a low-flow will not be exceeded for any given period. It is then possible to calculate the amount of storage required to ensure supply for any given level of desired system certainty.

Nonsequential analysis using a computer program to calculate desired releases and inflows over an extended period is a more complicated and accurate mode of analysis. Such a program might be a simulation of the physical system, including the generation of demand, or it could repre-sent a mathematical programming analysis in which the computer model would analyze the system without attempting to reproduce the inflow sequence over the planning period (Hydrological Engineering Center 1975).

An important consideration in making supply projections for a given system is that the projections of yield from the different surface water sources within the system may differ significantly. Because the low-flows of the various sources will generally not coincide, they will tend to cancel each other. For example, in a study of Boulder, Colorado, it was shown that by disaggregating the supply sources and then projecting their yield independently, the actual certainty of supply was far higher than shown by previous calculations (Dworkin 1975).

Groundwater Yields

In the United States, groundwater provides approximately 25 percent of the municipal water supply. Like surface water, groundwater is unevenly distributed. Unlike surface water, groundwater is usually of relatively high quality. In a few areas, however, quality may be poor due to the presence of dissolved salts, as in the groundwater underlying certain arid regions of the southwestern U.S. where water "age" has been estimated in terms of tens of thousands of years.

Groundwater is essentially in long-term storage and thus requires different concepts of yield than surface water. The long-term sustained yield of groundwater is equal to the long-term rate of infiltration. However, the development of groundwater resources for water supply has generally ignored the question of aquifer recharge, and withdrawal rates have as a rule been considerably in excess of rates of replenishment. This process is considered as water mining. Thus, short-term supply projections may be far in excess of the long-term projections—a fact which has obvious and serious consequences for those responsible for water planning.

In some places these consequences have been recognized, as in the Texas High Plains, which overlie an extensive fresh water supply in the Ogallala formation. Here, projections of the exhaustion of the aquifer have led water managers to view their chief task not as the provision of new supply sources, but rather as an attempt to optimize the use of the dwindling groundwater reserves.

> The "ultimate fate" of the Ogallala aquifer can be delayed for several decades if those irrigators still blessed with large capacity wells heed the teachings of history, and abstain from all forms of waste of their present supplies (Rayner 1974, p. 24).

In areas where surface water is available, artificial recharge of aquifers is sometimes practicable. Artificial recharge is, however, only a sophisticated method of storage which may improve sustained yields but generally will not significantly alter the total projected supply.

Groundwater is important not only in the arid regions of the country; many smaller communities in areas of high rainfall rely heavily upon groundwater for their supply. Furthermore, well fields near a river may provide higher-quality water from seepage than direct withdrawals from the river itself.

It has proven difficult to develop general methods to predict future groundwater supplies. Even if recharge rates are known, projections of the potential supply available from an aquifer are contingent on gathering a large amount of data about the geology of the aquifer and its boundary conditions. Accurate forecasts of supply from groundwater are thus more time-consuming and generally more expensive than those for surface water. Nonetheless, highly sophisticated models have been developed for both long- and short-term supply projections from groundwater. These projections can provide predictions not only of practicable withdrawal rates but also of potential total withdrawals and the effects of alternative well configurations or pumping rates. The impact of sustained pumping on water quality and on land subsidence may also be projected.

Use of Supply Projections

Projections of water supply, no matter how detailed and sophisticated, become meaningful only when evaluated in relation to projections of demand. It is important to remember that both supply and demand projections are, within certain boundaries, "elastic." Furthermore, for the purposes of planning, it is not the projections of supply from existing tapped sources that are of greatest interest, but rather the projections regarding the yields of various potential new sources of supply. At a time when such new sources are growing increasingly scarce, it is important to analyze the costs of a marginal water supply increase in terms of the effect these costs will have on demand. In addition, it is useful to explore the effects on supply projections of such system modifications as reduction of leakage or evaporation from reservoirs.

Supply projections have traditionally been concerned principally with water quantity. However, aspects of water quality should not be neglected. The water quality requirements for household, agricultural, and industrial uses differ markedly. These differences may in turn influence the consideration of sources when calculating potential supply. Along the same line, the potential of water reuse is now being extensively studied, and reuse can have a dramatic influence on supply projections. From these considerations it becomes evident that planning for water resources is no longer simply a matter of creating supplies to keep up with demand, but rather a careful balancing of the projections of supply and demand.

BALANCING SUPPLY AND DEMAND

In the past, water management has concentrated on adjustments to the supply side of the supply-demand equation, with major emphasis on the construction of new waterworks to increase total system capacity. Extensions of the water supply capacity have frequently been related to times of system stress, such as drought, or to expectations of a continued, unbridled increase in demand.

While extensions of system capacity continue to be of great importance, the growing economic, political, and environmental problems associated with this approach have led to a search for alternative methods to balance supply and demand. Generally speaking, in addition to augmenting supply, three other approaches emerge: (1) increasing system efficiency; (2) reducing or controlling system demand; and (3) wastewater reuse. These alternatives are not mutually exclusive; in fact, combinations of alternatives are beginning to take precedence over reliance on single-method approaches in municipal water management.

Recently another factor has gained wide attention in water system planning: the treatment of municipal wastewater. If new water quality standards for effluent discharges are to be met, the treatment costs for many municipalities are bound to rise. These costs may well become a decisive factor in economic calculations of planning alternatives aimed at balancing supply and demand in municipal water systems.

The practicability of the various alternatives is evaluated in the following sections, according to the criteria of economic efficiency, environmental consequences, legal constraints, and effects on public health. A discussion of the acceptability of the various alternatives to both water management professionals and the public at large is also of considerable importance and is presented in a later section.

INCREASING WATER SUPPLY

Increasing overall system capacity has been an avowed goal of many municipalities, especially those with growing populations. The technologies involved are well tested, and relatively accurate predictions can be made about expected results. However, this approach is, in fact, no longer the obvious solution for many communities. Furthermore, increasingly complex planning considerations, including those involving

23

environmental impact and economic efficiency, must be considered in most system expansion efforts.

Surface Water Diversion

The major source for municipal water supply in the United States is water from the diversion of rivers and streams. While diversions accounts for 75 percent of total supply, recent projections indicate that surface water flows may represent a slightly higher proportion of the total water used to satisfy future demands. Expanding urban areas have already captured the water available from the best local sources; those sites remaining are generally less favorable and their development more costly. As a result, many larger cities, especially those in areas susceptible to water shortage, have turned to interbasin transfers to increase their supply (Wollman and Bonen 1971).

Economic aspects. The cost of water from diversion of surface flows will almost certainly continue to increase. The reasons for this go beyond the often-cited rises in labor and construction costs. They include increasing costs of storage, decreasing returns from storage, and increasing costs of transmission.

The average storage costs for new reservoirs can be expected to rise since most sites with the greatest potential for storage, and consequent lower costs per unit of storage, are already in use. Size is critical in calculating capital investment: dams impounding 10 million acre-feet or more, cost on the average $26 per acre-foot of storage, while those storing less than 20,000 acre-feet cost an average of $186 per acre-foot of storage (Wollman and Bonen 1971). Furthermore, storage costs are increasing because, as data collected over the last two decades indicate, the cost of undeveloped land, in general, is rising (Clawson 1973).

As the amount of storage is increased for any stream, a decreasing yield is available from any further increase in storage (Löf and Hardison 1966). As a result of providing increasing levels of yield in critical water areas of the country, many streams are approaching maximum levels of storage where any additional increase in storage would reduce net flow to evaporation. As previously noted, the Colorado River, the Rio Grande, and the Upper Missouri have all exceeded the point of maximum useful development (Wollman and Bonen 1971). If the costs of providing storage are constant, the decreasing yield for each new unit of storage causes the resulting flows to be more costly.

A third factor affecting the economics of surface water diversion is that any increase in distance between the source of supply and the point of use raises the cost of water transmission. Some areas of the country, which have captured the total available local supply, have become dependent upon interbasin transfers for more water. If transmountain diversions are planned, expensive tunnels and high energy inputs may be required. While most transmountain developments are only partially for municipal use, some cities, such as Colorado Springs and Aurora, Colorado, have built and now operate such diversion projects solely for municipal use. As part of the increasing cost of diversion, transmission losses can become a major factor in rising costs. The Fryingpan-Arkansas Project calculates a 7 percent loss for every hundred miles of transmission (Southern Water Conservancy District, n.d.).

Environmental considerations. In recent years proposals involving planned diversions of surface water have often met with criticism from those representing what is loosely known as the "environmental movement." Arguments to protect unique natural environments prone to water development, such as the Grand Canyon and the Everglades, are not new. More recently, however, almost every major water engineering project has met with opposition from those concerned with protecting wildlife or the ecology of a river valley. Broader conflicts over ways in which land should be used are also hindering the implementation of large-scale water development projects.

Apart from a few extreme examples, it is not possible to resolve environmental controversies on economic grounds alone. The arguments ultimately rest upon conflicting societal values which may not be quantifiable. Whatever the merits of the arguments in individual cases, these controversies emphasize the need for new approaches to municipal water planning.

Legal constraints. In discussing governmental intervention in water management, Hirschleifer, DeHaven, and Milliman have noted, "With the possible exception of nuclear energy, no other basic resource is subject to more public and centralized control" (1960, p. 223).

State governments have long been intimately involved in the legal aspects of water. In most of the western U.S., where water rights are tantamount to development rights, the legal issues surrounding water have been a continuing focus of political controversy. Until recently, however, the federal government traditionally limited its legal involvement to assisting the resolution of interstate and international water rights controversies.

Since the passage of the Federal Water Pollution Control Act Amendments of 1972, the federal government has become increasingly involved in a wide range of water issues, especially in the area of water quality standards and environmental impact. Throughout the country, state and local agencies must now comply with new federal laws and directives, and many controversies are now resolved in federal courts. Thus, the legal difficulties to be encountered in any attempt to expand water supply through new surface water diversions are likely to become more complex. On the basis of potential legal delays alone, it may be more attractive for a municipality to examine less traditional strategies to balance supply and demand.

Groundwater Developments

Groundwater may be viewed, although often it is not, as water stored in a natural reservoir that need not be constructed, but only "tapped." This view has subtle but extremely significant effects on the economic and political aspects of the exploitation of groundwater. The issues involved in this exploitation are probably as complex as those in surface water diversion, but are generally less widely known and understood. Nonetheless, approximately one-third of the U.S. population served by public water systems is dependent upon groundwater, and about four-fifths of those not served by municipal supplies depend upon subsurface water (Fair, Geyer, and Okun 1971). Thus, the importance of groundwater development for municipal supply is already apparent and will become even more so in the future.

Economic aspects. Unlike the behavior of surface water, which is very similar under almost all conditions, the behavior of groundwater is closely tied to the geology of both the aquifer and the overlying strata. Thus, the economics of exploitation may vary radically within a given region. It is consequently impossible to determine development costs from the generally known physical and chemical properties of water. Rather, it is necessary to gather highly specific data about the geology of the area under study.

Certain other characteristics of groundwater development are distinctly different from those of surface water diversions. First, although the number of groundwater installations is far larger than that of surface water works, their size is considerably less. Thus, in contrast to the big jumps and large capital investment associated with the expansion of surface water supplies, groundwater may be developed incrementally.

Second, groundwater is usually available at or near the point of demand, and thus involves very low transmission costs. On the other hand, while surface water may be transported by gravity flow, groundwater nearly always needs to be pumped, sometimes from considerable depths.

Thus, groundwater exploitation is intrinsically energy-consumptive, sometimes extremely so, while the hydroelectric plant associated with the impoundment of surface water often represents a bonus in the form of a net energy gain.

Third, and perhaps most important, the fact that groundwater is stored naturally on a long-term basis means that exploitation considerably in excess of replenishment rates can continue for decades. In arid regions where heavy exploitation has taken place, severe economic dislocations resulting from the ultimate exhaustion of the aquifer can be predicted with some assurance.

Environmental and legal aspects. The broad range of environmental controversies surrounding the diversion of surface water is largely absent in the area of groundwater development. This is probably due in large part to the fact that activities carried out hundreds of feet below the earth's surface may not have a perceptible influence either on ecological cycles or on human amenity. Certain serious local effects do occur, such as land subsidence, seawater intrusion, and the drying up of rivers due to overpumping. In general, however, such phenomena have received less attention than is given to the effects of surface water diversion.

On the other hand, there is considerable concern among professionals in the field about the potential for and consequences of the pollution of groundwater sources. It is common practice for municipalities to dispose of their wastes in ways that might ultimately contaminate an aquifer, and large quantities of brackish water are deliberately injected into aquifers during oil drilling operations. In addition, underground disposal of radionuclides, if not properly controlled, could have a potentially disastrous impact on groundwater. Such sources of pollution may produce "long-term and sometimes irreversible effects" which reduce the utility of the groundwater source and thus "place greater demands on other sources of water" (U.S. National Water Commission 1973, p. 243).

The legal aspects of groundwater have been of less concern to the federal government than have those of surface water. However, the U.S. National Water Commission did express concern about the ultimate depletion of groundwater reserves and recommended such measures as pump taxes and quota restrictions on a state level, and cautioned Congress about the probability of future proposed "rescue projects" for areas which have exhausted their groundwater reserves (1973, p. 242). The commission also recommended that federal laws on pollution of surface water be expanded to cover groundwater as well (1973, p. 249). Thus, further legal involvement of the federal government in groundwater issues seems probable.

Conjunctive Use

In many places it has been possible to integrate ground and surface supplies into a single water supply system. Typically, aquifer capacity is used during periods when water levels in surface reservoirs are low. No matter how large the reservoir or how small the pumping capacity, integrated operation provides a larger sustained yield than separate operations. Thus, the assured storage capacity of an aquifer may be utilized to reduce the margin of uncertainty in predicting supplies:

> The basic attractiveness of integrated ground and surface water use resides in the characteristic differences between streams and aquifers as sources of water supplies. Through judicious co-ordination of these resources the strength of each overcomes the weaknesses of both. The abundant, but fluctuating surface water versus the lower (quantity) but steady (assured) delivery of ground water . . . are all factors to be considered in integrated use (Gert et al. 1975).

It should be emphasized, however, that increased exploitation of groundwater may reduce the total volume of surface water available because the two sources are interconnected. Integrated use may in some cases be viewed primarily as a method for achieving a higher degree of certainty about available supplies and greater flexibility in system construction. It may not, however, provide more than a marginal increase in total system capacity.

IMPROVING SYSTEM EFFICIENCY

Maximizing the physical efficiency of water systems has always been of interest to those concerned with their design, construction, and maintenance. However, the dwindling prospects of being able to tap new sources, the increasing costs of developing new sources, and the growing importance of water quality considerations all contribute to a continuing modification of the economics of system efficiency improvement. Whether such modifications involve relatively small increases in maintenance costs or significant new capital outlays, the investments involved must be weighed against the costs of other alternatives. It may be that, in the short run, an inefficient system will be cheaper than an efficient one. There are few areas of the country, however, where this is likely to remain true indefinitely.

The following sections examine the improvement of system efficiency by limiting losses due to evaporation and seepage, and losses due to leakage. These sections are followed by a brief discussion of the implications of improving the management of watersheds and aquifer recharge zones.

Evaporation and Seepage

Evaporation of water is a function of a number of variables including water temperature, amount of incident solar energy, air temperature, relative humidity, and wind speed. It has been calculated that losses due to evaporation range up to 100 inches per year in some extremely arid portions of the West (Meyer 1942). Although the average loss is rather less than half that figure, evaporative losses can amount to a significant portion of a year's catchment, especially for large, shallow reservoirs. It is also important to note that during evaporation, all contaminant elements remain in the reservoir, thus contributing to a net reduction in the overall quality of the stored water.

There are relatively few ways to reduce evaporative losses. One is to transfer some portion of the reservoir water into groundwater storage. One obvious precondition of this alternative is the presence of a suitable geological formation. Although groundwater is not 100 percent recoverable, the total reduction in water losses may be considerable and may justify the costs of the operation. This process may be especially attractive for regions of marked seasonal or annual fluctuations in rainfall, as previously noted in the section dealing with conjunctive use.

Evaporation of reservoir water is heavily dependent upon reservoir geometry. If the ratio of reservoir depth to surface area is increased, the ratio of the percentage of water lost to the percentage of water retained will decrease. While this factor is generally important in selecting sites for new reservoirs, dredging is the only means of improving the depth-to-surface area ratio of an existing reservoir. Thus far, the high cost of dredging has rarely made it a viable alternative on the basis of evaporation reduction alone.

One proposal for reducing the loss to evaporation has been the spreading of monomolecular films on water surfaces. However, an evaluation of the effectiveness of such films has shown that they are subject to destruction by small organisms and even moderate wind levels, and that they tend to raise water temperature, which in turn promotes evaporation (NAS 1968). Monomolecular films have therefore found no widespread application.

Seepage from reservoirs is another potential source of system loss. Although the permeability of area soils is taken into consideration in the original siting of a reservoir, potential losses may be high enough to justify linings to reduce seepage. The rising value of water may make such measures attractive as a part of future planning.

Leakage

In many municipalities loss of water from the distribution system is significant (see table 5). It is not uncommon that 15 percent of the water produced in a municipal system is unaccounted for (Simmons 1966). Leakage may also occur after the water is metered and enters a residential, commercial, or industrial structure. Significant reduction of system leakage may be an expensive undertaking, and once again must be weighed against the costs of increasing the amount of water that enters the system.

Land Use

The relationship of land to water has always been a significant constraint in determining the use of land. This is illustrated by the impact, often on a regional scale, of the construction of major waterworks on the patterns of land use. Such changes have, in fact, long been the avowed goal of much flood control work. In the western U.S., where water is scarce, the development of the concept of "water rights" is a result of the recognition of the importance of water in land development.

After examining the issues involved in the relationship of land to water, the U.S. National Water Commission (1973) formulated a series of recommendations designed to free water rights from certain institutional restrictions and to make possible the buying and selling of these rights on a kind of market basis. The intent of the recommendations was to promote

Table 5

FREQUENCY DISTRIBUTION OF UNACCOUNTED-FOR WATER IN CITIES, IN PERCENTAGE OF WATER PRODUCED

Unaccounted-for Water (% of production)	No. of Cities
5.0	130
5.0– 9.9	52
10.0–14.9	72
15.0–19.9	55
20.0–24.9	33
25.0–29.9	17
30.0–39.9	13
40.0 or more	7
TOTAL	379

Source: Seidel and Baumann 1957, p. 1535.

the allocation of water to more valuable uses, typically shifting water from agricultural to municipal or industrial uses.

Recommendations along these lines may be more acceptable politically than those directed towards large-scale modifications of the environment or the controlling of development rights in order to influence catchment. A wide range of such possibilities exists, including, for example, the clear cutting of large areas of timber to increase runoff from watersheds, the manipulation of land over aquifer recharge areas to increase permeability, and the periodic elimination of phreatophytes from river valleys. Proposals involving the last example have generated opposition in the West.

All proposals about land management ultimately involve the political acceptability of regional land use planning. Obvious conflicts develop around traditional concepts of property rights. In addition, serious questions are raised about the kinds of institutions most appropriate to conduct such planning.

> The wetlands illustrate one example where important resources have actually been in State ownership and subject to public trust rights, but where drainage and development have caused much damage because some States were simply not aware of what they owned and what the public rights were (U.S. National Water Commission 1973).

It is clear that the development of policy tools for the comprehensive management of catchment areas, both to increase the quantity of water available and to ensure certain levels of quality, involve some reevaluation and modification of current decision-making processes. If such developments occur, the optimum management of land for water supply and waste disposal will remain in conflict with a variety of other, equally important goals such as forestry, recreation, and food production. Thus the needs of municipal water systems must be brought into balance with many other issues beyond those factors directly concerned with water supply itself.

REDUCING WATER DEMAND

Proposals to make the management of water demand an integral part of planning procedures have predictably met with considerable suspicion, not only on the part of the public, but among those professionals involved in the planning process. This is understandable in view of the fact that conscious decisions about controlling water demand have important consequences for the growth and development patterns of whole sectors of the economy. Because of complex political implications, most measures to control demand for water have been associated with response to emergencies and have usually been imposed on a temporary basis.

Despite traditional opposition to policies aimed at controlling demand, the growing problems involved in increasing supply are forcing those responsible for municipal water management to examine demand-related measures. These measures, as discussed in the following section, include metering, pricing policy, restrictions on use, and public conservation strategies. Such measures may be useful not only in reducing overall consumption, but in redistributing patterns of peak system load.

Metering

The introduction of metering into a water system has a major effect on the consumption of residential and commercial water. For example, with only 25 percent of New York City water users being metered, it has been estimated that complete metering could reduce consumption by 125 mgd, or about 10 percent of average daily use (D'Angelo 1964). However, since most public and private systems in the United States are metered (Hirschleifer, DeHaven, and Milliman 1960), the potential of this particular alternative for increasing efficiency in water use is relatively limited.

The effectiveness of metering in controlling water demand is fairly clear. A study of Boulder, Colorado, showed that "Per capita consumption dropped about 40 percent over the period from 1960, when Boulder was only 5 percent metered, to 1965 when it was fully metered" (Hanke and Flack 1968, p. 1365). Thus, the effect of complete metering gave Boulder the capability to serve an additional 11,000 persons with the same water supply.

While the 40 percent drop in Boulder may be unusually high, the literature reveals a consistent pattern of reduced water consumption after adoption of metering. In Kingston, New York, a universal meter installation program was initiated in 1958. By 1963, 98 percent of the system was metered and average water use had decreased more than 20 percent (Cloonan 1965). When Philadelphia completed universal metering from 1955 to 1960, the demand among the previously unmetered customers was calculated to have dropped by at least 28 percent (Cloonan 1965).

The effect of metering on water demand is also demonstrated when a comparison is made between metered areas and flat-rate areas (see table 6 on page 33). The average consumption was 458 gallons per day per dwelling unit in metered areas as compared to an average of 692 gallons per day in flat-rate areas. The difference is largely attributable to reduction in lawn sprinkling.

The effect of metering in lowering demand for water appears to have a long-term effect. As meters were implemented over a thirty-year period

Table 6

WATER USE IN METERED AND FLAT-RATE AREAS
(October 1963–September 1965)

	Metered Areas	Flat-rate areas
	(gallons per day per dwelling unit)	
Annual average		
Leakage and waste	25	36
Household	247	236
Sprinkling	186	420
TOTAL	458	692
Maximum day	979	2,354
Peak hour	2,481	5,170

Source: Howe, Charles W. and Linaweaver, F. P. Jr. 1965, p. 14.

in the Boston Metropolitan District Commission, the demand for water continued to decline from 130 gallons per capita per day to approximately 100 gallons per capita per day (see figure 5).

Pricing

Pricing policies for both energy and water have traditionally had many similarities. With recent concern about anticipated shortages in energy supplies, new pricing approaches long advocated by economists have received serious consideration and in some cases have been adopted. Similarly, with the future need to conserve water resources, new pricing

Figure 5

EFFECT OF INTRODUCTION OF METERING ON WATER CONSUMPTION
BY METROPOLITAN DISTRICT COMMISSION CUSTOMERS

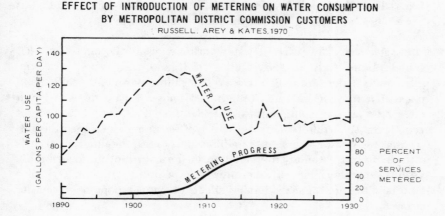

approaches will undoubtedly become an important tool in water management.

Since municipal water systems are usually a "natural monopoly," the price of water is not necessarily determined by market forces. A pricing or rate structure is developed in order to distribute the costs among the users of water. Rate structures inevitably favor, explicitly or implicitly, certain uses or users. Thus, water rates involve issues of social equity as well as system efficiency. This fact may help to explain the resistance frequently encountered by proposals to modify rate structures.

Another important cost is involved in municipal water systems management: the cost of wastewater treatment. This cost is currently rising and already represents a significant proportion of total system cost. Obviously, varying pricing policies may be applied to wastewater just as they are to supply water. In the area of household use, where the kinds of effluents are limited and volumes are roughly proportional to the amount of water supplied, pricing for both supply and disposal should probably be similar. Thus, most of the arguments concerning the modification of rates for water supply would be valid for wastewater disposal.

The treatment of industrial wastes can be an entirely different matter. In many industries the volume, and particularly the kind of effluents released, may make a tremendous difference in the treatment cost. Here a much more differentiated set of effluent charges might be levied. Such a policy would serve not only to allocate the real costs of waste treatment more fairly, but also to encourage the industries concerned to develop their own methods of treatment or to reduce the total amount of effluent.

Much of the extensive literature on the effectiveness of effluent charges for industry is directed toward the setting of national policies for pollution abatement (Kneese and Schultze 1975). Approximately one-third of U.S. cities have already adopted such charges (Seagraves 1973). The potential savings from these policies would vary widely among communities, but they should be kept in mind in the following discussion.

Rate schedules. The price of water varies enormously among municipalities. In a study of 485 utilities in Illinois, Afifi noted that the price ranged from zero to $10.95 for 5,000 gallons per month (Afifi 1969). In a similar study in Kansas, Gottlieb (1963) observed a wide variation in water rates among communities and identified five factors that might account for such differences: the effect of economies of scale, the differential costs of water drawn from different sources, the differential costs in the type of treatment, the variation in the nature of the distribution systems, and the effect of differential use of utility taxation. It is also important to note the considerable effects of average population density on price.

There are basically five types of water-pricing policies: (1) flat-rate or fixed monthly charge; (2) constant rate (per unit) schedules; (3) declining block-rate or promotional pricing; (4) summer differential rate; and (5) incremental block pricing.

A *flat-rate schedule* involves a fixed charge, usually on a monthly basis, which is unrelated to the amount of water used. Such pricing is relatively rare. In a survey of 123 water utilities, only 3 cities utilized a flat-rate schedule; ironically, two of these three are located in the arid western states: Aurora, Colorado, and Reno, Nevada (Gysi and Loucks 1971). Flat-rate charges are, of course, characteristic of unmetered systems.

Constant rate schedules are somewhat more common, although Gysi and Loucks calculate that less than 5 percent of urban water supplies rely on a constant rate structure. Simply put, after a minimum charge, the price per unit of water remains constant, no matter what volume of water is used. From one perspective, constant rate pricing is fair in that everyone pays the same price for water.

The *declining block rate*, often described as "promotional" pricing, is the most common schedule now in use. It is estimated that 94 percent of municipalities rely on this rate. Usually there is a minimum charge followed by lower rates as the volume of water purchased increases.

Summer differential rates may be used in conjunction with other rate structures; unlike flat, constant, or declining block rates, such structures represent a conscious attempt to modify demand. In some places during the summer months, the demand for water results in pressure loss or reduced reserves; consequently, higher rates are imposed during this period in order to lessen peak demands. The practice of summer differential rates is not widespread but does occur in the drier areas of the United States.

Incremental block pricing is a relatively new concept in pricing that has not gained widespread acceptance. Water rates increase as the amount of water purchased increases; thus, incremental block pricing is a reversal of the declining block-rate schedule. It is principally intended to encourage water conservation and also provides lower unit rates to low-volume water users, which include low-income groups.

Economic analysis.   The American Water Works Association noted in 1958 that in practice, the pricing policies of most systems are widely at variance with even roughly optimal policies. Traditionally, the price of water has been determined by dividing the total system costs by the amount of water delivered. This is called *average cost pricing*. An alternative approach favored by many economists is *marginal cost pricing*. In this method, the price of water is determined from the cost of supplying an additional unit of water. With the trend toward increasing costs, marginal cost pricing will almost always lead to higher prices charged for water than average cost pricing.

An examination of average cost pricing from the point of view of economic theory has led to severe criticism on the grounds that it encourages overinvestment in system capacity. Average cost pricing thus contains a bias in favor of system expansion—a bias left over from a day when water was regarded as a free good.

More recently, as noted by Hanke and Flack, a shift has occurred from the "requirements approach to water, that is, viewing water use in terms of an absolute amount of water demanded by a projected population for a municipality, to viewing demands of water as the willingness of consumers to pay" (1968, p. 1360). Many economists have long maintained that a shift to marginal cost pricing would significantly affect the demand for water, especially in the commercial and residential sectors. According to Gysi and Loucks, "Marginal cost pricing policy could save a much larger percentage than any policy of meeting demands at all times by always increasing capacity in advance of demands" (1971, p. 1372). Moreover, Riordan's study (1971) concluded that multistage marginal cost pricing might result in a 10–20 percent saving over average cost pricing policy.

It has also been proposed that utilities abandon the traditional fixed rate schedules of the past, and allow prices to fluctuate with short-term marginal cost (Hirschleifer, DeHaven, and Milliman 1960, p. 98). Thus any cost or savings involved in system operation or expansion, or resulting from fluctuations of supplies, would be passed directly to the customer. Such fluctuating rates would involve only minor administrative expense, but could be expected to meet with opposition from both the public and professionals in the field. A further problem in implementing marginal cost pricing involves the accurate determination of the marginal cost and of the cost increments to be used. Thus, while marginal cost pricing is theoretically attractive, its practical utility remains somewhat unclear.

Policy aspects.   In the context of the rising water costs and increasingly serious legal and environmental conflicts involved in system expansion, pricing policies will undoubtedly be more closely scrutinized in the future as "a means of not only adjusting revenues, but in increasing or decreasing average and maximum day demands" (Howe and Linaweaver 1967, p. 500). The effectiveness of increased water rates in modifying demands is well documented. Nonetheless, as already indicated, the reallocation of water implied by this method is not simply a matter of system efficiency; for example, altering the pricing structure may seriously affect the rate or kind of economic development. There are also significant social considerations involved: Hanke notes that "Those customers who reside in low-density areas farthest from the water system's load center are being sub-

sidized by those who reside in high-density areas closest to load centers"
(1974, p. 210). The subsidy elements contained in rate schedules have
heretofore gone relatively unnoticed. This is not likely to remain the case
in the future.

Pricing policies for water, like pricing policies for energy, are sure to
become more important as management tools. Their chief advantage lies
in their adjustability to a wide range of goals, since they are subject to
modification without great capital outlay or significantly increased system
operating costs.

Restrictions on Use

While restrictions and rationing of agricultural water have been traditionally practiced in the more arid regions of the country, such measures have never been popular. As a policy tool for municipal planning,
restrictions on water use are generally regarded as a last resort in coping
with severe system stress or the threat of serious water shortage. A variety
of restrictions has been imposed in different parts of the country, usually
in response to prolonged drought.

One great advantage of the restriction strategy is its flexibility. Restrictions may be voluntarily or legally imposed; they may be based on hours
of use or types of activity; they may be confined to peak demand periods;
or they may be general in nature. Indeed, in some communities, restrictions have been imposed on all uses, with water shut off for all except for a
few hours each day (Symposium, Journal American Water Works Assn.
1955). One drawback to restrictions is that their effectiveness appears to
be severely limited unless the public is convinced that a crisis situation
exists.

From a review of the literature, it appears that communities faced with
potential water shortages are quick to formulate and impose programs of
water-use restrictions. For example, at least 64 of the 75 communities in
Illinois that suffered shortage at some time during the drought of 1952–55
enacted restrictions on use (Hudson and Roberts 1955). In a study of 48
communities in Massachusetts during the drought of the early 1960s,
restrictions were adopted in 34 communities (Russell, Arey, and Kates
1970). Table 7, on page 38, summarizes the choices made among a variety
of restrictions by these cities and towns.

As a matter of policy, it is possible that publicizing the cost implications
of system failure would increase public tolerance for and cooperation with
restrictions, as Turnovsky's data imply (1969). It has been suggested that
one rational and effective way of promoting customer acceptance of water
use restrictions and of the idea of a planned failure rate for a municipal
water supply would be to publish, in advance, lists of planned restrictions

Table 7

NATURE OF RESTRICTIONS ADOPTED
BY 34 COMMUNITIES

Sector applied to and description	Number of towns adopting	Percentage of all towns imposing any restrictions	Percentage of those towns imposing restrictions on particular sector
Domestic sector:	34	100	100
Lawn-sprinkling	34	100	100
Car-washing	26	76	76
Swimming pool (re)fill	17	50	50
All outside use	10	29	29
Industrial sector:	13*	38*	100
Cooling water recirculation	9	26	69
Air conditioning	9	26	69
General cooling	2	6	15
Process water recirculation	1	3	8
Restrictions on air-conditioning use (hours, temperature)	2	6	15
Car and truck washing (including commercial establishments)	5	15	38
Public sector:	19	56	100
Ponds, fountains	13	38	68
Hydrant flushing	12	25	63
Swimming pool (re)filling	6	18	32

*Several towns took measures with reference to the industrial sector which did not seem to qualify as voluntary restrictions for the purposes of this table. Specifically, 7 towns "requested" industries to recirculate one or more streams (generally air conditioning). Two other towns "recommended" such recirculation. If these are included, 22 towns, or 65 percent of the restricting towns, took some action with respect to industry.

Source: Russell, Arey and Kates 1970, p. 75.

to be applied under various threatened levels of shortage. Thus, for example, the system's customers would know that in the face of a possible 10 percent shortage, all outside water use (sprinkling, car-washing, and so forth) would be forbidden and no nonrecirculating air conditioners would be permitted to operate. If the potential shortage were 15 percent, swimming pools could not be refilled. A 30 percent shortage might involve slowdowns or shutdowns of local water-using industries.

The limits of public acceptance of restrictions cannot be precisely defined, and are probably subject to some degree of modification through education campaigns. However, the imposition of restrictions has been shown to be an effective management tool for relatively short-term problems (Russell, Arey, and Kates 1970).

Public Conservation Strategies

Whereas the effectiveness and limitations of short-term restrictions are relatively easy to evaluate, little is known about the effectiveness of publicity directed toward long-term reduction in water use. When the prospect of eventual improvement in the supply situation is no longer operative, efforts to promote conservation may be ignored or even resented. Nonetheless, there exists a range of opportunities to reduce demand through heightened public awareness of the possibilities of and need for reduced consumption.

Public conservation opportunities include such small but cumulatively important measures as repairing leaking faucets or installing water-conservative appliances. In view of the relative inflexibility of indoor domestic uses, it might be expected that the greatest potential savings would result from modifying landscaping techniques, as in reduction of lawn size or in alteration of vegetation types.

The fact remains that the types of incentives, other than pricing, that might be effective in modifying demand are not presently known. The issue clearly deserves further research. However, regardless of this lack of knowledge, a first critical step can be identified: that of educating the public about municipal water supply problems. Ideally, these problems would be approached by combining conservation measures with technological modifications or improvements.

WATER REUSE

Renovation and reuse of municipal water is not a new concept; it is already occurring, if only in an inadvertent and unplanned manner. On the average, approximately one-third of the U.S. population relies upon municipal withdrawals from streams containing one gallon of previously used water for every 30 gallons withdrawn. In some instances, the ratio of previously used water is as high as one-fifth (U.S. National Water Commission 1973). On the other hand, water reuse can be direct and planned, as in a factory where water from one process is directed with or without treatment to another process in a series of cascading uses. In the municipal system, planned reuse involves the collection and treatment of sewage and the use of the effluent for irrigation, recreation, or industry, or for return to the supply system through an intervening body of water or aquifer.

The potential for water reuse has been recognized at the federal level. The U.S. National Water Commission recommended in its final report (1973) that the use of renovated wastewater "should occupy a prominent spot in future planning for overall water resources utilization." The Federal Water Pollution Control Act Amendments of 1972 stipulated that "the U.S. Environmental Protection Agency provide for the application of the best practicable waste treatment technology, including reclaiming and recycling of water. . . ." The Safe Water Drinking Act of 1974 called for a program to "investigate and demonstrate health implications involved in the reclamation, recycling and reuse of wastewaters for the preparation of safe and acceptable drinking water." As a result of such legislation, the federal mandate for studying the practicability of wastewater recycling is clear. Nevertheless, even though substantial research efforts in this area have been undertaken, water reuse remains, for the most part, only a potential source of available water for municipalities.

The Practicability of Reuse

In general, reuse of water is an attractive concept, but its *practicability* is a serious issue. At present, the practicability of reuse for most U.S. cities involves three major factors: health risks, economic feasibility, and public acceptance. The first two factors are discussed in the following section, while the issue of public acceptance of reuse is considered in a later section.

Public health.   Public health concerns are, for the most part, restricted to those uses in which drinking of or bodily contact with treated effluent is planned. Windhoek, South-West Africa, has provided the only long-term example of direct introduction of effluent into the municipal supply. At Windhoek, the sewage is treated to a tertiary level, including a final filtration through activated carbon, before being mixed with the conventional surface flow. During periods when the chloride content of the waste water is not excessive, up to one-third of the effluent in Windhoek is recycled for potable supply (U.S. National Water Commission 1973). The water produced meets all the use standards set by the World Health Organization (Cillie et al. 1966, and Stander 1969).

At present, no cities in the United States are processing effluent for direct potable use. One of the few U.S. experiences in this area occurred from October 1956 to March 1957, when Chanute, Kansas, treated and reused water for its municipal supply. While the quality of the renovated water met the standards established by the U.S. Public Health Service (1962), the chemical composition deteriorated markedly, the water had a pale yellow color and an unpleasant taste and odor, and foaming occurred when the water was agitated (Metzler et al. 1958). In late 1939 and 1940, another community, Ottumwa, Iowa, also recycled renovated waste water; again, no health problems were observed (Brown 1940).

In a pilot project, plans are being made to recycle renovated waste water in Denver, Colorado, for all uses including water for drinking. Currently a small demonstration plant (1 mgd) is under construction and a substantial research effort concerning water quality and health has been launched. Within ten years, it is possible that Denver may be recycling renovated waste water at the rate of 100 mgd.

In an experiment in Santee, California, recreational lakes were developed with treated effluent. The lakes served as a scenic background for picnicking, boating, fishing, and swimming, in successive stages. The swimming experiment was closely investigated and, although viruses were commonly isolated from raw sewage, none was ever measured in the input to a final contact chlorination process which preceeded discharge into the lakes.

Although promising, the conclusions drawn from these experiences should not lead to undue confidence concerning the effect of renovated waste water on health. While bacteria and viruses appear to be controlled under proper filtration and chlorination, little information exists concerning the occurrence and distribution of such heavy metals as chromium, mercury, and lead, and of such organochlorine compounds as carbon tetrachloride, DDT, aldrin, dieldrin, and chlordane, which are known to be potential carcinogens.

On the other hand, the lack of definitive information on water quality and health should not preclude serious consideration of water reuse in planning for municipal water supply, since the same problems exist for most other alternative sources of municipal supply. In a U. S. Public Health Service survey of 969 communities (1970), for example, only 50 percent of the communities produced drinking water that was acceptable under the recommended standards of the U.S. Public Health Service. The point is simply stated: the answers to questions regarding health and water quality are unknown for both water reuse techniques and for the currently operating conventional water supply treatment technologies.

With the passage and implementation of the 1974 Safe Drinking Water Act, progress should be made toward improving the quality of drinking water. In addition, with the completion of the Denver water reuse project, the finished product will undoubtedly be significantly higher in quality than the tap water presently available in most U.S. communities. As Dean noted as early as 1965:

> We can make a better quality of water by treating sewage than is available in many of our cities. Controlled treatment of a known hazardous raw material can produce a safer product than routine treatment of a deteriorating source. Viruses can be removed from heavily polluted water by suitable treatment and the cost is not unreasonable (p. 470).

In sum, any accurate evaluation of the public health risks associated with water reuse involves further research to determine relative toxicity of all pollutants in both conventional supply and treated effluent. Of course, the entire question of health is circumvented in those situations where water can be reused for purposes other than ingestion; for example, industrial cooling, irrigation, and recreation. Indeed, it is these noningestive uses where reuse will probably first be adopted. However, savings to the community might be foregone if water reuse is not also considered as a potential source for potable use.

Economic feasibility. If reuse is not currently a least-cost method of supplementing the capacity of municipal systems, its economic appeal will increase in the future. The reasons for this fall into two major categories: the growing cost of providing conventional flows, which has been discussed in an earlier chapter; and the decreasing cost of providing renovated water.

The differential costs of providing reused water are declining primarily because of the required upgrading of effluent discharged by municipal systems. Under the 1972 Federal Water Pollution Control Act Amendments, the federal government established standards that mandate secondary treatment of all municipal sewage and, in certain areas of special need, additional treatment to the advanced level. Whether secondary or advanced treatment is required, the additional costs involved in further treatment for distribution and reuse may not be substantially higher than the costs for treatment of water from other sources.

The current economic practicability of water reuse can be discussed in light of the experiences of Colorado Springs, Colorado, and Whittier Narrows, California. These are special cases which may, however, come to represent more general trends characterizing the future of water reuse in municipal supply systems. In Colorado Springs, reuse is viewed as a relatively inexpensive source of supply costing approximately one-third as much as deriving the city's potable water supply from extensive transmountain diversions of water (City of Colorado Springs 1970). Whittier

Narrows, which is using treated sewage to recharge an aquifer, has calculated the cost of providing secondary treated effluent as approximately equal to the cost of buying its potable water from the Los Angeles Metropolitan Water District (MWD).

In both Colorado Springs and Whittier Narrows, only three cost factors were utilized to determine the efficiency of reuse. These were the costs of (1) an alternative source of water; (2) the necessary treatment to provide an effluent of suitable quality; and (3) the provision and operation of a plant to produce the effluent. The costs of reuse were then compared with the costs of the alternative source. Generally, for such analyses, only a comparison with the costs of providing water from conventional sources is used to indicate the efficiency of reuse.

James Johnson (1971) provided the first challenge to the method of comparing costs of reuse directly with costs of conventional supply. His study points out that some of the necessary treatment costs would be required for pollution control whether or not water was reused. Along these same lines, the U.S. National Water Commission (1973) stated that a calculation of the true cost of reuse would be based on the following sequence of factors:

1. The cost of advanced treatment to make waste water suitable for reuse,

2. minus the cost of pollution control treatment measures otherwise necessary to achieve water quality standards,

3. minus the cost of water treatment of the supply being considered as an alternative to reuse,

4. plus or minus the difference in conveyance costs between the reusable supply and its alternative, including allowance for the cost of separate supply lines if reuse is contemplated for industrial water supply only.

In light of this procedure, the common method of evaluating the economic efficiency of reuse by comparing the costs of reuse and an alternative supply is misleading. Calculation of the costs of the final unit of water delivered in a system with and without reuse should be the criterion of any evaluation of the system.

The Role of Reuse

While reuse of water for return to potable water supply systems has proven feasible, most currently planned reuse is for nonpotable purposes, with the water supplied directly from the treatment plant to the user.

Most of the present uses for irrigation, industry, and recreation are supplied in this way.

No matter how it is employed, reuse provides a source of water which can delay or obviate the need for tapping new sources of supply. Any consideration of reuse efficiency must start with the concept of an integrated system which will furnish either treated effluent or potable water to users. This concept allows water managers flexibility in deciding whether to produce and distribute treated effluent, or to rely only on the normal potable supply for all uses. System integration thus eliminates unnecessary costs in producing and distributing effluent during periods when other sources of unused capacity exist.

The concept of system integration relies on a general relationship between reuse and storage of flows, a relationship which provides a guide to the optimal use of treated effluent. According to this relationship, reuse systems cost less to build but are more expensive to operate than systems designed to divert and store flows. Thus, the relationship suggests that reuse systems should be used only when water from storage is unavailable to meet demand. In this way, reuse functions most efficiently as a source of peak supply while storage, with its low operating costs, provides the necessary normal capacity. However, where treated effluent is not an acceptable source of potable supply, a separate system for its distribution is required.

Reliance on reuse as a standby source not affected by periods of low flow can increase system yield and provide planning flexibility in three major ways: (1) by achieving the high levels of assurance required in municipal systems; (2) by mobilizing any oversupply in the system; and (3) by shortening the planning cycle.

Reuse to assure supply.   The yield of a water supply system, based on storage of flows, is usually expressed as a quantity of water available or assured ninety-five percent (or more) of the time. To achieve this level of assurance, some storage must be provided which will be required less than 5 percent of the time. Because yield increases as assurance declines (Löf and Hardison 1966), the yields from a system could be increased by allowing the levels of assurance in a system to be relaxed. Reuse could furnish the additional water necessary to maintain the desired level of assurance.

Mobilizing excess supply.   Because many engineers find a potential shortage of even 5 percent to be unacceptable, engineering and reference handbooks urge the use of conservative calculations in planning for municipal water supply systems. Social scientists, on the other hand, assert that yields are often, if not always, understated. Furthermore, there is indication from cities experiencing periods of drought that rationing of water has not caused undue hardship. Renovation and reuse can play a constructive role in resolving this ongoing debate over levels of assurance. Thus, reliance on reuse as a standby source allows the continued use of a conventional supply source until accurate evaluations of yield can be made.

Shortening the planning cycle. The time required for the development of new water sources requires long-term estimations of future demand for water. In the past, because accelerated use of water utilized excess capacity, there was little concern if the future demand was overstated and if subsequent projects based on such inflated demand resulted in temporary oversupply. There is evidence, however, that this rapid growth in demand has slowed. Furthermore, certain factors, such as the low birthrate and the replacement of the single family house with apartments and cluster homes, indicate that the present reduction in demand will continue. Consequently, excess capacity added now under lower rates of growth will be utilized more slowly, with a consequent investment in idle capacity for a longer period. Reuse thus becomes significant since it allows for the evaluation of change in demand, and helps reduce reliance on long-term predictions as a basis for planning water supply systems. As a result, system adjustments and construction of water supply projects can proceed in stages undertaken according to pragmatic evaluations of changes in demand.

TECHNOLOGICAL INNOVATIONS IN WATER SUPPLY

Two other alternatives, desalinization and weather modification, are sometimes proposed for increasing water supply. These are discussed separately because they are relatively new technological alternatives which do not as yet provide generally practicable solutions to the problems of municipal water management.

Desalinization has proven to be a technologically feasible but generally uneconomical source of municipal water. Its use has so far been confined to small-scale operations where other sources are unavailable or prohibitively expensive. Since much of the cost of desalinization operations is a function of energy consumption, existing technologies cannot be expected to become less expensive, even for large-scale operations. It is therefore to be expected that, at least for the foreseeable future, desalinization will be useful in relatively few operations, and will not be a viable alternative for municipal water planning.

Attempts to modify weather by increasing precipitation under certain meteorological conditions have been successful. The possible advantages of such operations for municipal water supply are, however, difficult to evaluate. First, weather modification effects have so far been highly localized and thus of benefit on a relatively small scale. Second, the full ramifications of any detrimental environmental impacts which might occur are unknown. Further, while the economics of weather modification have been considered for a few locations, they have not been adequately determined at a more general level. Finally, the political implications of weather modification technologies at national and international levels are complex and may supersede consideration of the water supply needs of any one community.

In conclusion, both desalinization and weather modification do not presently represent widely feasible additional sources of municipal water supply. However, these technologies certainly deserve further research.

PUBLIC AND PROFESSIONAL RESPONSE

Faced with rising demands, dwindling sources of supply, and growing difficulties regarding quality, the professionals responsible for water system management are finding it necessary not only to justify their decisions but to enlist public support. No planning alternative or set of alternatives is truly viable without public acceptance. It cannot, however, be expected that the complexities and tradeoffs involved in water system management will be widely understood by the general public. Furthermore, professionals themselves must study and understand the alternatives before they can reasonably expect informed and effective input from the public.

In this context it is interesting to examine the issue of professional bias among decision makers. Decisions regarding water supply and waste water treatment are generally reached through the interaction of elected officials, departmental personnel, and outside consultants. However, as indicated in a study of 48 Massachusetts communities by Russell, Arey, and Kates (1970), "In the planning process, the scope of the debate is generally set by the consulting engineers. They define the alternatives, make the demand projections, and provide cost information" (p. 175). Hence, in planning for municipal water supply, the values and biases of the engineer appear to be extremely influential.

The potential effects of professional socialization on choice of resource management alternatives has been generally known, but until recently has been the focus of only a few studies. Sewell and Little suggest that, unlike government officials and special-interest groups, engineers are more likely to concentrate on physical problems, and choose physical construction alternatives from among a set of possible solutions (1972). As a result, while planners or engineering consultants may strive for objectivity and seek to identify the optimum strategy, their formulation of plans and recommendations may become an exercise in rationalization which selects evidence to support a preconceived and preferred choice of action.

In another study (1971), Sewell demonstrated that distinct differences may occur among various types of professionals in the water resource area. Both public health officials and consulting engineers, for example, reflected their particular professional biases: in the area of water quality, public health officials most frequently emphasized health problems, while

47

engineers usually focused on increasing production costs. Furthermore, when concerned with solutions to environmental problems, public health officials relied upon issuance of a warning followed by litigation, whereas engineers emphasized construction of facilities. Hence, the reliance on a few alternatives in the management of urban water supply is strongly related to professional socialization and past experience.

Another facet of acceptability relates to how professionals perceive the public's perception of various alternatives. This can best be illustrated in terms of the alternative of reuse. Recalling the debates over fluoridation of public water supplies, and aware of the heightened need for public participation in current water planning, water resource managers are especially concerned about public acceptance of recycled waste water. From an unpublished survey by Baumann (1969) of 300 municipal water managers in the United States, the most common reason cited by the 50 percent who opposed waste water reuse was anticipated rejection by the public. Similarly, Johnson (1971) found that "It would appear that water managers know very little of consumer responses concerning renovated waste water, but generally consider the public would not accept it" (p. 92). If this is the case, it could be that the public becomes a scapegoat for the reluctance of engineers, water managers, public health officials, city councils, and local water boards to change the established procedures of municipal water supply provision.

The recent experience in Denver, Colorado, seems to support the contention that the public may be more supportive of new water management alternatives than the professionals assume. In a survey of 500 people, the initial response to the concept of recycling renovated waste water was primarily negative. However, as the respondents were provided additional information concerning the implications of water reuse planning, the rate of public acceptance increased until 85 percent of the respondents expressed a willingness to drink renovated waste water (Heaton et al. 1974). In view of this evidence, a key obstacle in the consideration and adoption of recycling renovated waste water for municipal water supply may lie not so much in the mind of the consumer as in the perceptions of consulting engineers, public health officials, and other involved professionals.

These arguments apply generally, not only to reuse, but also to such alternatives as public adoption of conservation strategies, or acceptance of altered rate structures. It is therefore clear that professionals will have to overcome not only public bias but also their own prejudices in making intelligent planning decisions and in finding support for those decisions.

The public will not necessarily accept those alternatives that are technically most efficient, and optimal economic solutions may be opposed on noneconomic grounds. In recent times, there has emerged a range of groups concerned with broad social and environmental issues. Whether well informed or not, these groups have already had considerable impact on public perception of issues as well as on the context in which decisions must be made. As Kneese and Schultze note, an important factor in developing the unprecedentedly strict requirements of the 1972 Federal Water Pollution Control Act

> seems to have been dedicated and highly effective work by a small number of conservationists advocating zero discharge. They seem to have felt that the more stringent the restrictions were, the cleaner the water would be, although there is absolutely no historical justification for this view (1975, p. 56).

No doubt public and congressional perceptions of the complexities of these and other environmental issues will become more sophisticated. Nonetheless, to date there has been little research on public preferences and the means by which they might be changed. It is also apparent that much public education is necessary concerning the implications of various issues and alternatives in municipal water management.

BIBLIOGRAPHY

Afifi, Hamdy H. H. 1969. Economic Evaluation of Water Supply Pricing in Illinois. *Journal of American Water Works Association* 61, (1).

Alvord, Burdick, and Howson 1937. *Report to the Indianapolis Water Company Upon an Additional Water Supply.* Chicago.

American City 1946. "What Water Meters Did for Elizabeth City, North Carolina." 61, (9).

American Water Works Association 1958. *Water Rates Manual.* New York: American Water Works Association.

AWWA Committee on Water Use 1973. Review of the Johns Hopkins University Research Project Method for Estimating Residential Water Use. *Journal of American Water Works Association* 65, (5).

Baumann, Duane D., and Dworkin, Daniel 1975. *Planning for Water Reuse.* Washington, D.C.: U.S. Army Corps of Engineers, Institute of Water Resources.

Baumann, Duane D., and Kasperson, Roger E. 1974. Public Acceptance of Renovated Waste Water: Myth and Reality. *Water Resources Research* 10, (4).

Bonem, Gilbert U. 1968. On the Marginal Cost Pricing of Municipal Water. *Water Resources Research* 4, (1).

Brown, Gardner M. 1968. Industrial Water Demands: A Critique. In *Forecasting the Demands for Water,* edited by W. R. Derrick Sewell et al. Ottawa, Ontario: Policy and Planning Branch, Dept. of Energy, Mines, and Resources.

Brown, H. A. 1940. Super Chlorination at Ottumwa, Iowa. *Journal of American Water Works Association* 32, (4).

Burns, D. R. J. et al. 1975. *The Effect of Price on Residential Water Demand: A Comparative Use Study.* In Project Report, Seminar in Water Resources and Development Management. Boulder: University of Colorado, Fall.

Chambers, John C.; Mullick, Satinder K.; and Smith, Donald D. 1971. How to Choose the Right Forecasting Technique. *Harvard Business Review* 4.

Cillie, G. C. et al. 1966. "The Reclamation of Sewage Effluents to Domestic Use." *Third International Conference on Water Pollution Research.* Washington, D.C.: WPFC.

City of Colorado Springs 1970. *1970 Annual Report.* Colorado Springs, Colorado: Department of Public Utilities.

Clawson, Marion 1973. *Suburban Land Conversion in the United States.* Baltimore: The Johns Hopkins Press for Resources for the Future.

Cloonan, E. T. 1965. "Meters Save Water." In *Modern Water Rates.* New York: Battenheim Publishing Company.

Comptroller General of the United States 1973. *Improved Federal and State Programs Needed to Insure the Purity and Safety of Drinking Water in the United States.* Washington, D.C.: General Accounting Office, B-166506.

Culp, R. L., and Culp, G. L. 1971. *Advanced Wastewater Treatment.* New York: Van Nostrand Rheinhold Co.

D'Angelo, Armand 1964. *Report on Universal Metering.* To Honorable Robert F. Wagner, Mayor of New York City, 7 October.

Dean, Robert 1965. *Transmission of Viruses by the Water Route.* New York: John Wiley & Sons.

Dworkin, D. 1974. "The Value of Water Reuse for Municipal Supply." Worcester, Massachusetts: Department of Geography, Clark University, Ph.D. dissertation.

————. 1975. Water Reuse: A Flexible and Efficient Management Alternative for Municipal Supply. *Water Resources Research* 11, (5).

Dworkin, Daniel, and Baumann, Duane 1974. *An Evaluation of Water Reuse for Municipal Supply.* Washington, D.C.: Institute for Water Resources, U.S. Corps of Engineers.

Fair, Gordon M.; Geyer, John C.; and Okun, Daniel A. 1966. *Water and Waste Water Engineering.* New York: Wiley and Company.

Federal Water Pollution Control Act Amendments of 1972, Public Law 92-500, 92nd Congress, S. 2770, 18 October.

Gert, Aron; Rachford, Thomas; Borrelli, John; and Stottman, Walter 1975. "A Method for Integrating Surface and Ground Water Use in Humid Regions." In *Economic Concepts and Techniques Pertaining to Water Supply, Water Allocation and Water Quality.* Ft. Belvoir, Virginia: Institute for Water Resources.

Gottlieb, Manuel 1963. Urban Domestic Demand for Water: A Kansas Case Study. *Land Economics* 39.

Gysi, Marshall, and Loucks, Daniel P. 1971. Some Long Run Effects of Water-Pricing Policies. *Water Resources Research* 7, (6).

Hanke, Steve H. 1970a. Some Behavioral Characteristics Associated with Residential Water Price Changes. *Water Resources Research* 6, (5).

————. 1970b. Demand for Water Under Dynamic Conditions. *Water Resources Research* 6, (5).

————. 1974. "Water Rates: An Assessment of Current Issues." In *The State of America's Drinking Water*. Raleigh, North Carolina: Water Resources Research Institute.

Hanke, Steve H., and Flack, Ernest Jr. 1968. Effects of Metering Urban Water. *Journal of American Water Works Association*.

Harris, Robert H., and Brecher, Edward M. 1974. Is the Water Safe to Drink? *Consumer Reports* 39, (6).

Hartman, L. M., and Seastone, D. 1970. *Water Transfer*. Baltimore: The Johns Hopkins Press.

Headley, Charles 1963. The Relation of Family Income and Use of Water for Residential and Commercial Purposes in the San Francisco-Oakland Metropolitan Area. *Land Economics* 39.

Heaton, R. D.; Linstedt, K. D.; Bennett, E. R.; and Suhr, L. G. 1974. "Progress Toward Successive Water Use in Denver." Mimeographed.

Heggie, Glen D. 1957. Effects of Sprinkling Requirements. *Journal of American Water Works Association* 49.

Hirschleifer, Jack; DeHaven, James C.; and Milliman, Jerome W. 1960. *Water Supply: Economics, Technology and Policy*. Chicago: University of Chicago Press.

Hittman Associates, Inc. 1969. *Forecasting Municipal Water Requirements*. Columbia, Maryland: Report HIT–413.

Howe, Charles W. 1968. Water Pricing in Residential Areas. *Journal of American Water Works Association* 60, (5).

Howe, Charles W., and Linaweaver, F. P. Jr. 1965. The Impact of Price on Residential Water Demand and Its Relation to System Design. *Water Resources Research* 1.

————. 1967. The Impact of Price on Residential Water Demand and Its Relation to System Design and Price Structure. *Water Resources Research*.

Howe, Charles W., and Vaughn, William J. 1972. In-House Water Savings. *Journal of American Water Works Association* 64, (2).

Hudson, H. E. Jr., and Roberts, W. J. 1955. *1952–55 Illinois Drought with Special Reference to Impounding Reservoir Design*. Urbana, Illinois: Department of Registration and Education, Illinois State Water Survey Bulletin no. 43.

Hutchins, W. A. 1971. *Water Law in the Nineteen Western States*. Washington, D.C.: U.S. Department of Agriculture.

Hydrological Engineering Center 1975. *HEC-4 Monthly Streamflow Simulation*. Davis, California: U.S. Army Corps of Engineers.

Journal of American Water Works Association 1919. Publicity in Water-Waste Prevention Work. 6, (8).

Johnson, James F. 1971. *Renovated Waste Water: An Alternative Source of Municipal Water Supply in the United States*. Chicago: University of Chicago, Department of Geography Research Paper no. 135.

Kahan, Archie M. 1972. Weather Modification Progress Report. *Water Resources Research* 64, (5).

Kneese, Allen V., and Schultze, Charles L. 1975. *Pollution, Prices and Public Policy.* A study sponsored jointly by Resources for the Future, Inc. and the Brookings Institution, Washington, D.C.

Krutilla, J. V., and Cicchette, C. J. 1972. Evaluating Benefits of Environmental Resources with Special Application to the Hells Canyon. *Natural Resources Journal* 12, (1).

Lee, Roger D. 1974. "The Development and Application of the 1974 Drinking Water Standards." In *The State of America's Drinking Water.* Raleigh, North Carolina: Water Resources Research Institute.

Linaweaver, F. P. Jr.; Geyer, John C.; and Wolff, J. B. 1966a. *Final and Summary Report on the Residential Water Use Research Project.* The Johns Hopkins University, Department of Environmental Science.

————. 1966b. *Report on the Commercial Water Use Research Project.* Baltimore: The Johns Hopkins University, Department of Environmental Science.

————. 1967. A *Study of Residential Water Use.* Washington, D.C.: FHA Department of Housing and Urban Development, U.S. Government Printing Office.

Linstedt, K. Daniel, and Bennett, Edwin 1975. *Research Needs for the Potable Reuse of Municipal Wastewater.* Cincinnati, Ohio: U.S. Environmental Protection Agency.

Löf, G. O. G., and Hardison, C. H. 1966. Storage Requirements for Water in the United States. *Water Resources Research* 2, Autumn.

McBean, E. A., and Loucks, D. P. 1974. *Planning and Analyzing of Metropolitan Water Resource Systems.* Ithaca, New York: Cornell University, Water Resources and Marine Science Center, Technical Report no. 84.

McDermott, James H. 1974. "Impact of the Safe Drinking Water Act." In *The State of America's Drinking Water.* Raleigh, North Carolina: Water Resources Research Institute.

McPherson, M. B. 1976. *Household Water Use.* ASCE Urban Water Resources Research Program, Technical Memorandum no. 28.

Malone, Thomas F. 1968. Weather Modification; Present and Future. *Journal of American Water Works Association* 60, (10).

Marx, Jean 1974. Drinking Water: Another Source of Carcinogens. *Science* 186, 20 November.

Merrill, John C. et al. 1967. *The Santee Recreation Project.* Cincinnati, Ohio: Federal Water Pollution Control Agency.

Metzler, Dwight F. 1956. Recommended Action Against Effects of Severe Droughts in Kansas. *Journal of American Water Works Association* 48.

Metzler, Dwight et al. 1958. Emergency Use of Reclaimed Water for Potable Supply at Chanute, Kansas. *Journal of American Water Works Association* 50.

Meyer, Adolph F. 1942. *Evaporation from Lakes and Reservoirs.* St. Paul, Minnesota: Minnesota Resources Commission.

Miller, E. F. 1972. Desalting As a Source of Water Supply. *Journal of American Water Works Association* 64, (12).

Mitchell, A.; Dodge, B. H.; Kruzic, P.; Miller, D. C.; Schwartz, P.; and Suta, B. E. 1975. *Handbook of Forecasting Techniques.* Fort Belvoir, Virginia: U.S. Army Institute for Water Resources.

National Academy of Sciences 1968. *Water and Choice in the Colorado River Basin*. Washington, D.C., Publication 1689.

National Science Foundation 1968. *Weather Modification*. 10th Annual Report, NSF 69-18.

Neiberger, M. 1969. "Artificial Modification of Clouds and Precipitation." World Meteorological Organization, Technical Note no. 105, W.M.O. no. 149, TP 137.

O'Riordan, T., and More, Rosemary J. 1969. "Choice in Water Use." In *Water, Earth and Man*. Edited by R. J. Chorley. London: Methuen & Co. Ltd.

Phillip, William II 1974. The Direct Reuse of Reclaimed Wastewater: Pros, Cons and Alternatives. *Journal of American Water Works Association* 66.

Rayner, Frank 1974. *Ogallala Aquifer Water-Level Data, With Interpretation 1956–1974*. Lubbock, Texas: High Plains Underground Water Conservation District No. 1, June.

Riordan, Courtney 1971. Multistage Marginal Cost Model of Investment-Pricing Decisions: Application to Urban Water Supply Treatment Facilities. *Water Resources Research* 7, (3).

Russell, C.; Arey, D.; and Kates, R. 1970. *Drought and Water Supply*. Baltimore: The Johns Hopkins Press.

Safe Drinking Water Act 1974. 93rd Congress, S. 433 and H.R. 1059.

Seagraves, James A. 1973. "Industrial Waste Charges." In *Journal of the Environmental Engineering Division*, ASCE, Proceedings, Paper 10203, December, pp. 873–81.

Seidel, H. G., and Baumann, E. R. 1957. A Statistical Analysis of Water Works Data for 1955. *Journal of American Water Works Association* 49.

Sewell, W. R. D. 1971. Environmental Perception of Engineers and Public Health Officials. *Environment and Behavior* 3, March.

Sewell, W. R. D., and Little, B. 1972. Specialists, Laymen, and the Process of Environmental Appraisal. *Regional Studies* 6.

Sewell, W. R. D., and Roueche, Leonard 1974. Peak Load Pricing and Urban Water Management: Victoria, B.C., A Case Study. *Natural Resources Journal* 14, (3).

Sherwani, J. K. 1964. "Urban and Industrial Water Supply: Prospects and Possibilities." *Proceedings of Annual Meeting of American Water Resources Association*.

Simmons, John 1966. Economic Significance of Unaccounted-for Water. *Journal of American Water Works Association* 43.

Simon, Herbert A. 1957. *Administrative Behavior*. New York: The Free Press.

Sims, John H., and Baumann, Duane D. 1974. Renovated Waste Water: The Question of Public Acceptance. *Water Resources Research* 10, (4).

Southern Water Conservation District, n.d. Pueblo, Colorado: Brochure no. 7.

Stander, G. J. 1969. Water Reclamation in Windhoek. *Scientiae* 10.

State of California 1974. *The California Water Plan: Outlook in 1974*. The Resources Agency, Bulletin 160-74.

Symposium 1955. Eastern Water Shortage and Drought Problems. *Journal of American Water Works Association* 47.

Taubenfeld, H. 1967. Weather Modification and Control: Some International Legal Implications. *California Law Review* 55.

Turnovsky, Stephen 1969. The Demand for Water: Some Empirical Evidence on Consumers' Response to a Commodity Uncertain in Supply. *Water Resources Research* 5, (2).

U.S. Federal Water Resources Council 1968. *The Nation's Water Resources.* Washington, D.C.: U.S. Government Printing Office.

U.S. National Water Commission 1973. *Water Policies for the Future.* Washington, D.C.: U.S. Government Printing Office.

U.S. Office of Water Resources and Technology 1974. *Water Reuse—A Bibliography.* Washington, D.C.: Water Resources Information Center.

U.S. Public Health Service 1962. *Drinking Water Standards.* Washington, D.C.: U.S. Government Printing Office.

U.S. Public Health Service 1970. *Community Water Supply Study.* Washington, D.C.: U.S. Public Health Service.

Weinberg, A. 1967. *Reflections on Big Science.* Cambridge: MIT Press.

Weisbecker, Leo W. 1974. *Snowpack, Cloud-Seeding, and the Colorado River.* University of Oklahoma Press.

White, G. F. 1970. *Strategies of American Water Management.* Ann Arbor: The University of Michigan Press.

————. 1973. "Public Opinion in Planning Water Development." In *Environmental Quality and Water Development.* Edited by C. Goldman; J. McEvoy III; and P. Richardson. San Francisco: W. H. Freeman and Co.

White, Gilbert F., and Haas, J. Eugene 1975. *Assessment of Research on Natural Hazards.* Cambridge: MIT Press.

Whitford, Peter W. 1972. Residential Water Demand Forecasting. *Water Resources Research* 8, (4).

Wolff, Linaweaver, and Geyer 1966. *Commercial Water Use.* Baltimore: The Johns Hopkins University.

Wollman, N., and Bonen, G. W. 1971. *The Outlook for Water.* Baltimore: The Johns Hopkins Press.

Wong, S. T.; Schaeffer, J. R.; and Gotaas, H. 1963. *Multivariate Statistical Analysis of Metropolitan Water Supplies.* Chicago: Northeastern Illinois Area Planning Commission.

PART TWO

Current Issues

THE CONTEXT OF
WATER PLANNING

The political and legal context in which planning is conducted inevitably determines not only the quality of a plan but also whether it can be implemented. Both the long lead times necessary for water-resource project development and growing worries over the effects on the environment and human health that may be associated with water have created pressures to improve the planning process. Nonetheless, considerable confusion exists about how this is to be done, and this confusion is reflected in recent federal legislation. Planning for water quality is now virtually mandated by federal statutes which, however, fail to provide an effective mechanism for accomplishing it.

Perhaps the most serious barrier to adequate water resource planning in the United States is the decentralization of authority. The existence of many small governmental units, each with significant planning powers, is clearly an integral part of the American political tradition, as is, for that matter, a general distrust of "planning." However, some sort of planning will take place, and the problem of developing a context in which that planning can be conducted properly is the subject of the following papers by Warren Hall and by Dan Okun. Both authors conclude that regionalization is crucial to effective water resource management.

Hall emphasizes the historical development of water management institutions in this country and describes how conflicts over natural-resource issues have been resolved in the past. After assessing the consequences of alternative approaches to water management, he finds that voluntary regional integration is the most desirable solution. He concludes with a brief discussion of how such integration can be achieved within the American political framework.

The short selection by Okun is directed toward the difficulties of achieving current water quality standards. He believes that the tens of thousands of small water companies across the country cannot hope to acquire the technical facilities or the trained personnel to do so, and there is consequently no alternative to regional water management. He goes on to describe the successful experience of Great Britain in achieving complete regionalization of the management of that country's water resources over a period of three decades.

REGIONAL INTEGRATION FOR EFFECTIVE WATER RESOURCE MANAGEMENT

WARREN A. HALL,
Elwood Mead Professor of Engineering
Colorado State University

Some years ago Garrett Hardin (1968) described a phenomenon which he called "the tragedy of the commons." He was talking about the inevitable deterioration or destruction of resources held not by individuals but as common property. The situation can be described as one in which the optimal policy for the total system is in direct conflict with the sum of the optimal policies of the individual decision makers concerned. Economists characterize such systems as having externalities (benefits and costs to others) which dominate over internalities (benefit and costs to self).

The classical "tragedy of the commons" is the common pasture. There is an optimal grazing rate for land (the number of animals per unit area) which returns the greatest sustained total benefit to the users. However, each individual has the right to determine the number of animals he will graze on the community land. If he puts only a few of his animals on the land he reduces his share of the benefits. Thus his "self-optimal" decision is to maximize his own interest by placing as many animals on the pasture as he can. However, when each individual employs "optimal strategy," the net result is overgrazing and the eventual destruction of the productive capacity of the pasture.

Overgrazing is but one among many such "tragedies" that can be cited in recent history. The exploitation of oil fields, such as the fabulous Signal Hill strike near Long Beach, California, in the early decades of this century, provides another example. At Signal Hill the overlying lands were subdivided into thousands of city lots, each owned by a different individual. To get one's share it was essential to get a well down fast and pump like hell, even though everyone knew that by doing so a smaller fraction of the total resource could be recovered then by a cooperative effort.

Since World War II, the development of groundwater in the Texas High Plains has followed a similar pattern, and provides yet another recent example of the tragedy of the commons. In fact, most groundwater development today typifies this situation. The only difference is the time scale in which degradation or depletion will occur.

59

On a national scale, the management of both the quantity and quality of our water resources is deeply involved with the tragedy of the commons, and this has occurred despite an almost incomprehensibly large commitment for funding of a "solution." In the case of water resources, the problem concerns both "putting in" and "taking out," but the fundamental principles are the same. In the case of surface water quality, the costly, well-intentioned actions of some individuals can be essentially negated by the more economically pragmatic actions of others on a stream or lake. My cleaning up my own waste discharges at high cost does not assure that my water quality objectives can be met or the situation even improved. If I mix a glass of pristine pure distilled water with a glass of filthy, polluted, undrinkable water I get two glasses of filthy, polluted, undrinkable water, regardless of how much I have spent to obtain the glass of pure water. Thus, the quantity and quality aspects of the resource are inseparable and both are inherently tragedies of the commons.

Only three types of mechanisms have yet been devised as effective solutions to such problems. These are (1) the "fence" approach—dividing the common property and distributing it among individuals; (2) the "thou shalt not" approach—a governmental "police-power" regulation of the actions of the individuals affecting the commons; and (3) the "can do" approach—the creation of an institutional "individual," an *authority*, to manage the resource system for the best interests of all concerned.

Very few community problems can be cured by the "fence" approach. Historically, one of the most important successes was the management of rangelands in the West. Only the invention of barbed wire at a time when steel was at a very low cost allowed its introduction to the western United States in time to avoid serious overgrazing. Even today this approach is not an economically feasible solution for most of the underdeveloped world's community pastures.

Although the second and third mechanisms appear very similar, there is an important distinction. The "thou shalt not" approach uses the police power of the government to specify exactly what each individual must not and/or cannot do. It is reasonably effective when costs of insuring compliance are minimal and when no significant economies of scale can be obtained by joint action on a problem. The "can do" approach, on the other hand, creates a governmental authority which accepts the responsibility for insuring that the common goals are equitably attained. It differs from the second mechanism in that it is positively oriented.

Each approach has its place in solving the problem of managing a common resource. Our objective here is to review some of the advantages and disadvantages of each approach and then to comment on some of the possible reasons why none of the approaches has yet been successfully applied to water quality management at the national level—even though these same approaches have proved very effective for some water quantity problems in the West. We will also consider some of the possible reasons why these approaches have not been effective for the joint management of water quantity and water quality.

The remarks I will make have a strict analogy to all other problems of urban resource management. The concept of a municipal water supply usually involves the "can do" approach to the problem of providing water for households, although in most instances it falls short of a true regional approach. Irrigation districts in the West are other examples of quasigovernmental institutions designed to manage the water supply resource to the economic advantage of all concerned.

In the history of the development of "can do" water supply institutions, particularly in the arid West, one can note a curious combination of conflict and cooperation (Hardin 1968). In virtually every case in which a community water supply problem was involved, conflict was the early dominating factor. Whether we are talking about six-guns at a water hole or California v. Arizona, the conflict seemed to be inevitable. It was always bitter, always costly, and usually violent. Yet, sooner or later, in virtually every instance, the water supply problems of all concerned were resolved by cooperative community action. The benefits of such action were usually far greater than could have been possible had each party resolved its own problems by itself, even if there were no scarcity of resource. Also, in virtually every case, the ultimate equitable solution through joint "can do" action not only would have been reached by reasonable men bargaining in good faith but usually had been proposed early in the game and rejected by all concerned.

Let us look at some of these established systems and the history of their development in order to identify the essential factors involved (Nadeau 1950). In the 1920s the "Owens Valley War" in southern California bankrupted the valley and ultimately cost the city of Los Angeles more than three times the original price of the engineering system for water supply. It also cost 387 lives. The dispute was finally settled on a basis much less satisfactory to all parties concerned than that proposed by Mr. William Mulholland well before the beginning of violence. During the war, the valley residents demanded that the city "buy us *all* out or leave us alone," including business properties in the valley as well as the ranches with water rights. After the valley was no longer in a position to demand anything, the city of Los Angeles did precisely that, paying the peak prices of ten years earlier instead of the 1933 depression prices which prevailed. Why weren't these reasonable and rational actions taken earlier?

The most obvious reason these actions were not taken—a reason that emerges from a review of the positions of the day—was a complete lack of mutual trust and respect. This one deficiency is probably the most important single factor responsible for the failure of people faced by a common problem to move to a "can do" solution *before* outsiders, disgusted with the fighting and bickering, impose a "thou shalt not" regulatory system policed by outsiders and generally insensitive to the totality of objectives of the region concerned.

There are a great many examples of conflicts which have led to the "thou shalt not" sort of solution. Labor–management relations are an instance in which the parties concerned may find themselves unable to reach a "can do" mutual agreement. As a result, federal authority has applied a solution consisting of a number of "thou shalt nots" to both sides and set up outsiders to enforce the regulations. In fact, virtually all such solutions to the "commons" problems have been imposed by a legislative authority considerably broader and more remote from the parties involved than should be necessary. Such solutions inject an undesirable amount of external control (and sometimes abuse) into the situation, and the objectives of the regulators are often not at all in harmony with the objectives of those being regulated.

Even more significant is the fact that in the U.S., "thou shalt not" authority has generally been imposed *only* when it became clear that a "can do" action could not be implemented by the parties concerned. Labor and management were allowed nearly 100 years to establish a suitable self-governing system before their rights to do so were suspended step-by-step by federal legislation (Phelps 1955).

There have been some suggestions for applying "the fence" approach to the water-quality management problem. Some economists have urged that the costs of pollution be transferred back to those releasing the discharges into the streams by means of "effluent charges." Presumably, if these charges were set equal to or higher than the cost of treatment, the pollution problem would be internalized to the firm, municipality, or other unit discharging the offending wastes. The idea has considerable theoretical merit, but has not been endorsed with any enthusiasm by either dischargers or legislative bodies. One possible reason for this is that an effluent charge implies that a right to pollute can be purchased. If any firm or city elects to pay the charge rather than treat the water, the quality objective is not attained.

Presumably, this problem could be prevented by raising the charge. The only question is, how much is necessary? Unfortunately, the charge is an *annual* cost, while the treatment system is primarily a long-term investment cost. The tradeoff point between these two noncommensurate dollar values will vary widely among polluters, depending on age of the plant, prospects for moving to new sites, current and future prospects for profit, available investment capital, and so forth. Some companies might prefer to pay the charges for a decade or more, even if they are nominally more expensive, rather than accept the financial risk of a large capital investment or of a disastrous effect on their credit caused by excessive bonding levels. The latter consideration is a particularly important problem for cities.

In order to make the charge system force *all* operators to provide treatment systems at adequate levels, the charge would have to be based on the "break-even" decision of the most reluctant operator. However, a charge set at this level is equivalent to a fine, and thus we are essentially facing the "thou shalt not" option. Furthermore, in this context a system of fines has some advantages. It eliminates, for instance, the need for precise daily measurement of residual effluent loads and the detailed economic and physical analysis required to establish rates.

From my point of view, the "can do" approach—that is, regional management through agreement of all parties concerned—offers some distinct advantages for everyone involved in water resources management. What are some of these advantages?

Probably the most important advantage is that this approach leaves the policy and decision-making power in the hands of those concerned with and affected by the water problem. This may sound somewhat contradictory, since these same people must transfer some of their present local authority to the regional management institution. However, one cannot expect the consequences of the "do nothing" approach to be a continuation of the status quo. If local authorities prove unable to manage responsibly the total water resource system with which they interact, then a higher level of authority, such as the federal government, will inevitably step in and dictate policies and actions to the local people whether they like it or not. Furthermore, because of the federal government's limited authority, its "dictation" must conform to the legal principles of equity— that is, all persons must be treated equally under the law. This in turn means that the standards of performance of *all* local entities must be set at the level which is required for mitigating the worst situation. This is an expensive overkill.

The only possible exception to this result might be for the federal government to go into the waste treatment and water supply business and, in effect, become the regional authority. This does not appear likely in the current political environment.

In any case, the responsibility and authority for establishing such things as water quality performance standards and the enforcement of those standards under current law must pass from local entities to a higher level of government *unless* these local entities can "agree to agree" on a community plan of action that will permit unified self-management of the water quality of the water resource. The question is not really a case of giving up local authority and control. Rather it is one of preventing the inevitably exercise of higher, non-local authority inherent in the powers of higher, more remote, and less responsive governments. There is absolutely no question of the federal authority to step in and mandate action. However, the current law specifically provides for and indeed encourages local acceptance of the responsibility for regional management and authorizes the intervention of the federal government *only if* that responsibility is not accepted.

What are some other advantages of the "can do" approach? Perhaps the second most important is that it permits water quantity and quality management at satisfactory levels at minimum cost. This does not mean that all supplies come from one source or that all wastes are collected and treated at one central location. Rather it means that the institutional authority created can be given the responsibility to assure the best overall management of the resource and to accomplish all *necessary* treatment at such levels, by such means and at such locations as may be most efficient in terms of costs. Furthermore, it can assure that every dollar expended for water quality will produce a measurable improvement in the water quality of the stream. There are simply not enough investment dollars, nor is there adequate engineering and construction capability, to permit a one-shot cleanup of any major stream and/or lake system. Despite expenditure of billions of federal and local dollars on waste treatment systems, there has been very little measurable improvement in stream-system water quality. This is largely because these expenditures to date have been haphazard and uncoordinated.

The "water quality plans" required by the law contain, more often than not, little more than lists of cities willing to start construction (with a federal grant) rather than a real plan. In effect, a major tax burden for interest and principal has been imposed on many well-intentioned cities, with little or no observable water quality benefits for anyone, except perhaps as a clean discharge may produce a clean conscience.

Regionalization of the management problem can result in major economies of scale. However, without a regional authority no one unit has the expertise, the funds, or the incentive to identify and evaluate these economies. Under regionalization, optimal advantage can be taken of the assimilative capacity of the natural system. In certain circumstances, instream treatment systems can also be very effective, but they are very unlikely to be evaluated, let alone implemented, under a fragmented system or a "thou shalt not" regulatory approach to quality management. The West has already fully documented the efficiency and effectiveness of regional solutions to water supply problems for the mutual benefit of all concerned.

The third most important factor should perhaps have been mentioned first. Indeed, it seems almost too obvious to be mentioned at all. Unfortunately, it doesn't seem to rank very high on the list of priorities of any of the agencies concerned. Simply stated, the objective of water quality management is the management of water quality. I apologize for the apparent redundancy, but we all seem to miss the forest for the trees. The obvious purpose of all water quality laws and regulations is to achieve the maximum level of water quality control that can be obtained under the limitations of cost and technical capability. This fundamental purpose seems to have been replaced by the objective of administering the regulatory system.

Requiring an industry to install a tertiary treatment system when at the same time a city is discharging primary treatment sewage a few miles upstream does not constitute water quality management. Often it contributes absolutely nothing toward achieving the water quality objectives for that stream. Yet, as attested by hundreds of cases, when we utilize the regulatory approach, the relative political and economic strengths of various dischargers of wastes have often resulted in precisely such situations.

This is not to assert that effective expenditures which actually improve the level of utility or aesthetic quality of streams have not been made. Rather, it is to point out that under the present regulatory approach to water quality control such results are quite fortuitous. They are more likely to be the happy-chance result that might be occasionally expected from any random policy of "muddling through," than the result of a rational management system. One cannot single out the worst problems for priority action and still maintain the required equality before law.

The final advantage of the regional approach is that, once water quality and quantity gains are accomplished, an institutional authority has the responsibility of maintaining those gains as conditions change in the future. A regulatory approach is not only a heavily inertial system with corresponding inflexibility and unresponsiveness to changing needs—but, more importantly, it contains the seeds of the inevitable "gamesmanship" that has accompanied most attempts at social regulation of economically important matters, including water quality laws, tax laws, and so forth. Thus we can be sure that loopholes will be found in whatever laws are passed. These loopholes will be managed for the economic benefit of a few and at the cost of defeating the water resource management objectives. This has occurred with every water quality law to date and there is no reason to believe that it will not continue.

There are of course negative factors to the regional approach. In order to create an authority for action, authority must be factually transferred from those who now possess it to the new entity. This transfer carries a concept analogous to that of mass balance in physics: if one grants such authority it is not retained; if it is retained it is not granted. The total authority is the sum of the parts.

Virtually everyone has a basic reluctance to surrender any authority which affects or might affect him directly. Persons presently holding delegated authority can be expected to be even more reluctant to pass some of it along to others. Thus we can expect that the process of granting authority will seldom be painless. This reluctance is exacerbated considerably by a lack of mutual trust and understanding that almost always exists between semisovereign entities such as two cities or two states. For example, when the proposal was announced to create a Potomac River Basin Commission with authority to restore and maintain water quality on this river and its estuary, there appeared a number of editorials in local newspapers to the effect that "we aren't going to let those people on the other side of the river (downstream, upstream, pick your enemy) tell us what we're going to do." This was the reaction despite editorials and comments in the same newspapers blasting the failure to produce satisfactory water quality conditions for the river.

Until and unless mutual distrust and suspicion can be overcome it will be difficult to achieve a "can do" resolution of either water quality or water quantity problems. Yet we can expect that in the absence of a "can do" agreement, all concerned can be assured that ultimately a "thou shalt not" solution will be imposed. Thus persons whom they know and trust even less than their upstream or downstream enemies will be telling them what they are going to do. It seems that even the ability to control one's own destiny is a "tragedy of the commons" problem for our communities.

Were the establishment of trust and understanding sufficient to solve problems, I could stop my dissertation. However, it is not. Lack of trust is not a fabrication of the mind; it is based on hard evidence. The saying "give him a inch and he'll take a mile" and the story of the camel inching into the tent are proverbial but based on long-standing experience. Regional authorities, however large or small, have a habit of using that authority to its limit—if not beyond. Thus a fundamental problem which must be resolved before the creation of a regional water-resource management authority is the precise definition, in a strict legal sense, of the necessary and sufficient authority to be transferred and the establishment of the limits thereof.

When individuals or groups of individuals determine that individual action can no longer suffice and a community action must be taken, before they can "agree to act" they must first pass through the process of "agreeing to agree." Usually the "agreement to agree" takes the form of a charter, a constitution, a set by bylaws, and so forth, containing (1) the scope of matters to which the "agreement to agree" shall apply, and (2) the definition of what shall constitute "agreement" with respect to any of those matters. Normally, there is a mechanism for amendment and ratification. The amendment process usually requires considerable consensus. Ratification is generally based on acceptance by enough parties to allow the charter to accomplish its objectives. This could be anything from 100 percent ratification, as in an interstate compact, to the minimum number of members necessary to take effective joint action (as was the case in the founding of most of our professional societies).

Most important to the process is recognition that once the defined authority has been transferred, it cannot be rescinded by individual action. The United States Constitution was a transfer of authority from the sovereign states to that institution known as the United States. In legal terms, the Civil War was really fought over the issue of the right to rescind that action rather than over the institution of slavery. The Union simply could not admit the existence of such a right, and hope to survive. Neither can a regional authority hope to accomplish its mandate if individuals and groups of individuals which grant it authority retain a right to secession at their own discretion.

Thus we see that regionalization of our water management problems must involve a sequence of four steps:

1. Identification of region which needs self-created community action. It must be carefully delineated and physically capable of unitization.

2. Development of the rationale for agreement. Before people can "agree to agree," there must be a clear-cut set of reasons why it is necessary to take this step.

3. Drafting of a charter as a candidate document for the agreement to agree. The charter should describe the scope of the agreement and the definition of what shall constitute agreement. The authority transferred must be obviously necessary in order to accomplish the range of objectives related to the scope. At the same time this authority must be carefully defined and limited in order to obtain the consent of the parties involved.

4. The above steps must be combined with such moral persuasion as can be generated in order to overcome the mutual distrust and suspicion that will inevitably exist among the parties concerned.

History is saturated with accounts of communities that bitterly maintained their local enmities until all the antagonists were subjugated by third parties. Thus there is no assurance that a clear-cut demonstration of the desirability of regionalization will be sufficient to allay distrust, fears, and jealousies that stand in the way of creating effective regional authorities. In most instances strong local leadership will be required to transform existing fragmented loyalties into a common regional loyalty in which local conflicts are subordinated to common needs.

REFERENCES

Hall, W. A. 1964. *Proceedings, Western Interstate Water Conference* (preface). University of California Water Resources Center.
Hardin, Garrett 1968. "The Tragedy of the Commons." *Science* 162.
Nadeau, R. A. 1950. *The Water Seekers.* Garden City, N.Y.: Doubleday and Company.
Phelps, O. W. 1955. *Introduction to Labor Economics.* McGraw-Hill.

FRAGMENTATION OF THE
WATER INDUSTRY IN THE U. S.

DANIEL A. OKUN,
Kenan Professor of Environmental Engineering
University of North Carolina at Chapel Hill

A municipal water supply should be esthetically pleasing and free from contaminants that might threaten the public health, and be continuously available in sufficient quantity and at adequate pressure. Unfortunately, the Safe Drinking Water Act of 1974 (SDWA) PL 93–523, does not address itself to one of the major problems facing those responsible for providing a municipal water service of high quality. That problem is that under existing institutional arrangements, the fragmentation of the water industry precludes sound management of the tens of thousands of small municipal systems that constitute the bulk of the water supply systems in the United States.

The 1970 Public Health Service (PHS) Community Water Supply Study (U. S. Environmental Protection Agency 1970) confirmed an opinion previously held by many water experts—that a large number of water supply systems were not meeting the PHS Drinking Water Standards, mainly because of their small size. In 1963, some 20,000 water supply systems were identified, half of them serving fewer than 1,000 persons. Prior to passage of SDWA, only those systems serving interstate carriers came under federal surveillance. With passage of SDWA, which placed all public water supplies under federal jurisdiction, the Environmental Protection Agency (EPA) attempted to determine the number of systems for which it bears responsibility. The first EPA estimate in 1975 of 37,000 was soon raised to 40,000; and now the EPA estimates that about 50,000 community water supply systems in the U.S. serve about 175 million people. This is an average of only about 3,500 persons per system; more than half the systems serve fewer than 1,000 persons.

The SDWA brings under federal purview, through the aegis of state programs in cases where the states are granted primacy, an additional 200,000 systems serving the public at highway rest stops, camps, and the like. If, as has been well demonstrated, surveillance cannot readily be provided to small community water supply systems, and in fact they cannot even be accurately counted, what is the likelihood of their being adequately monitored?

The elegant theories for balancing supply and demand and the innovative pricing schemes that have been suggested by many economists should be extremely valuable to the larger water systems; but how useful are they likely to be to the 99 percent of the systems serving almost half the U.S. population reached by public systems? These small systems serve fewer than 50,000 persons each, and they do not now have, or are they soon likely to be able to afford, the necessary professional staff for efficient planning, management, and financing. Nor can they afford to use many of the tools now becoming available to help provide a high-quality water service.

Contributing to the difficulty in solving these problems are the approximately 50,000 public sewerage and wastewater disposal agencies, only a few of which are combined with the water supply services. The need to plan for wastewater collection and disposal on a regional basis has been recognized in the Federal Water Pollution Control Act Amendments of 1972, PL 92–500; but, at best, implementation has faltered, and no incentive is provided for combining water supply and wastewater disposal operations. If wastewater reuse is to be a viable option in meeting increasing demands for water in the future, and I believe that wastewater is a resource, then joint enterprise between water supply and wastewater disposal agencies is essential.

Considerable attention has been given to regionalization in the water industry in the United States, and some notable examples have demonstrated the benefits of yielding local political sovereignty in the interest of better and more economical service. For instance, the Metropolitan Water District in California manages regional water supply, and the Metropolitan Sanitary District of Greater Chicago manages wastewater treatment and disposal. Yet even among these successful efforts toward regionalization there are few examples of joint management of water supply and wastewater disposal.

Despite all that has been written about the proliferation and fragmentation of local government services, and despite strong advocacy for regional approaches, very little has been accomplished in overcoming local parochialism. I pursue this subject because I see no hope of addressing the water problems of most of the people of the United States without regionalization, and because I have seen successful regionalization, in a setting little different from ours, which provides the inspiration to persist. In this context, it should be clear that a regional service does not necessarily require the physical interconnection of systems that are widely scattered, but rather their common management.

In 1945 in England and Wales, some 1,200 systems served 40 million people. The Water Act of 1945, initiated during World War II, called for massive regionalization or regrouping of water supply systems throughout the country. One objective was the agglomeration of systems in order to achieve a minimum of population of about 150,000 persons per system. This was believed to be a population large enough to support for each system a qualified clerk, or manager, an engineer and a chemist (Okun

1967, pp. 153–54). By 1974 the number of separate systems had been reduced to 187, serving 50 million people, with more than 99 percent of the total population being served from public systems.

The success of these regionally managed water supply systems, I am convinced, made it possible for the ultimate regionalization to be undertaken. Under the Water Act of 1973 (Okun 1975, pp. 918–23), ten water authorities were created for the entire country.[1] Each authority was based on hydrologic boundaries and assumed responsibility within those boundaries for the planning, design, construction, operation, finance, and ownership of facilities for:

— Water resources development, including dams, reservoirs, ground water supplies, transmission mains, treatment plants, and distribution systems

— Provision of sewerage and treatment of wastewaters and their disposal

— Restoration and maintenance of the quality of the nation's waters

— The use of waters for recreation and the enhancement of amenity values

— Flood prevention and land drainage

— Fisheries and navigation in inland waters.

With complete ownership of all water-related facilities in a basin, the water authorities can optimize their investments. They can locate intakes and outfalls most advantageously with no concern for political boundaries. If, for example, a particular contaminant such as nitrates needs to be reduced in concentration, rather than requiring a uniform effluent standard for all outfalls, the removal facilities might be located at only one or two critical sites, thus minimizing the overall cost. Another important advantage is that not only can basin models be created, but the solutions they suggest can be implemented!

Without any national subsidy for water services, each consumer receives a bill that covers the costs for all his water services. Thus, the water authority can be expected to weigh very carefully each investment which will need to be paid for by its customers. The kind of wastefulness inherent in investments under PL 92–500, where the federal government pays for 75 percent of construction costs, is unlikely.

One concern with the creation of the water authorities was the fear that

1. The studies of the reorganization of water management in England and Wales were sponsored by the Rockefeller Foundation and the RANN program of the National Science Foundation.

their distance from the consumer would make them less responsive than local governments had been. Originally it had been proposed that the water authorities be directed by appointed specialists in the field of water management. As a compromise, to balance technical and managerial competence against local accountability, each water authority is made up of both appointed and locally elected members. By law the latter must constitute a majority.

After less than three years of existence, it is clear that the water authorities have been a success. They have dealt effectively with the most severe drought to hit England and Wales since records were initiated in 1727. It is extremely doubtful that the fragmented and conflicting water management system which formerly prevailed could have accomplished this. Furthermore, the water authorities have proved able to cope with the serious economic perturbations now facing the nation.

While it is not to be expected that we in the U.S. can or should emulate the regionalization effort of the British, we can learn from their experiences in preparing and implementing this revolutionary legislation. The British recognized early that the serious economic and technical problems associated with balancing supply and demand cannot be solved without first paying attention to the institutional context of water management.

In the U.S. the adoption of many proposals for planning and management is severely constrained by archaic institutional arrangements for managing municipal water supply, particularly the fragmentation into many small systems. Many of these are barely viable and in no position to explore options that would provide better service at lower cost. An early order of business, therefore, is an examination of methods available for the stimulation of regionalization of water management and the integration of the management of water supply with wastewater collection and disposal. A conference dealing with institutional alternatives for municipal water management might well be in order.

REFERENCES

Baumann, D. et al. 1976. *Planning Alternatives for Municipal Water Systems*. Indianapolis: Holcomb Research Institute, Butler University.

Okun, Daniel A. 1975. Water Management in England: A Regional Model. *Environmental Science and Technology* 9, October.

———. 1967. Regrouping of Water Supplies in the United Kingdom. *Public Works* 98, 206, June.

U.S. Environmental Protection Agency 1970. *Community Water Supply Study*.

PLANNING METHODOLOGY: MODELING AND FORECASTING

In an important sense, rapid advances in technology can be viewed as the cause of most current urban water problems. The construction of large-scale water diversions, the accelerated growth of metropolitan areas, the ever-rising per capita consumption of water, and the introduction of thousands of chemicals into our waterways are all the results of growing technology. On the other hand, the powerful new analytical tools associated with technological development can be utilized to solve the problems that technology creates.

The solution of water problems is requiring a growing share of society's economic resources. Partly because of the vast expenditures involved in the construction of waterworks and partly because of the extremely long planning horizon for such projects, the efficient allocation of economic resources has assumed new importance. Two important analytical tools directly relevant to this allocation are computer modeling and demand forecasting; these are treated respectively in the following papers by Jerome Milliman and John Boland.

Milliman begins by reemphasizing the need for regional institutions for water management. He points out, however, that regionalization alone will not solve problems. Management at a regional scale will require sophisticated new techniques. He notes that even those regions which have succeeded in creating the necessary political structure for effective management have failed to utilize new techniques associated with economic analysis, and he expresses serious doubts about the efficacy of much current regional water planning. He concludes by describing the elements of a regional econometric model which he believes can provide the basis for sound management.

Boland presents a careful discussion of the many factors related to forecasting urban water demand. He follows a review of the inadequacies of past approaches with a summary of recent developments in forecasting and of the conditions under which various techniques ought to be applied. He surveys the range of current research and concludes with a description of a research project he is now conducting in the Washington, D.C., area.

PLANNING FOR METROPOLITAN
WATER RESOURCE DEVELOPMENT

JEROME W. MILLIMAN,
Department of Economics
University of Florida at Gainesville

We all know that federal and state water agencies are rapidly developing plans for major water basins and other regions. At the same time, relatively little effort has been directed toward the formulation of comprehensive water plans to guide the development of metropolitan regions or major urban areas. There is, however, growing recognition of inadequate current planning at this scale.

The objectives of this paper are three-fold:

1. To point to the growing need for regional planning of water resource development for metropolitan areas.

2. To analyze some of the deficiencies in present metropolitan water resource planning.

3. To suggest some approaches for making this planning more meaningful and effective.

Clearly, many metropolitan water systems now in operation were planned in bits and pieces—for limited subregions and for partial subsystems. Therefore, it is important to consider how this planning might be improved by a systems approach which integrates multiple water resources, demographic, and economic variables into a metropolitan regional framework.

THE PRESENT SITUATION

An important prerequisite to effective metropolitan water resources planning is the creation of an adequate metropolitan and regional structure to conduct this planning. In recent years, the need for such a structure has become apparent, as reflected in a report by the American Society of Civil Engineers (1968):

Urban water resources planning and supporting research are at levels well below those for river basins and large regional complexes. Deliberate and systematic study of urban water problems from an overall point of view has long been neglected (p. 1).

In 1973, the National Water Commission highlighted the concern:

Regionalization of water supply systems appears inevitable and the process will be accelerated by the need to resolve environmental as well as economic problems—problems that are dealt with most effectively at the regional level (p. 454).

The National Water Commission also recognized (1973) that the practice of having federal–state agencies do the planning for river basins may create conflicts unless metropolitan interests are adequately represented:

Many metropolitan areas extend into more than one State's jurisdiction. The State government and the metropolitan area are sometimes political and economic rivals. Faced with choices, State representatives to basin planning bodies will tend to give priority to statewide interests. It will, therefore, not always be adequate to rely upon State representatives to define and defend the interests of the metropolitan area where competitive choices are being made on a regional level. Whatever body may be empowered to make allocations of regional water supply, it is important that metropolitan areas be given a more direct voice than they have at present in the regional water planning process (p. 455).

Recently, the push to regionalize water-resource planning for urban areas has been accelerated by the requirements of the Federal Water Pollution Control Act of 1972, PL 92–500. Sections 201 and 208 contain provisions for the planning of area-wide wastewater and water quality programs for metropolitan areas. However, it is possible that this legislation may actually hinder efficient regional water-resource management if there is a separation of planning for water quality from planning for water supply. In addition, the emphasis placed by this act on "end-of-the-pipe" treatment programs may be a poor approach to the attainment of regional water quality. Finally, without some metropolitan structure for coordination of water planning, the coming of a multitude of federal–state grant programs for water plans and facilities for specific purposes can be an invitation to waste and chaos.

I believe that considerable lip service has been paid to the need for regional water resource management in the United States, but very little has been done to promote the development of institutional arrangements that will allow for efficient water management. This point of view has been continuously presented by Allen Kneese (1975) for at least a decade.

> Virtually nothing has been done to create permanent regional agencies for continuous water quality management. If anything, our national policy has in practice hindered the construction of regional institutions. If one could realistically foresee the development of institutions capable of efficiently implementing the full range of technologies (including point discharge and nonpoint discharge), anticipated costs of water quality improvement could be greatly affected (p. 190).

Thus, although I see a real need for metropolitan planning for water resources, it is clear that an adequate institutional framework will not in itself be sufficient. Closely related to the issue of the adequacy of institutional arrangements are questions of whether the planning will be carefully done, using both qualified personnel and the best techniques available. It has long been a basic article of faith in regional planning that planned development will be superior to unplanned development—that is to say, we often assume that the planning will be "wise." This assumption may not be justified.

At least two other major problems may impede adequate planning for water resources in metropolitan regions. First, our ability to forecast the future is limited. Therefore, our confidence in planning for the future will depend upon our ability to make forecasts with reasonable accuracy, or to provide sufficient flexibility in our plans to deal with a range of possible outcomes. This is an important point, and I will return to it later.

Second, it is usually assumed that the development of plans and area-wide programs for water supply and water quality will be carried out using the best information, procedures, and personnel. Too often this is not the case. Most of us know of plans now being formulated by regional water agencies and consulting firms using untrained personnel, outmoded techniques, limited budgets, and short deadlines.

Environmental impact statements provide an excellent example of this latter phenomenon. The general quality of much current environmental impact analysis is poor. Attempts to define the socioeconomic impacts of regional water-quality plans have hardly progressed beyond a laundry list of primary impacts. Projections of demographic and economic activity for metropolitan areas are often no more than linear extrapolations of historical trends. As confusion abounds, the size of impact statements and the bulkiness of plans increase. Many planning documents now resemble large encyclopedias which catalogue a wide variety of facts and often obscure the real tradeoffs between alternative choices.

I fear that efforts to develop plans without proper personnel, budgets, and techniques could lead to waste and possibly harm.

CHANGING METROPOLITAN GROWTH TRENDS

Three current demographic trends in the United States should strongly influence water resource planning. These are the decentralization within metropolitan areas, the national shift of population toward the South, and the decrease in the overall growth rate of the population in general. The fact that these trends were not predicted serves to highlight some of the inadequacies of forecasting. Furthermore, the fact that these trends have now been documented does not necessarily offer any assurance that they have been incorporated into water resource plans. Nonetheless, the trends have important implications for the planning process, and they deserve individual attention.

Decentralization within metropolitan areas has been a major aspect of population movement in the United States, particularly over the past two decades. Although at the beginning of the century central cities were growing at a spectacular rate, since 1920 the suburbs have grown faster than the central cities. Between 1960 and 1970 the suburban population grew 27 percent while the population of central cities increased only about 6 percent. Currently, 75 percent of the U.S. population live in metropolitan areas, and over 50 percent live not in central cities but in suburbs.

Most of the largest central cities are in fact experiencing a decline in population. In 1960, 21 U.S. cities had populations over 500,000. By 1970, 15 of these had lost population. For example, Cleveland's population declined by 14 percent, even though its suburbs grew by 27 percent; St. Louis lost 17 percent of its inhabitants while the surrounding suburbs grew by 29 percent. In recent years, the most rapid growth rate in the U.S. has been experienced by communities of 25,000 to 100,000 located on the fringes of large cities.

A second major aspect of population settlement affecting metropolitan planning for water resources has been the recent surge of urban growth in the "Sunbelt" regions. Since 1970, the states in the South and Southwest have grown six times as fast as those in the Great Lakes region and ten times as fast as the combined Middle Atlantic and New England states.

In 1974 the Bureau of Economic Analysis of the U.S. Department of Commerce published projections (1972 Obers Projections 1974) for the U.S. Water Resources Council for 1980, 1990, and 2020. These projections were based on 1972 data and included figures for population, personal income, and employment for each of the 50 states. By the end of 1975, nine states—Arkansas, Louisiana, Mississippi, South Carolina, Arizona, Texas, Utah, Alaska, and Hawaii—had already exceeded their 1980 projections, and New Mexico had gone above the 1990 forecast. By the same token, the shortfall in slower growing regions has been large. For example, New York State was projected to grow by 1.1 million people from 1970 to 1980. By the end of 1975, it was estimated that the state had lost 100,000 people.

These changing growth trends are notable in themselves; but even more important is the fact that they were not anticipated by the Bureau of Economic Analysis, whose inaccurate projections have been used by many water planning agencies. It can be pointed out that these population movements have an influence far beyond the estimation of future water demands. They may also reflect regional changes in economic growth, migration of jobs, and shifts in regional incomes. Many of these movements, once under way, create multiplier effects and self-sustaining economic momentum. Related to these economic flows are the changing fortunes of local governments in terms of tax base, tax revenues, and the ability to support adequate levels of public services.

A third aspect of urban population growth is related to trends in the United States as a whole. The growth rate of the U.S. population has decreased sharply since 1957. In that year, the growth rate was estimated to be 1.7 percent per year, which implied a doubling of the U.S. population every 40 years. By 1973, the population growth rate had declined to 0.72 percent per year; and recently the total fertility rate has dropped below 2.1 births per female, which is the rate necessary for the U.S. population to reproduce itself, assuming no net immigration. This does not mean that zero population growth for the U.S. will be achieved immediately. For several generations the population will continue to increase because of the present large number of females of childbearing age. However, if the fertility rate remains at its present level. the total U.S. population will grow at a diminishing rate for about 70 years before reaching zero growth. On the assumption that the fertility rate will remain at present levels, the census bureau has revised sharply downward its projections for U.S. population for the years 2000 and 2020.

The upshot of this declining rate of U.S. population growth is that urban planners now perceive that the need for new cities and new urban development will be much less than was envisioned only a few years ago. Although we can never be sure that underlying factors affecting growth rates will remain stable, it now appears that urban growth in the U.S. will result chiefly from shifts in population within and between regions rather than from an overall population increase. This factor makes it extremely important to employ the best available techniques in forecasting regional demographic and economic trends.

Planning for metropolitan water resource development must also reflect these changing growth trends. I suspect that much of the water resource planning for existing metropolitan areas—planning done only a few years ago—is in need of reassessment because it was based upon population and economic growth projections which are now outdated. Moreover, when pricing policies for urban water supply and wastewater systems begin to reflect actual water scarcities and rising construction and energy costs, there may be a leveling-off in water use per capita and per unit of output because of the pressure to cut down on the wasteful water use, so long a feature of growing metropolitan regions. Such a leveling-off has rarely been contemplated.

PRESSING METROPOLITAN WATER MANAGEMENT PROBLEMS[1]

Three basic water utility services must be provided in metropolitan areas: water supply, wastewater collection and treatment, and stormwater disposal. In addition, water planners are increasingly being asked to help augment facilities for water-based recreation and to help improve the general quality of the urban environment. It is well recognized that the provision of urban water services involves investment expenditures of large capital, long lead times in planning and construction, and heavy fixed costs. Furthermore, much construction must be undertaken well in advance of the market because of the need for large plans to take advantage of economies of scale and the need for coordination of policies across service areas and coordination of various services within service areas. Clearly, pricing, investment, and management policies for water resources can affect the form, location, and amount of urban growth. Thus, decisions about water resources development play a pivotal role in long-term regional planning.

This is a rather formidable set of responsibilities, and metropolitan water planners and water managers encounter many obstacles in attempting to carry them out. The National Water Commission (1973, p. 442) has identified some of the most serious problems in metropolitan water management. I shall mention them only briefly, but it should be remembered that planning from a regional point of view can only set the framework for

1. For an extended discusison, see National Water Commission 1973. *Water Policies for the Future*, chap. 12, and American Society of Civil Engineers 1968, *Urban Water Resources Research*.

dealing with these problems. It is doubtful that they can ever be truly solved.

According to the National Water Commission, the most frequent water management problems are:

1. Inadequate or unnecessarily costly service because too many different water agencies operate within the same metropolitan area.

2. Poor integration of water supply, wastewater treatment, and [storm] drainage services with each other and with planning for the use and occupancy of land.

3. Insufficient attention to the nonutility aspects of providing metropolitan water services—including neglect of recreational, esthetic, and environmental values.

4. Inadequate data, particularly on current water management practices in metropolitan areas.

5. Inability to finance future water needs of metropolitan areas.

6. Inadequate institutions for managing metropolitan water services and for determining and representing metropolitan viewpoints in federal, state, regional and multistate water resource management.

7. Water pollution, a substantial portion of which comes from nonpoint-sources outside current pollution control programs, particularly in growing communities.

8. The encroachment of urbanization upon watersheds and the resulting deterioration of the quality of water supplies.

Each of these metropolitan water management problems is worthy of extended analysis, but I suspect that number 6, the deficiencies in current institutional arrangements for management of metropolitan water resources, is the most critical of the problems identified. It should be made clear, however, that there is no common solution for proper institutional arrangements which can be applied to all of the diverse regional situations. Metropolitan areas will demonstrate wide differences in size, hydrology, political arrangements, climate, and economic and social structures. Each metropolitan area must therefore fashion the particular institutional and organizational arrangements suitable for its own situation. It is clear that federal authorities must not only be sensitive to the need for metropolitan planning, but must also recognize that new planning arrangements must preserve accountability to the regional electorate.

DEFICIENCIES IN METROPOLITAN WATER POLICY ANALYSIS

With the growing awareness of the need for metropolitan water resource planning have come efforts to implement more broadly based approaches. However, there are not many examples of joint administration of water, wastewater, and storm water services for an entire metropolitan area. Philadelphia is one of the few cities that has combined these three services into a single department and supported them through service charges (Committee for Water and Wastewater Operations 1971). Planning for joint regional water supply or for joint wastewater systems is being carried out in a number of major metropolitan areas including Seattle, Dallas–Ft. Worth, Boston, Denver, and Houston.

Many states are developing statewide water-use plans and regional supply plans. For instance, New York State has, at a cost of $4.4 million (Bumstead 1976), completed 61 comprehensive public water supply studies to develop area-wide master plans for water supply. The U.S. Army Corps of Engineers is continuing the massive Northeastern United States Water Supply Study (NEWS). The scale of such studies is impressive, but I believe that much of the planning work falls short of its goals through failure to use the best techniques and properly trained personnel.

In particular, I am concerned that the economic input in current water-use and regional supply plans may not be as strong as we might hope or expect. For example, I know of a major state which has some of the best legislation on the books for developing statewide and regional planning for water resources. This legislation recognizes the need to relate water planning to land-use planning, to combine management of ground and surface waters, to provide adequate protection of the environment, and so on. Yet, the planning actually being conducted leaves a great deal to be desired in terms of economic analysis. Only one of the five major water districts in that state even employs a person trained in economics, and there is not a single trained water economist at the state level. In several major metropolitan areas of the state the economic impact analysis required for the granting of water permits is being carried out without competent economic consultation. Some of the water planning studies in the state are being performed under contract by major consulting firms whose qualifications are questionable. As far as I can judge, their strengths in economic analysis are greatly inferior to their technical expertise in physical sciences and engineering. I believe that my observations concerning this particular state are probably also applicable to others across the country.

Perhaps the best-known comprehensive plan for water supply in the U.S. is the Northeastern United States Water Supply Study being conducted by the U.S. Army Corps of Engineers. This project was initiated as a response to the drought of 1961–67, which reduced historic yields in the Northeast by approximately 30 percent (Russell, Arey, and Kates 1970). Five metropolitan regions are being examined by the Corps: Boston, Providence, the New Jersey–New York City–Connecticut complex, Baltimore–Washington, D.C., and the York–Harrisburg–Lancaster area of Pennsylvania.

To date, the NEWS study has accumulated a massive data base. It is claimed that a methodology has been developed both for total impact assessment and for evaluation of potential systems and projects (Schilling 1976). To my knowledge neither the methodology for impact assessment nor the methodology for evaluation of potential systems and projects has been given careful outside review by water resource analysts and regional economists. I am very skeptical that the framework developed produces water use projections as part of an overall regional growth model. Moreover, I suspect that possible feedbacks of water resource costs upon water use projections were not considered.

Preliminary reports on the NEWS study state that the projected demands for many problem areas for 1980 exceed the present system capabilities. Yet, I strongly suspect that these projected demands were developed independently of prices and costs of present and expected water supplies and wastewater treatment. That is to say, I suspect that the Corps has used the outmoded requirements approach for the development of demand projections for metropolitan water services and thus has neglected the need to take price elasticities of the demand for water and wastewater services into account. It is not correct to assume that the burden of heavy costs for metropolitan water supply augmentation and additional wastewater treatment facilities will not influence future use projections and metropolitan growth patterns. Even to this day the installation of metering devices in New York City, which might save approximately 125 mgd, is a controversial issue which apparently is no further toward resolution than in 1960 when Hirschleifer, DeHaven, and Milliman (1960) documented the need to make better use of existing water supplies for New York City by sensible price policies.

My point here is not just that pricing and investment policies for metropolitan water services must be more rational and that wasteful water use should be discouraged. I am also emphasizing that metropolitan growth analysis and future projections of population, employment, and incomes must be done concurrently with metropolitan water-resource planning. The widespread practice today is to separate the two activities. Metropolitan water-resource planners are given projections of future water demands that are developed independently of water-resource cost constraints. These water planners then view their task as one of minimizing the costs of augmenting the water services that will be required; and these requirements are, in turn, based upon growth projections which may also be suspect.

Effective water resource planning cannot be done in isolation. Demographic and economic growth projections for metropolitan regions should not be made independently of costs of supplying water services; and by the same token, water resource planners should not operate outside the framework of analysis of regional growth trends. Metropolitan planning can be better served by regional policy analysis which integrates demographic, economic, and water resource sectors in a systematic framework. It is ironic that many regional water agencies have developed highly sophisticated computer models for simulation of the water resources sector alone, yet have made very little use of the capabilities of computer simulation to incorporate the economic, demographic, and water resources sectors in a common system or framework.

In short, I believe that the greatest difficulties in metropolitan water resource planning arise from the failure to employ well-trained economic analysts and the failure to use the best economic techniques.

More specifically, in regard to methodology, two major weaknesses in the planning process can be identified. First, in the typical plan, water use is projected as a need, or requirement, independent of water supply constraints. The implicit assumption is that water supplies are unlimited or costless. This means not only that the demand projections are suspect but also that inadequate consideration is given to the economics of reallocating existing supplies or to reduction in use. Conservation in use and possible reallocation among uses should be explicitly considered in conjunction with the alternatives of new development and supply augmentation. New development cannot be justified on economic grounds unless incremental (marginal) values in use are equalized among competing uses and are sufficient to justify the incremental costs of the new investment. Demand projections for metropolitan water services have generally failed to do this.

Second, current regional economic projections for metropolitan areas often employ noncausal techniques such as trend extrapolation or shift–share analysis. These techniques cannot replicate cyclical behavior and are not useful for policy analysis because they do not contain behavioral parameters. The problem is not just that current trends may not hold in the future. The point is that all three sectors—the demographic, the economic, and the water resource sectors—are interdependent. Policy analysis cannot be either one-dimensional or linear. Clearly, economic policies have water resource effects, environmental effects, and demographic effects; demographic changes have economic effects and water

resource effects; and water resource policies have economic and demographic effects. What is needed is an analytic system for relating the
demographic, economic, and water resource sectors to each other in
order to assess systematically many alternative assumptions and policies
for the future in a multidimensional framework.

COMPUTER MODELS IN WATER RESOURCE PLANNING

There is a growing interest on the part of both government and business in the use of computer models to increase the understanding of
socioeconomic systems at the metropolitan level. This understanding is
essential to efficient planning decisions. Increasing evidence indicates
that regional demographic and economic behavior can be systematically
explained and simulated. I want to suggest that planning for water resource development for metropolitan regions can be improved by the use
of regional-policy computer simulation models.

A conjunction of events now has made it possible to build regional
econometric models for projections of population, employment, and income on a metropolitan basis. The potential usefulness of such models has
been apparent for some time. However, the capability to construct such
models on a sound conceptual and empirical basis has developed only
recently. Two factors are responsible for this capability. First, substantial
progress has been made in obtaining intercensual data on the distribution
of employment and incomes by detailed SIC (Standard Industrial
Classification) industries for metropolitan areas. Without these data the
requirements for a regional econometric model could not be met.

The second factor has been the development of regional modeling itself
in the last decade. In 1971, Milliman's review of large-scale regional
forecasting models concluded that the state-of-the-art had advanced significantly from the pioneering New York regional study to the Susquehanna River Basin simulation model, which integrated demographic,
employment, and water sectors for eight major subregions in the Susquehanna River basin (Milliman 1971). Glickman's review of small-area
econometric models (1972) showed that the field had come of age. No
longer are urban and regional economists confined to the simple, community economic-base framework as popularized by Tiebout (1962). It
is also clear that econometric models provide a flexible alternative to the
expensive data requirements of regional input–output models as
exemplified by Hirsch's 1959 St. Louis input–output model (Hirsch 1973)
and Isard's Philadelphia input–output model (1967).

Regional econometric model building is now possible at reasonable cost in terms of the required data, the computer programs, and the regional economic theory. The time is right to construct such models for metropolitan water resource planning.

SPECIFICATION OF A REGIONAL ECONOMETRIC
MODEL FOR METROPOLITAN WATER PLANNING

I would like to outline in nontechnical terms the framework of a general regional econometric model which could be used for forecasting and for policy simulation in planning metropolitan water services. To my knowledge no such model exists at the present time. However, the objectives could be accomplished through the modification or extension of existing regional models. One of these is the Susquehanna River Basin simulation model (1969), which for the first time combined demographic, economic, and water resource sectors within a single model (Hamilton et al. 1969). Most other regional water-planning models have either modeled the water resource with the economic factors being generated outside the model, as in the Lehigh Basin simulation (Hufschmidt and Fiering 1966), or modeled the economy with the water resources assumed to have no constraints, as in the Ohio River Basin study (Arthur D. Little 1964).

A metropolitan water-planning model would have at least three sectors: demographic, economic, and water resources. As figure 1 illustrates, the demographic and economic sectors should be tied together by feedback loops which include population, labor force, unemployment rate, regional income, and migration variables. In addition, each of these sectors is tied to the water resource sector so that changes in the level and composition of economic activity and in the size and composition of population affect the demand for water resources. In turn, the effect of changes in the supply, costs, and quality of water resources feed back into the demographic sector. Thus, changes in the supply or demand for water at critical locations could change effective prices of water, and costs of pollution control might alter the amount and location of industrial and population growth.

The economic sector provides forecasts of employment and income for perhaps 60 industry groups. These groups can be divided into three categories. First are the externally-oriented industries, which serve markets external to the area, are subject to external demand forces, and have the ability to compete in national markets. Second are the locally-oriented ancillary businesses which serve industries in the export sector. In the third category are the locally-oriented industries which provide all types of goods and services to the resident population.

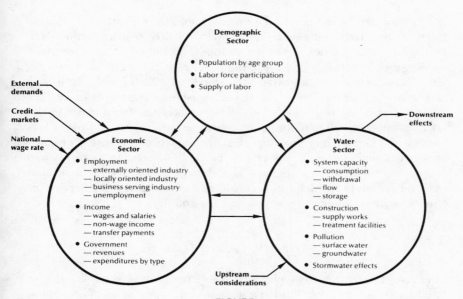

FIGURE 1
ELEMENTS AND LINKAGES FOR
A METROPOLITAN WATER RESOURCES MODEL

Income is generated from three sources. The first source is income from wages and salaries, which depend upon wage rates and local employment levels. The second source is nonwage income in the form of rents, intercepts, and dividends. The third source is transfer incomes, which represent social security payments and other government income transfers.

The demographic sector includes population, perhaps initially disaggregated into four age groups with separate equations for births, deaths, migration, and labor force participation for each age group. Disaggregation by age groups is important because economic and environmental factors affect the groups differently; and, in turn, different age groups make different demands upon the water resource and economic sectors. For example, low levels of economic activity may repel working-age people while they might attract retirement-age people looking for a high level of environmental amenities. Differing population trends thus affect the labor force and the employment sector, and the demands for water resources.

One essential feature of the water sector involves the ability to simulate potential effects of constructing projects such as dams, reservoirs, and wastewater treatment plants. The model could thus illustrate (1) the effects of alternative augmentation or water quality policies upon water quantities and qualities at various locations; (2) the effects of alternative pricing and investment policies in the water resource sector on economic activity and population; and (3) possible feedback effects from water-based recreation activity or environmental enhancement upon the economy.

In my opinion, responsible federal water agencies could make an important contribution to metropolitan water resource planning by sponsoring the development of prototype regional models of this sort in order to make detailed midterm and long-term studies of water demands and supplies for metropolitan regions. The ultimate goal would be to develop several prototypes which can be made operational and cost-effective for numerous metropolitan regions across the country.

CAUTIONS FOR THE FUTURE

Because of the size and complexity of the systems involved in planning for metropolitan water policy, I have suggested the application of econometric computer simulation. I believe that the application of simulation methodology is particularly well suited to bridging the gap between planning and prediction. Regional econometric forecasting models have come of age. It is time that they be applied to metropolitan water service planning.

However, here are some cautions that should be observed.

1. There will be a continuing need to monitor individual regional modeling efforts. Criticism by outside observers is always a healthy experience for all planning exercises. It is even more important when the complexities of computer simulation are involved.

2. In the past many of the regional planning efforts involving large-scale models have concentrated on the initial model building effort. In most cases, the report, the model, and the projections were turned over to the sponsor and the model-building teams were disbanded or shifted to new tasks. Virtually no funds were set aside for verifying projections or for rerunning the model with new data to see how the model could be improved or revised. This is not just a matter of needing to provide revised sets of projections for planning agencies under alternative assumptions and changing conditions. A major rationale for keeping complex computer models operative is internal model validation. Model builders need to become familiar with the dynamic properties of their own models. Proper policy would require continuing funding

for model validation and revisions as well as provision for periodic outside consultation and review.

3. Models should not be too big. I think it a far wiser strategy to build less expensive models that can be updated and extended rather than embark upon a massive attempt to construct an extremely sophisticated model that may be too expensive to use on a continuing basis.

In conclusion, I suspect it is fair to say that the adoption of improved planning techniques such as modeling and the employment of more highly trained personnel, both of which are needed to improve metropolitan water planning, will not be achieved unless the institutional arrangements for decision making are altered. It is necessary to provide the proper incentive structures if various public agencies are to adopt new techniques and policies. Perhaps the search for dramatic improvements will always prove somewhat frustrating until these institutional incentives and arrangements are changed.

REFERENCES

American Society of Civil Engineers 1968. *Urban Water Resources Research*. Sponsored by Office of Water Resources Research, New York City, September.

Arthur D. Little, Inc. 1964. *Projective Economic Study of the Ohio River Basin*. Prepared for U.S. Army Corps of Engineers. Washington, D.C.: U.S. Government Printing Office.

Bumstead, J. 1976. "Comprehensive Water-Supply Study for New York State." *Journal American Water Works Association* 68, January.

Committee for Water and Wastewater Operations 1971. "Joint Administration of Water/Wastewater Works." *Journal of American Water Works Association* 68, April.

Glickman, N. 1972. "Son of the Specification of Regional Econometric Models." *Papers and Proceedings of the Regional Science Association* 28.

Hamilton, H. et al. 1969. *Systems Simulation for Regional Analysis: An Application to River Basin Planning*. Cambridge, Massachusetts: M.I.T. Press.

Hirsch, W. 1973. *Urban Economic Analysis*. New York: McGraw Hill.

Hirschleifer, J.; DeHaven, J.; and Milliman, J. 1960. *Water Supply: Economics, Technology and Policy*. Chicago: University of Chicago Press.

Hufschmidt, M., and Fiering, M. 1966. *Simulation Techniques for the Design of Water Resources System*. Cambridge, Massachusetts: Harvard University Press.

Isard, W. 1967. *Philadelphia Region Input–Output Study*. Working Papers, vols. 1 and 2. Philadelphia: Regional Science Research Institute, March.

Kneese, A. 1975. "Costs of Water Quality Improvement, Transfer Functions, and Public Policy." In *Cost–Benefit Analysis and Water Pollution Policy*, edited by H. Peskin and E. Seskin. Washington, D.C.: The Urban Institute.

Milliman, J. 1971. "Large-Scale Models for Forecasting Regional Economic Activity: A Survey." In *Essays in Regional Economics*, edited by J. Kain and J. Meyer. Cambridge, Massachusetts: Harvard University Press.

National Water Commission 1973. *Water Policies for the Future*. Port Washington, N.Y.: Water Information Center.

1972 Obers Projections of Economic Activity in the U.S. Volume 4 States, 1974. Washington, D.C.: Bureau of Economic Analysis, U.S. Department of Commerce and Economic Research Service, U.S. Department of Agriculture for U.S. Water Resources Council, April.

Russell, C.; Arey, D.; and Kates, R. 1970. *Drought and Water Supply: Implications for the Massachusetts Experience for Municipal Planning*. Baltimore: The Johns Hopkins Press.

Schilling, K. 1976. "Water Supply for the Greater New York Metropolitan Area." *Journal American Water Works Association* 68, January.

Tiebout, C. 1962. *The Community Economic Base Study*. New York: The Committee for Economic Development.

FORECASTING THE DEMAND FOR
URBAN WATER

JOHN J. BOLAND,
Department of Geography and
Environmental Engineering
The Johns Hopkins University

The water industry—the public supply of potable water and removal of wastewater—is, in terms of capital investment, the second largest industry in the United States. Comprehensive data are difficult to find but those available suggest that the water industry invests at least $5 billion per year in new facilities, more than 80 percent of which is funded locally.[1] This sum is exceeded only by the electric utility industry, which spends some $15 billion per year on new plants,[2] and compares to the total new investment by *all* private sector industry, which is of the order of $100 billion per year.[3]

Furthermore, the service provided by the water industry is one of critical importance. Without minimizing the importance of other public utility services such as electric energy or communications, it is safe to say that the standard of life and health to which we are accustomed would be unattainable in the absence of properly functioning systems for the supply of water and the removal of waterborne waste. The water industry, then, is both relatively large and essential; it follows that issues which are important to the water industry are important to the nation as well. One issue which is demonstrably important to the water industry, and therefore to the nation, is the subject of this paper: the problem of forecasting future demands for water and wastewater services.

The emphasis universally accorded to the forecasting problem reflects not so much the absolute size of contemplated investments, but the in-

1. The National Commission on Water Quality (NCWQ 1975) reported 1974 total sewer system contract awards at $3.2 billion; water supply investments make up the balance. Federal cash outlays in 1974 are reported by the commission (NCWQ 1975, p. III-47) at $605 million. Federal grant commitments associated with reported contract awards were not available on a consistent basis, nor were state outlays or commitments. The 80 percent local funding estimate reflects recent, not future, funding patterns. The federal share can be expected to grow to nearly 50 percent under current legislation.

2. The Edison Electric Institute (1974) gives new investment for the industry at $14.9 billion for 1973.

3. The Council of Economic Advisors (1974) reports total business expenditures for new plant and equipment at $98.7 billion in 1973.

herent capital intensiveness of the industry. Water services are available only as a result of large investments in fixed plant—source works, treatment works, transmission lines, distribution systems, and so forth—investments which are frequently committed many years in advance of the resulting services. Investments may precede the demands which induce them by five, ten, fifteen, or even twenty years. The facilities themselves, once built, may have useful service lives of 25, 50, 75, or more years.

These circumstances affect the type of forecasts required by the water industry. All properly managed industrial activities require reliable short-term forecasting—ranging from one month to several years in time coverage—so as to facilitate the orderly and efficient allocation and scheduling of resources. The water industry is no exception in this regard. What is unique, however, is the requirement for reliable long-range forecasting covering periods ranging from several years to several generations. As much as 50 percent or more of the operating budget of a water or wastewater utility may be allocated to servicing debt incurred as a direct consequence of long-range forecasts. It is clear the the reliability of such forecasts is a matter of serious concern, and it is this concern which I address here.

The topics discussed in this paper apply generally to long-range forecasts of the various measures of water and wastewater services rendered in urban areas. Of these measures, three can be singled out for comment, although the analysis remains relevant to other measures not specifically mentioned. Three important measures of service are:

1. Average day water use, also expressed as annual water use

2. Maximum day water use

3. Average day contribution to wastewater flow.

Average day water use is the most common expression of the magnitude of the water services provided, and may be relevant to the design of certain source works, such as large impoundments. Maximum day water use is the measure most closely related to water supply system capacity; it determines the design of many types of source works, major transmission lines, and most treatment works.

Similarly, major wastewater interceptors, treatment works, and outfall works tend to employ a forecast of maximum day wastewater flow as a basis of design. This measure is the sum of two components: the net inflow to the sewer system from ground water infiltration, connected storm water inlets, and other nonsanitary sewage sources; and the contributions by water users. The former component tends to vary widely in magnitude among various sewer systems, and to fluctuate with weather and season. Suitable techniques for forecasting this component are not likely to be of general applicability, and such techniques are not discussed in this paper. The second component of sewer flow, contributions by water users, is amenable to systematic forecasting approaches, and is discussed.

In order to place this review of long-range forecasting techniques for these measures of water and wastewater service into a proper context, I first briefly review certain past and present approaches to this problem. Included in the review are several advanced approaches not yet in wide use by the industry. Against this background I attempt to clarify the nature of the problem, and suggest criteria by which candidate forecasting techniques can be judged. Finally, I review the state of knowledge of the nature of water and wastewater services, and describe how this knowledge is currently being used to develop improved forecasts for a portion of the Washington metropolitan region, and indicate what results might be expected from such efforts.

PAST APPROACHES TO FORECASTING

A recent article in a British journal (Herrington 1976, pp. 67–84) reviewed water use forecasting methods in use in Great Britain and elsewhere, organizing techniques into four categories:

1. Judgment methods, where future water use is simply predicted, based on the experience and opinion of the individual making the prediction

2. Survey methods, where the opinions of various individuals are sought, including, perhaps, those of selected major water users

3. Extrapolations, which are further divided into unsophisticated extrapolations—graphical extensions of historical data—and sophisticated extrapolations—including trend and regression analysis

4. Analytical methods, which are based on causal-type models of water use and require prediction of both explanatory variables and of model coefficients.

Herrington notes that judgment methods are now "irrelevant to the industry's needs," relying as they do on the intuition and subjective observations of one or more individuals. He also suggests that survey methods are primarily "useful in establishing forecasts for important water-using industries." In his survey (1970) of forecasting methodology in major U.S. cities, Gilbert White described practices in only a few cities which suggest the use of judgment or survey techniques. It can be assumed that these approaches are widely considered inadequate and obsolete.

If there is a "standard" technique for forecasting water use in the United States, it is the practice of extrapolating per capita usage observations. Most utilities observe average day water use and service area population, producing a historical record of average day use in terms of gallons per capita per day. Maximum day use is characterized by calculating maximum/average day ratios, while average day contributions to wastewater flow have largely gone unnoticed. The methods employed to extrapolate, or forecast, these measures typically fall into the category Herrington has classified as "unsophisticated."

Because per capita methods ignore all influences on water use save one—service area population—and in particular because they exclude consideration of the economic factors of water price and user income, they are often termed "requirements" methods. They imply that the chosen per capita use level is a fixed requirement exerted by each individual, unresponsive to changes in other, especially economic, factors. This philosophy often carries over into the closely allied process of supply facility planning, where the water use forecast may be taken as an absolute requirement for future supply capacity, to be met regardless of cost.

Still, the per capita approach has much to recommend it. For one thing, it is clearly the simplest, quickest, and least expensive forecasting method which still retains any degree of credibility. Fair, Geyer, and Okun (1966) point out that historical per capita figures "generalize the experience" of a water utility and that they "are useful in comparing the records of different communities. . . ." They possess as well a certain rudimentary logic: water use is assumed to be perfectly correlated with population, and it is evident that it is people who use water. Once we accept this reasoning, forecasting future water use becomes a matter of extrapolating population, extrapolating per capita use, then calculating the product of the two factors.

However, the results of this simple process have scarcely been encouraging. Per capita use has displayed considerable variation, both over time and among various communities at the same time. Clemens Herschel, the inventor of the Venturi tube, calculated the per capita water use in Imperial Rome at 38 gallons per capita per day (gpcd) in A.D. 97 (Herschel 1973). Linaweaver, Geyer, and Wolff (1966) summarized other observations of per capita use prior to this century, reporting levels for Paris ranging from 0.25 gpcd in 1550 to 65 gpcd in 1890.

An early attempt to apply the per capita approach to forecasting average day wastewater contributions is the effort of the sewerage commission of the city of Baltimore (1897). The commission observed that per capita water use in Baltimore had been rising, and had reached a level of 95 gpcd by 1895. It expressed concern over the fact that water use in a nearby city, Philadelphia, had risen from 72 gpcd in 1885 to 162 gpcd only ten years later. At about that time, the noted water supply pioneer Allen Hazen studied the Philadelphia situation on behalf of the Woman's Health Protective Association of Philadelphia, and concluded that elimination of wasteful use would restore per capita usage to the vicinity of 100 gpcd (Hazen 1897). On the basis of this rather unsatisfying historical record, the Baltimore group decided to plan a municipal sewerage system on the assumption of sewer flows equal to 150 gpcd. Water use in Baltimore today is on the order of 175 gpcd, but average contributions to sewer flow may be as little as 130 gpcd.

Time and economic development have not dampened fluctuations of this type. National averages of per capita use are reported to have risen from 90 gpcd in 1900 to 140 gpcd in 1954 (Symons 1954, pp. 222–26). The 861 utilities which responded to the 1965 AWWA survey (AWWA, n.d.) averaged 156 gpcd use, while the 768 utilities which responded to the 1970 survey reported an average of 189 gpcd. In the latter survey, water use for individual utilities ranged from 31 gpcd to 552 gpcd. Fifteen percent of all utilities reported per capita use less than 100 gpcd, and seven percent reported use in excess of 300 gpcd. In contrast to the generally upward trend in per capita use seen throughout the early decades of this century, some utilities are beginning to experience level or declining per capita use, especially since 1970 (Patterson 1976, p. 6).

Altogether, per capita methods lead to long-range forecasts of the crudest sort. They rely on a suitable historical record for the community in question, since very little consistency can be observed among various utilities. They deal with only one of the many possible explanatory factors, population; per capita forecasts contain the implicit assumption that all other factors will continue to act on water use exactly as they have done in the past, or will change in exactly the same manner as in the past. Where these assumptions cannot be reasonably granted, per capita forecasts are likely to be significantly, even seriously, in error. Although most applications of the per capita approach are concerned with average day water use forecasts, estimates of maximum day water use and average day wastewater contribution based on this method would clearly suffer the same disabilities.

IMPROVED FORECASTING APPROACHES

Increased scarcity of high quality water sources and rising real costs of supply have directed considerable attention to forecasting techniques, especially since 1960. More recently, a greatly expanded federal water pollution control program has highlighted inadequacies in existing methods of forecasting wastewater flows. As a result of these and other stimuli, a number of forecasting approaches have been proposed which represent significant improvements over the time-honored per capita technique. I describe here two such approaches, in order to illustrate the range of innovation already attempted.

Perhaps the most fully operational forecasting technique which departs significantly from historical approaches is the MAIN II system developed by Hittman Associates, Inc. (1969). This forecasting system is, in turn, based on earlier work at The Johns Hopkins University, at Hittman Associates, and by other investigators. The basic feature of MAIN II is the disaggregation of water users, which forms the basic structure of the underlying model. This disaggregation reflects the obvious fact that different classes of water users make use of water for different purposes, and therefore respond to different stimuli. The MAIN 2 system divides urban water users into residential, commercial–institutional, industrial, and public use classes.

Each use class is further disaggregated for purposes of actual use forecasting. The residential class is separated into those user groups with and without water meters, and into those with and without public sewers. Commercial, institutional, industrial, and public users are categorized by the nature of their activity, with up to 280 different categories available. A mixture of forecasting techniques is employed: some classes are forecast by means of analytical models containing a number of explanatory factors including economic variables; others are estimated by means of more simplistic requirements models. For example, industrial water use is treated on a per employe basis, while residential water use is estimated by means of the demand models developed from the Johns Hopkins residential water use study and reported by Howe and Linaweaver (1967).

The various parameters, variables, and coefficients which must be projected to produce a water use forecast are subject to three alternate forecasting techniques: (1) they may be predicted individually by any method and the forecast values provided; (2) they may be extrapolated from an historic time series; or (3) they may be forecast by means of an analytic model. All water use calculations, including the last two forecasting calculations, are performed by a computer program. The results of the computer calculations include forecasts of average day, maximum day, and peak hour water use. Simple modifications to the system would result in forecasts of average day wastewater contributions as well.

The MAIN 2 system has been employed a number of times to forecast water use in various urban areas. By their very nature, forecasts are difficult to evaluate in a quantitative sense, and, to the author's knowledge, no attempt has yet been made to critique the forecasts developed using the MAIN 2 approach. During the development of the model, however, the approach was used to "backcast" water use for several communities, that is, to estimate the water use based on known values of explanatory variables, but without using historical water use data. These "backcasts" are summarized in table 1, taken from an earlier discussion of

Table 1

APPLICATION EXPERIENCE WITH MAIN 2 SYSTEM

Location	Actual Demand (mgd)	MAIN 2 Estimate (mgd)
Baltimore, Maryland (1963 data)		
Residential	97.3	95.2
Public-Commercial	19.6	19.2
Industrial	42.0	45.1
TOTAL	158.9	159.5
Park Forest, Illinois (1959 data)		
Residential	1.68	1.49
Commercial	0.15	0.15
Park Forest, Illinois (1961 data)		
Residential	1.70	1.58
Park Forest, Illinois (1962 data)		
Commercial	0.18	0.15
Park Forest, Illinois (1963 data)		
Residential	1.72	1.58
Commercial	0.19	0.17
Park Forest, Illinois (1965 data)		
Residential	1.91	1.75
Commercial	0.21	0.19
Park Forest, Illinois (1967 data)		
Residential	1.91	1.84
Commercial	0.21	0.20
Baton Rouge, Louisiana (1965 data)		
Residential	n/a†	14.0
Commercial	n/a	5.20
Public & Unaccounted	n/a	4.36
TOTAL	23.8	23.6
Kings Heights District Anne Arundel County, Maryland (1968 data)		
Residential & Commercial	0.31	0.32

†n/a = not available.

Source: Boland 1971.

this model (Boland 1971, pp. 295–316). The MAIN 2 system was quite successful in estimating water use in communities having widely different characteristics and per capita use histories; errors on aggregate use range from 0.4 percent to 10.4 percent.

After the development of MAIN 2, a different but equally interesting approach to forecasting methodology was taken by Peter W. Whitford (1972, pp. 829–39). His analysis was confined to residential water use and incorporated an analytical model of water use, with principal explanatory variables explicitly included. Whitford's contribution, however, is his direct treatment of the inherent uncertainty surrounding the future behavior of any of the explanatory variables, ranging from population to weather.

A system of alternate futures, or scenarios, is employed with accompanying estimates of the probabilities of occurrence of each of the constituent assumptions. Water use is calculated for each alternate future, and the calculations, when combined with their associated probabilities, produce an estimated probability distribution of future water use, rather than a point estimate. Such a result is a significant step away from the older methods, which generate a single estimate but do not provide information as to the relative likelihood that actual water use will fall within a given amount above or below the forecast level.

These and other methods, whether based on extrapolative or analytical techniques, seek to remedy the deficiencies of the much simpler per capita approach by introducing additional factors known to affect water use. In this way it is hoped that variations between communities as well as changes over time can be explained; the more complete the explanation, the more reliable the resulting forecast. All such methods, however, are inevitably orders of magnitude more complex, time-consuming, and expensive than the familiar per capita method. The required level of effort is not unreasonable when weighed against the importance of the problem, although the resulting forecasts must still justify their cost in terms of proven improvements in reliability. It may be too early to make this judgment, even as the search for still better methods continues.

A CRITERION FOR SELECTION OF A FORECASTING METHOD

It is self-evident that significant improvements in forecasting reliability will be made only at the expense of increased complexity and cost. The advanced techniques proposed thus far require observation and analysis of trends in many factors, and some techniques impose the further requirement of analyzing changes in water use coefficients. Housing type, population per household, irrigable area, family income, water price, and price structure: these are only a few of the factors which have been used to explain residential water use. Consideration of other categories of use adds many more factors to the list. Elasticities of water use with respect to these factors must not only be understood for the current time period but also be predicted for future time periods.

Since the range of available techniques is likely to continue expanding, some means must be available to permit the selection of the particular technique appropriate to a given forecasting problem. Requirements differ, and the use of an excessively sophisticated technique in a given application is not only wasteful but may prove confusing as well. The proper criterion for selecting techniques is readily determined in principle, if not yet in practice. It requires only that the results of an inaccurate forecast be considered:

1. A forecast which proves too high, and which results in unused supply capacity, creates overinvestment.

2. A forecast which proves too low, and which results in insufficient capacity being provided, leads to inadequate service or to water shortages.

The optimal forecasting technique is the one which strikes the balance between these two possible outcomes and which is, in some sense, the best compromise.

While such considerations apply to all three measures of water service discussed in this paper, experience has shown these considerations particularly relevant to forecasts of maximum day water use. It is for this type of forecast that investment decisions are most closely tied to forecast results, and that the possibility of a complete supply failure is most closely correlated with underinvestment. Past practice within the industry suggests that overinvestment has been considered preferable to supply failure, and most forecasts of maximum day water use have overstated future use levels. Actually, such behavior has probably been appropriate, given the unknown but large uncertainty associated with past forecasting techniques and the lack of information as to the impact of supply shortage. Ordinary prudence would dictate making every attempt at reduction in the probability of occurrence of events whose consequences are unknown, that is, incorporating generous "safety margins" into forecasts of maximum day water use.

With the advent of improved forecasting techniques, especially those which deal explicitly with uncertainty and with the continued development of improved understanding of the nature of water, this risk-avoiding approach is no longer necessary, nor is it acceptable. Forecasts need not be blind guesses; they are expected future levels of use, given numerous explicit assumptions regarding future conditions. The possibility of water use, in the actual event, being higher or lower than the forecast value will be increasingly understood in a quantitative sense, so that probabilities associated with each of the results of inaccuracy given above can be assessed.

The cost of either type of inaccuracy can be predicted as well. The cost of overinvestment is evident and well understood. The cost of underinvestment is represented by the lost benefits to consumers from water services which they do not receive. It has long been realized that the value of lost benefits which result from water shortage may be substantially in excess of the value expressed by the price of water; thus the historic aversion to possible shortages. This is a matter of simple economics, reflecting not only a consumer surplus in the consumption of water services, but the fact that, during shortages, consumers are not free to shed only the lowest-priority uses—they must refrain from all uses, whatever their importance, during the time of shortage. Still, techniques are being developed to evaluate such lost benefits; a pioneering effort is the work of Russell, Arey, and Kates (1970), and further investigation has been conducted by the U. S. Army Corps of Engineers, among others.

Ultimately, then, we might imagine having available forecasts which take the form of probability distributions of future levels of maximum day water use, and reliable data on the actual social cost of various levels of water shortage. The cost of overinvestment would, of course, also be well understood. Various forecasting techniques would provide forecasts having various probability distributions. Each forecast would carry with it a cost of uncertainty—the sum of the expected value of overinvestment and the expected cost of underinvestment.

Choosing appropriate forecasting methodology is then a simple matter of selecting the technique which minimizes the sum of the cost of forecasting and the cost of uncertainty. Where the consequences of error are minor, a low uncertainty cost may be associated with a low-cost forecasting method. As the impact of drought losses, or the size of capacity investment rises, more and more sophisticated forecasting methods—along with higher and higher forecasting cost—may be justified by reductions in the cost of uncertainty.

THE NATURE OF WATER USE IN THE UNITED STATES

All forecasting techniques have at their base certain assumptions regarding the nature of water use. The per capita methods, when applied to aggregate data, assume that water use is perfectly correlated with service area population, that the quantity of water used is always proportionate to the number of persons using it. More advanced methods, such as the MAIN 2 system, assume that the nature of water use differs among user categories and that one or more factors influences use in each category. Others, including Whitford's approach, view many water use factors as probabilistic phenomena which may assume any of a range of values in the future.

The sources of these assumptions, and others like them, are empirical observations and analyses of water use which have been conducted both inside and outside the water industry for many years. At one time, such observations were quite cursory, but as the industry matured, more careful analysis became the rule. Measurements of the sensitivity of water use to price—the price elasticity—date back to 1926, for example Metcalf (1926, pp. 1–22). Limited studies of other determinants of residential water use occurred at various times, including the notable work of Dunn and Larson (1963, pp. 441–50). The first and so far only comprehensive national study was the Johns Hopkins residential water use study, which occurred during the period 1961–1966 and which was most usefully reported by Howe and Linaweaver (1967, pp. 13–32).

A review or even a listing of the many investigations of water use of all types that have been reported in recent years would be far too lengthy for this paper. I will attempt, however, to summarize, briefly and without full attribution, the major findings of these studies which bear on forecasting methodology, especially as they diverge from traditional views.

In some cases, specific investigations have been carried out for the service area of the Washington Suburban Sanitary Commission (WSSC). As I will describe shortly, the results of these investigations are now being used to develop a forecasting method appropriate to the needs of this utility. The following discussion of major aspects of water use is illustrated by examples drawn both from the literature and from these specific investigations in the Washington metropolitan area.

The WSSC serves the Maryland suburbs of Washington, D.C., consisting of Montgomery and Prince Georges counties (see figure 1). This is one of the most affluent and rapidly growing residential areas in the nation. The WSSC serves more than 230,000 customer connections, 99 percent of which are residential in character. The remainder of the customers are engaged in commercial, institutional, and governmental activities. No significant process industry exists within the service area. The largest users are federal government installations such as the National Institutes of Health, the National Bureau of Standards, and other government owned establishments, including the University of Maryland. Water supply is obtained from the Potomac and the Patuxent rivers. The Potomac, which is the major source, is a run-of-the-river supply with no actual

FIGURE 1
SERVICE AREA OF THE WASHINGTON SUBURBAN
SANITARY COMMISSION

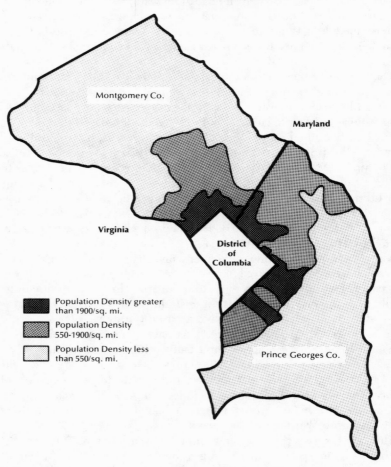

impoundment; the Patuxent is controlled by two commission-owned dams. Wastewater is collected by the commission and treated at several locations, principally the Blue Plains Wastewater Treatment Plant, owned by and located in the District of Columbia.

Per Capita v. Per Customer

Although per capita approaches to water use have been traditionally used, the fact is that water use is better correlated with the number of customer

Table 2

CORRELATIONS BETWEEN WATER USE, POPULATION AND CUSTOMER CONNECTIONS

Description	Sample Size	Coefficient of Correlation
1970 data, utilities serving 100,000 or more persons, at least 95% metered:		
Metered water use vs. population	12	0.6877
Metered water use vs. connections	13	0.8023
1970 data, utilities serving 50,000 or more persons, 100% metered:		
Metered water use vs. population	25	0.7959
Metered water use vs. connections	25	0.8773
1970 data, utilities serving 50,000 or more persons, 100% metered:		
Residential water use vs. population	10	0.8412
Residential water use vs. residential connections	10	0.8708

Source: AWWA, undated.

connections than it is with resident population. This assertion can be demonstrated on an aggregate level by use of data obtained from the recent AWWA surveys of water utilities (AWWA n.d.). Table 2 summarizes the results of several calculations of simple correlations. In every case, the correlation of water use with number of customer accounts is noticeably higher than that with resident population. If this observation is coupled with consideration of the difficulty in obtaining reliable population data, let alone forecasts, for water service areas, and the fact that some water utilities actually estimate population on the basis of customer connections, it is evident that population is markedly inferior to customer connections as an indicator of water use.

Water User Classes

Even while per capita forecasting methods have been employed, it has long been recognized that significant differences exist among the water uses of various types of customers. Aggregate per capita use is a weighted average of residential water use, commercial water use, industrial water use, even of leakage and waste, all expressed on a per capita basis. Obviously, any change in the level of water use by a nonresidential class of customers, without accompanying changes in population, would alter the per capita water use. In fact, such changes and variations are the major cause of the considerable scatter observed in calculations of per capita use.

Table 3

WSSC WATER USE BY CUSTOMER CLASS
September 1973 through August 1974

Customer Class	Number of Observations	Mean Use (gdc)[1]	Standard Deviation	Coefficient of Variation[2]
All Customers	**424,697**	**523**	**5,734**	**10.96**
Single family residential	406,130	274	341	1.24
Garden apartment residential	3,645	11,904	23,448	1.97
High-rise apartment residential	639	25,124	40,194	1.60
Industrial, commercial	13,307	2,146	10,938	5.10
Government, institutional	976	23,203	89,954	3.88

1. gdc = gallons per day per connection
2. coefficient of variation = standard deviation/mean
Source: Boland et al. 1975

This fact may be illustrated by considering data collected for WSSC during the period September 1973 through August 1974 and summarized in table 3 (Boland 1975). A total of 424,697 observations of water use resulted in a mean water use of 523 gallons per day per customer (gdc). This estimate is accompanied by a very high variance, more than ten times the mean, indicating considerable scatter among individual uses. Dividing the customers into five customer classes, however, results in widely different mean levels of water use for the various classes and in variances which are much lower relative to the associated means. This indicates that an important fraction of the variance, or scatter, has been removed by the classification scheme. Forecasts which deal with each class explicitly will be much less vulnerable to errors caused by undetected hidden trends.

Variability Among Individual Water Users

Whatever level of disaggregation is chosen for analysis of water use, there is a tendency to neglect consideration of the variability that exists within each user class, as though each class consisted of identical users. Such an assumption is a serious error. When the water use observations collected in the WSSC service area were subjected to statistical analysis, it was found that each class and subclass of use, no matter how narrowly defined, exhibited unexpectedly high variances and positive skewnesses. The variances observed by major customer class are given in table 3, and further disaggregations failed to reduce these significantly. Skewnesses were found to be on the order of +20 to more than +70 for various subgroups within the single-family residential class, and were generally between +1 and +6 for other groups of users.

The implications of these analyses can be illustrated with the aid of figure 2. Curve A is a normally distributed group of water users, characterized by low variance and zero skewness. Most customers use water at or near the mean rate for the class. Curve B is a normal distribution with high variance and zero skewness, where individual water use varies widely, but is as likely to be below the mean as above it. Curve C shows high variance and moderate positive skewness. Individual water use varies widely, but the likelihood of a particular customer being below the mean is somewhat greater than that of being above it. The patterns of water use observed in the WSSC service area for apartment houses and all nonresidential groups of customers tended to fit this pattern.

The single-family residential groupings, however, exhibited very high positive skewness, too high to be explained by a distribution of type C. The only conclusion that appears consistent with the data is one of a multimodal distribution; customers are clustered about two or more modal points, and scattered thinly between them. Such a pattern of usage

FIGURE 2

EFFECT OF VARIANCE AND SKEWNESS ON WATER USE DISTRIBUTIONS

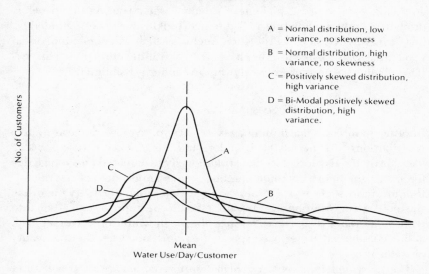

A = Normal distribution, low variance, no skewness

B = Normal distribution, high variance, no skewness

C = Positively skewed distribution, high variance

D = Bi-Modal positively skewed distribution, high variance.

No. of Customers

Mean
Water Use/Day/Customer

Source: Boland, Hanke, Church, and Carver, 1975

is suggested by curve D. If this is indeed the case, it suggests that residential water users could be usefully disaggregated still further, according to an as-yet-undiscovered distinction among patterns of water use. Each of the modal points may be the single mode of a subdistribution, one that would possess much reduced skewness and possible lower variance.

These statistical properties of individual water use have received little attention in the literature. One study of particular relevance, however, was conducted in Ames, Iowa, by Harris F. Seidel (1969, p. 490), who developed actual distribution curves for winter residential water use in Ames for the years 1955, 1961, and 1968. He observed high variances and moderate positive skewnesses, although his sample distributions were unimodal. Of greatest interest is the fact that Seidel's samples exhibit increasing variance and skewness over time; the 1968 distribution is substantially "flatter" than the 1955 distribution. He notes: "Perhaps the much broader frequency pattern for 1968 reflects the greater range in size and character of single-family residences now as compared to 15 years ago."

Based on these findings, it appears that further analysis of residential water use may produce increased knowledge of the parameters and explanatory factors related to such use. A much wider variation in individual use exists than was previously expected, and this variation may be associated with clustering of use about several modal points. The factors which explain this clustering, if it indeed exists as a general feature, would go a long way toward explaining residential water use. As this paper is drafted, a study is beginning at The Johns Hopkins University, funded by the U. S. Environmental Protection Agency, which will obtain individual residential water use data from a number of utilities throughout the nation, for the purpose of exploring this and other possibilities.

Seasonal Water Use

In order to forecast maximum day water use, or average day wastewater contributions, it is necessary to understand the seasonal nature of water use. Maximum day forecasts have traditionally been based on average day forecasts, the most common method being application of a "rule-of-thumb" ratio such as 1.5 times average day (Fair 1966). Average day wastewater contributions are usually taken to be approximately equal to winter day water use. The differences between winter day, average day, and maximum day water use express, in a simplistic way, the seasonality of water use.

The most widely accepted explanation for seasonality of urban water use is the practice of irrigating lawns and gardens during the summer growing season. Certain other uses may be seasonal to some degree, but irrigation is presumed to dominate. The Johns Hopkins residential water use study provided the first thorough analysis of seasonal use by single-family residential users, showing it to be positively correlated with residential-lot irrigable area, summer-season moisture deficit, and home value, and to be negatively correlated with the price of water (Linaweaver, Geyer, and Wolff 1966). According to this analysis, when other factors are equal the seasonality of residential water use would increase with decreasing housing density (larger lot sizes).

In order to test this assumption in the WSSC service area, and to explore seasonality in other categories of use, the term "fraction seasonal" was defined as the fraction of total annual water use which is seasonal in nature. A small "fraction seasonal" indicates that summer usage is only slightly greater than winter; a large fraction indicates large increases in summer usage. The service area was divided into three density zones, as shown in figure 1. The fraction seasonal was calculated for each customer class, and for each customer class in each density zone. The significant results appear as table 4.

Table 4

SEASONALITY OF WATER USE IN WSSC SERVICE AREA
September 1973 through August 1974

Customer Class	Number of Observations	Mean Use (gdc)	Fraction Seasonal[1]
All customers, all density zones	424,697	523	0.20
All customers, high density[2]	133,392	503	0.23
All customers, medium density	232,121	538	0.19
All customers, low density	59,184	500	0.15
Single-family residential, all density zones	406,130	274	0.14
Garden apartment residential, all density zones	3,645	11,904	0.15
High-rise apartment residential, all density zones	639	25,124	0.11
Commercial, industrial, all density zones	13,307	2,146	0.23
Government, institutional, all density zones	976	23,203	0.20
Single-family residential, high density	125,933	255	0.12
Single-family residential, medium density	222,568	273	0.15
Single-family residential, low density	57,629	322	0.18

1. Fraction seasonal is the excess of average annual use over average winter use, divided by average annual use.
2. High density zone: more than 1,900 persons per square mile. Medium density zone: less than 1,900 persons per square mile, but more than 550 persons per square mile. Low density zone: less than 550 persons per square mile.

Source: Boland et al. 1975

The results show that the single-family residential class displays exactly the seasonal characteristics expected: increasing average use and increasing seasonality with decreasing density. Apartment water users show seasonality comparable to that of single-family residential users. This no doubt reflects the use of water to irrigate apartment building grounds, as well as swimming pools, and so forth. No significant differences in apartment water use seasonality were found among density zones.

Completely unexpected, however, were the seasonalities displayed by the nonresidential users. Both major nonresidential classes proved to be more seasonal than any residential group. Furthermore, these seasonalities were not significantly correlated with density, depending instead on the location of specific installations. The overall effect of these results is to produce a total system seasonality which varies *directly*, rather than *inversely*, with density. Total system seasonality is noticeably greater than residential seasonality, as well.

Several problems are introduced by this analysis. The forecast of maximum day water use and average day wastewater contributions cannot be based on analysis of residential user patterns alone, since other users may evidently greatly change the seasonal characteristics of aggregate water use. Further, forecasts of these measures for portions of a utility service area cannot meaningfully be based on overall relationships, since the degree of seasonality may differ significantly among the various areas. Further study of these relationships may produce an estimating procedure for maximum day or winter day water use which takes these problems into account, but no such procedure exists at this time.

Price Elasticity

Since the pioneering work of Metcalf (1926), numerous investigators have analyzed the sensitivity of water use to price. One review of this literature identified five studies of consequence reported during the 1950s and nine more during the 1960s (Feldman 1965). Further studies have appeared during this decade and will doubtless continue to appear. Most studies have addressed either aggregate municipal use or residential sector use. Very few have examined other customer classes individually. Most studies have been cross-sectional in nature, although several have employed time series or pooled cross-sectional/time series data. The widespread use of block-type rate structures by the industry has complicated the proper identification of the price variable, a problem that affects individual studies in varying degrees.

Altogether, it appears that the elasticity of aggregate municipal water use is relatively inelastic, as one would expect, probably in the vicinity of -0.4 or -0.5. Lower elasticities appear to be the rule when price level is very low, with greater sensitivity accompanying higher price levels. Analyses of residential water use have shown it to be similar to total use in price elasticity, unless, as in the Howe and Linaweaver study (1967), seasonal uses are treated separately. In this case, residential seasonal uses exhibit much higher elasticities, well into the elastic range in some parts of the country. Very little is known of elasticities for other classes of customer, but it is evident that price level is an important factor in explaining water use and an essential component of any forecasting method.

Income Elasticity

Related to the phenomenon of price elasticity is income elasticity: the sensitivity of water use to changes in the income of the user. Studies of the income elasticity of total municipal water use have appeared from time to time, and some later studies have focused on the residential sector alone. Howe and Linaweaver (1967) employed home value as a surrogate for income, since income data were not available from the Johns Hopkins residential water use study.

The consensus of the available studies is that income elasticity is positive and rather small, of similar or lower magnitude to price elasticity. This suggests that water use may be slightly less responsive to changes in income than to changes in price, but that income effects are still quite important. Accordingly, income is yet another factor that must be taken into account if useful forecasts of future water use are to be prepared.

THE WASHINGTON AREA STUDY

At the present time a study is under way to develop a forecasting method appropriate to the needs of the Washington Suburban Sanitary Commission. This effort, conducted by Ecological Analysts, Inc., of Baltimore, Maryland, must address a number of particular circumstances of water supply and wastewater disposal which exist in the Washington area. WSSC obtains the greatest percentage of its water supply from the Potomac River, which it shares with the District of Columbia. The combined withdrawal of the two jurisdictions has, on occasion, exceeded the historic low flow of the river, but withdrawals have not yet exceeded available flow on any given day.

Much of the wastewater collected by WSSC is passed to the District of Columbia wastewater treatment plant, where strict flow quotas have been established. Present flows are close to maximum allowable levels, in spite of an active program of locating and correcting ground water infiltration problems. The commission has experienced considerable difficulty in obtaining sites for additional wastewater treatment plants, which will be required if wastewater flows continue to increase.

It seems clear that increasing water use in all parts of the metropolitan region will soon result in the inability of the Potomac to support withdrawals at summer season rates, so additional water supply seems an eventual necessity. Such sources of supply as are available appear limited to large impoundments on the Potomac River or to interbasin transfers; all alternatives proposed thus far require major expenditures, long lead times, and significant environmental impacts.

It is a matter of critical importance to the commission to know exactly when supply augmentation must occur, taking proper account of the expected costs of water shortage as well as those of supply augmentation. For these reasons, it was decided to develop a forecasting approach which utilizes the best available methodology and information, and to prepare new demand forecasts for the WSSC service area. These forecasts would include average day water use, maximum day water use, average day wastewater contribution, and the water shortage frequency and severity expected to be associated with various supply augmentation alternatives.

An extensive program of data analysis is now under way, utilizing data gathered from the WSSC and from the Fairfax County Water Authority, a similar service area located in suburban Virginia. Total water pumpage data have been obtained for a number of years, by day, by month, and by year. Numbers and types of customer connections, socioeconomic data, weather data, and other information have been obtained for both jurisdictions for the same period of time. Also, many hundreds of thousands of individual meter readings have been obtained from the computer files of the utilities and are being processed to yield a data file containing observations of water use together with the type and location of customer, time of year, water rate schedule in effect, and other potential explanatory information. Historic records of daily flow in the Potomac River are also available.

Following preparation of the data files, the analysis will proceed in three phases: (1) development of demand models; (2) development of forecasting scenarios; and (3) forecasting. Statistical analysis similar to that described in this paper will be used to disaggregate the WSSC service area by customer class and by geographic area. The objective is to develop subclasses of water users which are as homogeneous as possible.

Demand models will be developed from historic data for each subclass, explaining as clearly as possible the variations in water use which have existed in the past. Separate models will be developed for each season, thus facilitating estimation of maximum day and winter day water uses. Water use in each subclass will be explained in terms of the relevant demographic, geographic, socioeconomic, and weather variables.

Likely future values for all of these variables except weather-related factors will be reviewed and the necessary assumptions made to permit formulation of one or more forecasting scenarios. Each scenario will consist of a set of predictions of future values of explanatory variables and a set of assumptions regarding extent and timing of supply augmentation.

The summer season moisture deficit, and any other weather-related factor which may be employed, will be treated as a stochastic variable, having a probability distribution similar to that observed in the past. Resulting water use forecasts will depend upon the values chosen for weather-related factors, because of the role of seasonal water use.

The available water supply from the Potomac River also fluctuates from year to year as well as from day to day, through the influence of weather variables, principally rainfall. These fluctuations may reflect weather changes as far away as several hundred miles from the service area, and changes in river flow may lag behind weather changes by a week or more transit time, but the potentiality for a perverse correlation appears to exist. Certainly a lengthy spell of hot, dry weather can be expected to result in abnormally low river flows and abnormally high water use.

As a result, the correlation or lag correlation between river flow and water use will be investigated, using historic data. Water use will be normalized by each year's average flow, and records of river flow and daily water withdrawal will be utilized. Based on the type of correlation found, a simulation technique will be developed to produce streams of paired estimates, one of water withdrawal, one of river flow. The time streams will reproduce the observed probability distribution of weather-related changes.

After adjustment for withdrawals by the District of Columbia, analysis of these time streams will produce expected values and probability distributions for future water use levels, as well as estimates of the duration and magnitude of predicted water shortages, if any. If this process is repeated for each forecasting scenario, the exact effect of alternate supply augmentation plans can be determined, as well as the consequences of various uncertainties surrounding the future values of explanatory factors.

CONCLUSIONS

It is expected that a forecast of the type just described will provide the information that is needed to plan a rational and prudent supply augmentation program, avoiding premature investment or unnesessary environmental disruption, while dealing explicitly and consistently with the possible impacts of supply failure. Some of the work described is innovative to the extent that it represents an attempt to deal with specific features of the forecasting problem in the WSSC area. The remainder, however, merely reflects application of what is known about urban water use, taking maximum advantage of that knowledge to produce the most reliable possible forecast.

It should be clear that traditional methods of per capita calculations and simple extrapolations would not suffice here. In fact, such methods have been used in the past and have consistently predicted imminent water shortages which have yet to materialize. Clearly, a water shortage will occur at some time if present trends continue, but it is critically important to know exactly when and how serious the shortage will be. To exaggerate the seriousness of the problem is, in this case, at least equally as damaging as to understate it. That old standby, conservatism, must give way to accuracy.

It should also be clear that the study I have described is expensive. Data collection of the scale and complexity required is time-consuming and difficult. The analysis itself may be intellectually more demanding, but accounts for a small fraction of the total project budget. My view is that as certain required research in this area is accomplished, such as the EPA study noted earlier, and that as experience with this type of forecasting approach is accumulated, data requirements for any given application will fall substantially. It may not be necessary to investigate certain relationships in each case, and much smaller randomized samples may suffice to characterize other relationships. Once the various factors of water use and the general nature of the relationships are known for a specific service area, subsequent studies may require only minor updating.

I have attempted to show that knowledge of the structure and explanatory factors in urban water use has advanced rapidly in past years. These advances have not yet been incorporated into conventional forecasting practices used by the water industry. In particular, a number of research findings are relevant:

1. Water use is better correlated with number of customer connections than with resident population.

2. Significant differences in the nature of water use exist among the various categories of customers.

3. Individual water use within a class is subject to great variability.

4. All classes of water use can be highly seasonal in nature.

5. Economic variables, including water price and water user income, are important factors in explaining water use.

Forecasts which neglect these factors must be considered to have less than maximum possible reliability, a deficiency which must be balanced against the expected cost of forecasting error in each situation. As further research is concluded and as experience with more advanced forecasting procedures is gained, the range of available forecasting options promises to expand even further, thus improving the potential long-range investment performance of the water industry.

REFERENCES

American Water Works Association (AWWA), (n.d.) "Operating Data for Water Utilities 1970 & 1965." Denver, Colorado: AWWA Statistical Report no. 20112.

Boland, John J. 1971. "The Micro Approach—Computerized Models for Municipal Water Requirements." In Albertson et al., eds., *Treatise on Urban Water Systems*. Fort Collins, Colorado: Colorado State University.

Boland, John J.; Hanke, Steve H.; Church, Richard L.; and Carver, Philip H. 1975. "An Examination of Alternate Rate-Making Policies for the Washington Suburban Sanitary Commission." Baltimore: Rivus, Inc.

Council of Economic Advisors. 1974. "Economic Report of the President." Washington, D.C.: U.S. Government Printing Office, February.

Dunn, Dorothy F., and Larson, Thurston E. 1963. "Relationship of Domestic Water Use to Assessed Valuation, with Selected Demographic and Socio-Economic Variables." *Journal of American Water Works Association* 55, (4).

Edison Electric Institute 1974. "Statistical Yearbook of the Electric Utility Industry for 1973." Publication no. 74-34. New York.

Fair, Gordon M.; Geyer, John C.; and Okun, Daniel A. 1966. *Water and Wastewater Engineering, Volume 1: Water Supply and Wastewater Disposal*. New York: John Wiley and Sons.

Feldman, Stephen L. 1975. "An Analysis of Residential Water Use in Israel." Ph.D. dissertation submitted to the Department of Geography, The Hebrew University of Jerusalem, Jerusalem, Israel, February.

Hazen, Allen 1897. "Report on the City's Water Supply." A report to the Woman's Health Protective Association of Philadelphia, Philadelphia, Pa.

Herrington, Paul 1976. "The Economics of Water Supply and Demand." *Economics*, vol. 12, part 2 (summer 1976).

Herschel, Clemens 1973. Translation of and commentary on Sextus Julius Frontinus, "The Water Supply of the City of Rome," (A.D. 97). Boston, Mass.: New England Water Works Association.

Hittman Associates, Inc. 1969. "Forecasting Municipal Water Requirements: The MAIN II System—vol. I. The Main II System." Columbia, Maryland: Available from National Technical Information Service, Springfield, Virginia 22151, as PB-190 275 .

Howe, Charles W., and Linaweaver, F. P., Jr. 1967. "The Impact of Price on Residential Water Demand and Its Relation to System Design and Price Structure." *Water Resources Research*, vol. 3, no. 1.

Linaweaver, F. P., Jr.; Geyer, John C.; and Wolff, Jerome B. 1966. "Residential Water Use: Report V, Phase Two." Final and Summary Report. Baltimore, Md.: The Johns Hopkins University, June.

Metcalf, L. 1926. "Effect of Water Rates and Growth in Population Upon Per Capita Consumption." *Journal AWWA,* 15, (1).

National Commission on Water Quality (NCWQ) 1975. "Staff Draft Report." Washington, D.C.: November.

Patterson, W. L. 1976. "Water Use Trends Since 1970." *Willing Water,* 20, (3).

Russell, Clifford; Arey, D.; and Kates, R. 1970. *Drought and Water Supply.* Baltimore, Md.: The Johns Hopkins Press for Resources for the Future, Inc.

Seidel, Harris F. 1969. "Trends in Residential Water Use." *Journal AWWA,* 61, (9).

Sewerage Commission of the City of Baltimore 1897. "Report of the Sewerage Commission of the City of Baltimore." Baltimore, Md.

Symons, George E. 1954. "Design Criteria: Part I, Water and Sewage Works. May.

White, Gilbert F. 1970. *Strategies of American Water Management.* Ann Arbor: The University of Michigan Press.

Whitford, Peter W. 1972. "Residential Water Demand Forecasting." *Water Resources Research* 8, (4).

WATER QUALITY LEGISLATION

From the point of view of many harried water system managers, the problems confronting them have not so much to do with water quality as with recent and proposed federal regulations. Considerable criticism has been leveled at the federal government for the way in which it has gone about protecting the nation's waters, but there is little disagreement that these waters do need protection. Although some of the states have been willing to accept full responsibility for water quality, the continued presence of the federal government in the field seems assured. The papers of this section focus on various aspects of the Safe Drinking Water Act (SDWA) of 1974, PL 93–523, the most critical piece of legislation for municipalities.

The development of acceptable standards is not easy. Robert Clark traces the history of water quality legislation in the United States and describes the background of the SDWA. He then discusses the process through which a regulatory agency must go before setting a standard, using as an example the presence of chloroform in drinking water supplies, an issue which has recently given rise to widespread concern.

Primary responsibility for overseeing the quality of the nation's waters is vested in the U.S. Environmental Protection Agency. Francis Mayo describes the problems that accompany any move by the federal government into a new and untested area. Perhaps the most important of these problems is the development of legally defensible regulations necessarily based on scientific understanding. He concludes with a description of the areas most urgently in need of further research.

THE SAFE DRINKING WATER ACT:
ITS IMPLICATIONS FOR PLANNING

ROBERT M. CLARK,
Systems Analyst, Water Supply Research Division,
Municipal Environment Research Laboratory
U.S. Environmental Protection Agency
Cincinnati, Ohio

INTRODUCTION

This paper discusses the Safe Drinking Water Act (Public Law 93–523) passed in December 1974, in terms of the historical development of water pollution and water quality legislation, as well as current implications for the water supply industry. The role of the courts in the development of early water law is discussed, and major water legislation is presented. The major components of the Safe Drinking Water Act are reviewed. An example of the kind of logic that might be followed for setting a standard under the act is presented and should provide insight into planning for the implementation of the act.

Figure 1 shows the major water-related legislation of the U.S., beginning with the Rivers and Harbors Act of 1899. The Oil Pollution Act of 1924 was replaced by the Water Quality Improvement Act of 1970. The Federal Water Pollution Control Act was enacted in 1948 and amended in 1956, 1961, 1965, 1966, and 1972. The National Environmental Policy Act was passed in 1970, and the Safe Drinking Water Act in 1974. These laws, of course, represent only a part of the environmental legislation currently in force in the U.S.

EARLY WATER LAW IN THE UNITED STATES

The basis for water law in the U.S., in large part, can be traced to English common law. Clause 33 of the Magna Charta commanded the king of England to remove weirs from the rivers throughout England to clear the

The writer would like to acknowledge the assistance of John A. Machisko, Gregory Trygg, Richard Stevie, and Dr. James M. Symons, all of the Water Supply Research Division, in the preparation of this manuscript.

117

streams for the passage of people and fish (Ciriacy–Wantrup et al. 1967, p. 180). English common law as applied in the U.S. emphasized riparian rights, but carefully distinguished between natural and extraordinary use. Extraordinary or business users could not use all water to the exclusion of other riparian users. Not only were the rights to surface waters assumed to go to the property owner, but he was entitled to all water underneath his land as well. In the water-rich eastern U.S., this approach worked reasonably well before large settlements had been established. In 1855, however, the supreme court of Pennsylvania observed, "Where a subterranean flow of water was so well defined as to constitute a regular and constant stream, the owner of the land through which it flows may not divert or destroy it to the injury of the person below on whose land it issues in the form of a spring" (ibid. pp. 83–84). This ruling began the development of the rule of reasonable use, which eventually would apply to both surface waters and groundwaters. The rule was to be applied extensively in the settlement of the arid West.

As the western U.S. became more densely settled, appropriative water

FIGURE 1
WATER LAWS AND THEIR AMENDMENTS

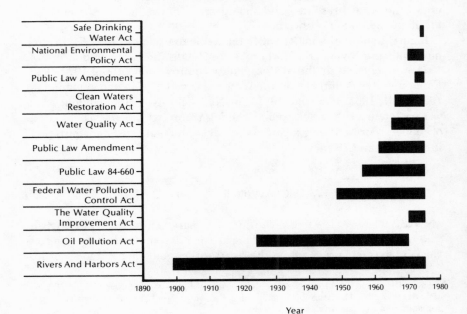

Year

rights evolved that depended not upon land ownership but upon the actual use of water. In the West, places existed in which water had to be diverted for drinking supplies and other purposes. Appropriative statutes were eventually developed which allowed water to be diverted from stream channels for irrigation.

The appropriative concept was developed because not everyone can live by a watercourse. The appropriative doctrine states that he who is first in time is first in right, as long as he continues to use the water in a beneficial way. When the riparian right and appropriative concept came into conflict, the riparian right was normally considered to hold sway.

Much water law has been made by court decisions. Two early cases illustrate the court's involvement:

The first case is *McNamara* v. *Taft* (1908, Massachusetts), in which a mill on riparian land was polluting a watercourse and causing damage to the plaintiff's drinking water (Ciriacy–Wantrup et al., p. 73). The court found for the plaintiff.

In a second case, *McDonough* v. *Russell* (1917, North Dakota), the defendant was using water from the Heart River to wash wheat in his mill but had installed a septic tank to handle waste (Grindler 1967, p. 85). The plaintiff was using water for watering his horses and making ice. The plaintiff found black specks on his ice and had to cut off the bottom five inches. The court awarded $100 for these small damages, but issued no injunction against the mill because the use was not unreasonable. The court found that the defendant had taken steps to avoid pollution.

These cases illustrate the rule of reasonable use. In the first case, the defendant's use of water was ruled as unreasonable, but, in the second, it was found that the defendant had made an attempt to comply with the reasonable use concept. Pollution has been defined by the courts as being an unreasonable use, but over the years an exact technical definition has proved difficult to establish.

Liability with respect to water quality also extends to water purveyors, although a municipal water department is generally held not to be liable for furnishing unwholesome water except on proof of negligence. A private water supplier is also not held liable unless negligence is proven. One means of establishing the liability of a water purveyor is through the development of drinking water standards which act in effect as a warranty or guarantee between the supplier and consumer of water. The development of drinking water standards is discussed in a later section of this paper.

It was inevitable, with the courts heavily involved in creating water law by decision and the states establishing water statutes, that the federal government would eventually become involved in water quality and pollution control. The development of federal legislation in this area is discussed in the following section.

FEDERAL WATER LAWS

The federal government has been active in controlling water pollution since the 1880s. Figure 1 illustrates the scope of its legislative activity.

The Rivers and Harbors Act of 1899 prohibits the creation of any obstruction on a navigable river unless authorized by Congress (Grindler, pp. 354–55). Section 13 of the act makes it unlawful to dump refuse into navigable water without a permit from the U.S. Army Corps of Engineers. In 1966, the U.S. Supreme Court used this provision to rule that the Standard Oil Company had violated Section 13 with an accidental oil spill into a Florida river (Hines, p. 495). The court interpreted the law as applying to both navigation and pollution nuisances.

In 1912 the U.S. Public Health Service was authorized to investigate the effects on health of pollution in navigable waterways. The 1924 Oil Pollution Act made it unlawful to dump oil into navigable coastal waters (ibid., p. 461).

The Federal Water Pollution Control Act of 1948 directed the Surgeon General of the U.S. Public Health Service to promote cooperation and participate in joint activities with state and interstate agencies (ibid., p. 465). An amendment in 1956 added a construction grants program, and another amendment in 1961 shifted responsibility for implementation from the surgeon general to the secretary of the Department of Health, Education and Welfare (DHEW) (ibid., pp. 470, 475). Still another amendment (the Water Quality Act of 1965) created a federal water pollution control administration and a program for the establishment of water quality standards, and an amendment in 1966 increased federal participation in the construction grants program. The most current amendments to the Federal Water Pollution Control Act were made in 1972 (ibid., pp. 478–79, 484–85). The Water Quality Improvement Act of 1970, which made additional provisions dealing with marine standards, replaced the Oil Pollution Control Act of 1924 (ibid., p. 488).

The National Environmental Policy Act of 1970 stated a national policy concerning environmental values and created a watchdog council within the executive branch to protect these values (ibid., p. 488). The act also provides for environmental impact statements.

In 1974 the Safe Drinking Water Act was passed. It strongly emphasizes the use of drinking water standards to protect the consumer. The drinking water standards concept does not originate with the Safe Drinking Water Act, however. The following section traces the historical development of drinking water standards and their importance in water supply.

DEVELOPMENT OF DRINKING WATER STANDARDS

The concept of standards for drinking water is not new. One of the first historical references to drinking water standards is 4000 years old, recorded in Sanskrit (McDermott 1973, pp. 469–70):

> It is directed to heat foul water by boiling and exposing to sunlight and by dipping seven times into it a piece of hot copper, then to filter and cool in an earthen vessel. The direction is given by the god who is the incarnation of medical science.

Hippocrates, the father of medicine, identified the need for sanitary surveys with the following statement:

> When one comes into a city to which he is a stranger... one should consider most attentively the waters which the inhabitants use, whether they be marshy and soft, or hard and running from elevated and rocky situations, whether it be naked and deficient in water or wooded and well watered. . . .

Waterborne disease was prevalent in the U.S. by the end of the nineteenth century; for example, in the 1880s, the typhoid death rate was 158 deaths per 100,000 in Pittsburgh in one year (McDermott 1973, pp. 470–71). However, the national typhoid death rate was 5 per 100,000 in 1935. Reductions in waterborne disease outbreaks were brought about by the use of sand filtration, chlorination-disinfection, and the application of drinking water standards. More recent epidemiological evidence by Craun and McGabe shows that the number of all waterborne disease outbreaks dropped from 45 per 100,000 in 1938–40 to 15 per 100,000 in 1966–70. The average annual number of outbreaks ceased to fall around 1951 and may have increased slightly since then for reasons unknown at this time.

The federal authority for drinking water standards originated with the Interstate Quarantine Act of 1893, which authorized the surgeon general to make and enforce regulations to prevent the introduction, transmission, or spread of communicable diseases in the U.S. (ibid., pp. 471–72). A provision in the act resulted in the promulgation of the Interstate Quarantine Regulations of 1894. In 1912 the first water-related regulation—the prohibition of the use of the common drinking water cup on interstate carriers—was adopted. Since that time a series of drinking

Table 1

DRINKING WATER STANDARDS

Date of Standard	Major Feature
1914	The first bacteriological performance standard was introduced.
1925	Standards were modified to include chemical standards.
1942	Bacteriological samples were taken from distribution systems.
1946	Standards were made generally applicable to all water supplies in the United States.
1962	Requirement was made that water supply systems be operated by qualified personnel.
	Recommended maximum concentration limits were added for
	alkyl benzene sulfonate barium cadmium carbon chloroform extract cyanide nitrate silver
	Temperature was considered in setting limits for fluorides and addition of section on radioactivity.
	Rationale used by committee in setting limits.

water regulations has been issued. The dates and major implications of the regulations are shown in table 1 (ibid., pp. 472–73).

The last set of drinking water standards was issued in 1962. In 1969 a technical committee was established to write a new set of standards. The committee's work was completed in 1972, but the new standards were held up pending the passage of the Safe Drinking Water Act of 1974.

THE SAFE DRINKING WATER ACT

Title 14 of the Public Health Service Act, entitled "Safety in Public Water Systems," is commonly called the Safe Drinking Water Act (Public Law 93–523). It applies to all public water systems as defined in the act, including federally owned or maintained water systems.

The act defines contaminants, maximum concentration levels, primary drinking water regulations, secondary drinking water regulations, public water systems, supplies, agency heads, and so forth. Some of the definitions are as follows:

> *Contaminant*—Any physical, chemical, biological, or radiological substance or matter in water
>
> *Maximum Concentration Level* (MCL)—The maximum concentration of a contaminant allowable in water delivered to a user
>
> *Public Water System*—A water system that has at least 15 connections and serves at least 25 individuals.

The more than 200,000 public water systems specifically included under PL 93–523 serve cities, towns, communities, Indian communities, and federal facilities. Public water systems include those in service stations, hotels, and other facilities where the public has access to water (noncommunity systems). Of primary interest to the U.S. Environmental Protection Agency (EPA) are the approximately 40,000 community systems.

Water systems not covered under the Safe Drinking Water Act include those that consist only of distribution and storage facilities, those that obtain all water from another public water system, those that do not sell water to any person, and those that do not supply an interstate carrier that conveys passengers.

Primary drinking water regulations specify contaminants that may have an adverse effect on health. They define a maximum contaminant level or treatment technique and contain criteria and procedures to assure a safe supply. Secondary drinking water guidelines specify maximum contaminant levels that are necessary to protect the public welfare and include such items as taste, odor, and appearance. These may vary according to regional circumstances and are not federally enforceable, but are guidelines.

Figure 2 shows the major tasks to be performed under the act and the milestones for three fiscal years after enactment. As we can see, the program emphasis changes from one fiscal year to another, although the primary drinking water regulations are of major importance over the entire time period. Interim primary drinking water regulations were to be proposed in March 1975 and were to be promulgated in September 1975. In fiscal year 1977, the revised national primary regulations are to become effective. Prior to the proposed regulations, the National Academy of Sciences must submit a study to Congress upon which these revised regulations will be based. The act has major provisions for state program grants.

FIGURE 2
SAFE DRINKING WATER ACT
(ENACTED DECEMBER 17, 1974)

	M A E †	National Primary Standards	National Secondary Standards	Exemptions and Variances	State Program Regulations	Underground Regulations	Reports to Congress
March 75	3	★ Propose					★ General Activities
April 75							
June 75	6	★ Promulgate			★ Propose	★ Propose ★ Publish List of States Needing Programs	★ Carcinogens Report
Sept. 75	9		★ Propose		★ Promulgate ★ Notify State Governors ★ Begin Review of State Program Applications		
Dec. 75	12		★ Promulgate			★ Promulgate	★ Waste Disposal Survey
March 76	15						
April 76							★ General Activities
June 76	18						
July 76							
Sept. 76	21					★ States Submit Applications	
Dec. 76	24	★ Adopt ★ NAS‡ Study					★ NAS‡ Study ★ Rural Survey
March 77	27	★ Establish MCLs††† ★ Propose Revised					★ General Activities
June 77	30						
Sept. 77	33	★ Promulgate Revised					
Dec. 77	36						
March 78	39			★ Begin Review			★ General Activities
June 78	42			★ Complete Review			

†Months After Enactment ‡National Academy of Sciences †††Maximum Concentration Level

EPA is authorized to make program grants if the state is willing to establish a program according to the act's provisions.

A much neglected area included in the act is underground water source protection, a provision that is sorely needed. EPA can award program grants to those states that will establish programs for receiving a grant and that will assume primary enforcement responsibility for the underground regulations. The state must establish a permit program in which each applicant will assure the state that underground injection will not endanger drinking water. The program requires inspection, monitoring, and record keeping in accordance with EPA requirements. The underground regulations apply to federal agencies and property owned or leased by the federal government. These regulations cannot interfere with underground injection of brine associated with oil and natural gas production, or in the secondary or tertiary operations of oil and gas producers.

EPA is authorized to conduct research on methods to identify and measure contaminants, treatment techniques, and protection of underground water sources. EPA is required to conduct studies on both the costs of carrying out primary regulations and waste disposal endangering groundwater sources and control methods, methods for underground injection which do not endanger groundwater sources, virus contamination, carcinogens, and contamination sources that endanger groundwater. EPA is authorized to make grants for the purpose of training water-treatment plant operators, inspectors, and supervisory personnel.

The act requires assurance of chemical supplies. Personnel in a public water supply may request the EPA administrator to issue certification of need for water treatment chemicals. The President or his delegate can then issue an order to supply the chemicals.

The act has a public notice requirement under which a utility must give notice to its consumers if it fails to meet a primary drinking water regulation, fails to perform required monitoring, has a variance or exemption (the possibility of variances or exemptions is provided for in the act), or fails to comply with a schedule for a variance of exemption. Notice must be given every three months in a newspaper of general circulation or on water bills. In the act there is also a citizens civil action provision under which any citizen may commence a civil action against any person for alleged violations of the act. No suit may be brought until 27 months after enactment.

Another important part of the act is the emergency powers and provisions under which the EPA administrator may take action in case a public water supply is contaminated and if the contamination presents an imminent and substantial threat to public health. The act contains provisions for the administrator to take various courses of action when a contaminant is detected for which no MCL has been established. The following section contains an example of the use of this provision in setting a standard for an organic compound. The particular case involves chloroform and provides insight as to the logic that might be followed in setting other standards under the act.

SETTING A STANDARD

Trihalomethanes in general and chloroform (recently determined to be a carcinogen in drinking water) in particular are examples of contaminants for which no MCL has yet been proposed (Symons 1976, pp. 1–5). Trihalomethanes are present in drinking water as a direct consequence of chlorination, a long-established public health practice for the disinfection of drinking water. Chlorine probably reacts with certain organic materials to produce chloroform and related organic byproducts. These compounds in drinking water escaped detection because of their low concentrations and because of their low boiling points, which allowed them to be lost in the procedures used for performing typical water analyses.

Recently, investigators have developed new sensitive analytical procedures that allow for more precise measurement of trihalomethanes. These newly developed procedures demonstrate that the concentration of chloroform and related compounds is generally higher in finished than in raw water, leading to the conclusion that they are being produced during the chlorination process.

Acting on these findings, on 29 March 1976, Russell Train, administrator of EPA, released a statement that said in part: "The recent test results and the fact that chloroform is prevalent in the environment have convinced me that the prudent course of action at this time is to minimize exposure to this chemical wherever it is feasible to do so" (Symons 1976, pp. 1–5). He also said, "EPA will work with cities and states to evaluate certain modifications to current treatment practices that can reduce the formation of chloroform during the water treatment process, without lessening the effectiveness of disinfection. EPA research has shown that changes in chlorination procedures practiced by some water systems can result in reduction in the levels of chloroform produced. EPA plans to share these initial findings on chloroform reduction with the states and some cities encountering high chloroform levels, in an effort to reduce human exposure as quickly as possible. This will also allow EPA to gain added information to support the development of national regulations to limit chloroform levels in water supplies."

As an indication of its desire to establish a standard for organics in general and for trihalomethanes in particular, EPA issued an Advanced

Notice of Proposed Rule-Making (ANPRM) (Federal Register 7–14–76).
The ANPRM proposed two regulatory options:

> Set Maximum Contaminant Levels in which MCL's would be established for
> specific compounds or for a general organics contamination indicator. It
> would designate the maximum amount of the substance that is permitted . . .
> in drinking water.

> Establish treatment technique requirements for substances that cannot be
> monitored feasibly.

Another possibility is to take no regulatory action, concentrating instead
on rendering technical assistance to those utilities that have immediate
need for such assistance. As of December 1976, no decision has been
made by EPA regarding its course of action.

However, this issue provides an opportunity to examine the kinds of
logic that a regulatory agency must use in making decisions for standard-
setting. A hypothetical example of possible standard-setting strategies
follows. The example is based on readily available data and is a gross
simplification of actual procedures that may be used if and when a standard is actually established.

The example centers around chloroform and focuses on the economic
impact of setting a standard for this contaminant. The example is approached in three steps:

1. Determine the general impact of the standard. Make preliminary estimates of the costs involved.

2. Determine the prevalence of the problem.

3. Estimate the final economic impact in annualized and per capita costs
   for those utilities affected.

Steps will be discussed in the following sections.

General Impact

In estimating the impact of a potential standard, it is important to analyze
for economic characteristics that are unique to water systems. One of
these characteristics is the effect of economies of scale (increasing unit
costs with decreasing system size). Because of economies of scale, the
impact of any regulations for organics will be great on small public water
systems, especially on those serving between 25 and 10,000 persons.
Installation, operation, and maintenance of sophisticated control processes together with monitoring requirements may result in substantial

Table 2

COSTS FOR LARGE AND SMALL WATER SYSTEMS BY FUNCTION

Utility Size	Billed Consumption mil gal/yr	$/mil gal					
		Support Services	Acquisition	Treatment	Distribution	Interest	Total
Large	31,227	99.04	54.34	48.00	118.25	86.94	415.66
Small	614	150.45	129.05	87.55	357.77	129.18	853.77

costs for small systems. Table 2 summarizes data collected by the water supply research division on both large and small water supply systems. As can be seen, the average cost for 12 large water supplies (averaging approximately 85 mgd) is $415 per mil gal. The average cost for 30 small supplies, averaging approximately 0.5 mgd, is $854 per mil gal.

Table 2 contains current costs for large and small systems. It is conceivable that these costs for small systems could increase dramatically as compared with costs for large systems, as many large systems already have sophisticated treatment, while many small systems do not.

An illustration of the costs for granular activated carbon is shown in figure 3 (Clark et al. 1976). As can be seen from this curve, the cost in cents per thousand gallons increases dramatically for systems smaller than

FIGURE 3
TOTAL OPERATING & MAINTENANCE COSTS
VARIABLE COMPONENT

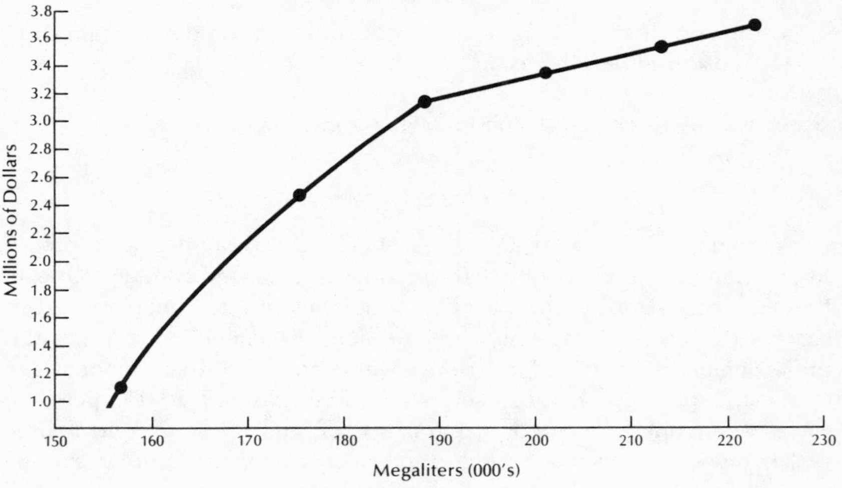

Table 3

NUMBER OF UTILITIES WITH GROUND AND SURFACE SOURCES

POPULATION CATEGORIES	NUMBER OF UTILITIES			
	Ground Source		Surface Source	
	Chlorinated	Nonchlorinated	Chlorinated	Nonchlorinated
100,000 to 500,000	52	8	124	0
500,000 to 1,000,000	5	0	24	0
>1,000,000	0	0	16	0

5 mgd. If these unit costs were added to an already high cost for water supply, the economic burden to small system users would be high. For purposes of this example, therefore, the minimum system size discussed for economic impact analysis will be for utilities serving no fewer than 100,000 people (10 mgd at 100 gal per capita per day). Such an argument could lead into discussion concerning equal protection for all consumers. The act, however, states that economics must be considered.

Fortunately, many small systems utilize groundwater sources while others may be able to switch to purer surface water sources which would not require extensive treatment. Because many groundwaters are low in organics, they also would produce very little chloroform (trihalomethanes) and, in many cases, minimal, if any, treatment for organics control would be necessary. Thus, a standard would most likely impact surface water supplies and shallow groundwater sources.

Table 3 summarizes the number of utilities in the U.S. serving over 100,000 people into three size categories by source. The hypothetical standard-setting exercise will concentrate on the 164 utilities with surface water sources which chlorinate.

Prevalence of Chloroform

On November 3, 1974, Russell Train, administrator of the EPA, ordered a nationwide survey to determine the concentration and potential effects of certain organic chemicals in drinking water. Designated as the National Organics Reconnaissance Survey (NORS), it included 80 cities in the

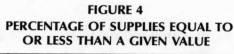

FIGURE 4
PERCENTAGE OF SUPPLIES EQUAL TO
OR LESS THAN A GIVEN VALUE

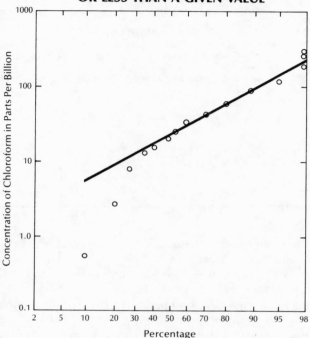

U.S., geographically distributed so that some of the cities were in each of EPA's 10 regions (Symons 1975, pp. 634–47). The supplies were chosen to represent as wide a variety of raw-water sources and treatment techniques as possible.

Figure 4 shows some of the results from this survey. It is a graph of chloroform concentration versus the number of utilities that when sampled had concentrations equal to or less than that level. For example, 91 percent of the utilities sampled had concentrations of chloroform in their finished water equal to or less than $100\,\mu g/l$ (ppb). If it were assumed that this distribution applied equally to all surface water suppliers chlorinating and serving more than 100,000 people, we could estimate the number of utilities that would be affected by a chloroform standard. Assume, therefore, that three potential levels are considered for a standard: $100\,\mu g/l$, $30\,\mu g/l$, and $5\,\mu g/l$. Table 4 shows the percentage of utilities that would be affected at each of these levels. Applying the factors in table 4 to the surface supplies that chlorinate (table 3) yields the number of utilities affected in each of the three size categories. These data will be used to

Table 4

SURFACE SUPPLIES AFFECTED BY STANDARD

Level	Percent of Supplies Affected
5 μg/l	92
30 μg/l	62
100 μg/l	9

assess the total economic impact of the standard. Note that the line drawn in figure 4 to derive the data in table 4 tends to overestimate the number of utilities that will be affected and, therefore, the magnitude of the total economic impact.

Total Economic Impact

Several technological approaches may be utilized for solving the trihalomethane problem. One is to use chlorine dioxide as an alternative disinfectant to chlorine. Chlorine dioxide reacts with organic material with lower levels of halogenation, but presumably achieves disinfection results equivalent to those of chlorine. A more elaborate approach would be granular activated carbon, which is much more expensive than chlorine dioxide in both capital and operating costs. It actually removes the precursors to chloroform and provides a more "polished" drinking water supply by removing organic compounds.

Both types of treatment are examined in this paper. The average service population for each of the three population categories (table 3) considered will be multiplied by the number of utilities affected at each standard level (columns 2, 3, and 4 in table 5). This product is then multiplied by 100 gal/capita/day (assumed water consumption) and by the cost in ¢/1,000 gal for each technology (calculated at the equivalent plant capacity for the average service population). These cost figures are shown in columns 5 through 10 in table 5. The unit costs are taken from the Interim Treatment Guide (Clark et al. 1976). For example, table 5 shows that implementation of a chloroform standard (100μg/l) using chlorine dioxide technology would yield an annual cost (Operating, Maintenance, and Capital) of $1.77 million. Using granular activated carbon to meet the same standard would result in an annual cost of $8.09 million.

These annual costs can be translated into per capita costs for the affected utilities, as shown in table 6. The estimates shown in tables 5 and

Table 5

COST OF COMPLIANCE FOR SURFACE WATER SUPPLIES
(assuming 100 gal/capita/day usage)

Population	No. of Utilities Affected			Cost of Chlorine Dioxide (mil dol)			Cost of Granular Activated Carbon (mil dol)		
	5 μg/l	30 μg/l	100 μg/l	5 μg/l	30 μg/l	100 μg/l	5 μg/l	30 μg/l	100 μg/l
100,000 to 500,000	96	65	10	13.57	9.13	1.27	86.45	58.40	8.85
500,000 to 1,000,000	20	13	2	6.08	4.02	0.51	31.80	21.17	3.29
>1,000,000	12	8	1	15.00	10.22	1.77	67.87	46.36	8.09

6 do not allow for capacity expansion or inflationary effects, but should provide some perspective on the annual costs required to meet a chloroform standard. Using the logic described herein, one could estimate the economic impact of other standards which will eventually be promulgated.

There are many arguments, both pro and con, regarding the need for setting an organic standard under the Safe Drinking Water Act. Some of these arguments will be examined in the following section.

Table 6

PER CAPITA COSTS FOR
AFFECTED UTILITIES

Level	Chlorine Dioxide ($/capita/yr)	Granular Activated Carbon ($/capita/yr)
100,000 to 500,000	0.51	3.28
500,000 to 1,000,000	0.48	2.55
>1,000,000	0.40	1.83

PROS AND CONS OF SETTING A STANDARD

In setting a standard, the arguments focus on the need for assessing risk (Lowrance 1976). Four steps that may be followed in assessing risk are:

1. Define the conditions of exposure.
2. Identify the adverse effects.
3. Relate exposure with effect.
4. Estimate overall risk.

Once a risk assessment has been performed, a decision has to be made as to the relative costs and benefits of removing the risk.

The conditions of exposure to chloroform have been reasonably well defined. Chloroform is known to be a byproduct of the interactions of chlorine with organic material.

The adverse effects are also reasonably well defined. The National Cancer Institute has identified chloroform as a carcinogen (Report on the Carcinogenesis Bioassay).

Relating exposure to effect is a more difficult task. Studies performed by the Environmental Defense Fund indicate a statistical relationship between cancer and the presence of chloroform in drinking water (Page 1976). The conclusiveness of these studies is still a matter of debate.

Despite imperfect knowledge, an estimate of the overall risk must still be made. The Environmental Defense Fund has estimated that perhaps as much as 10 percent of the cancer in areas served by surface water may be caused by drinking water. This estimate is also a matter for debate.

Assuming that the technology is 100 percent effective in removing chloroform and if, in fact, chloroform in drinking water causes cancer, then the cost figures in tables 5 and 6 provide some rough estimates as to what chloroform control costs will be. The public must then decide if it is willing to make the investment to minimize the risk of cancer from drinking water.

A valid argument against setting a chloroform standard is that the cancer to chloroform-in-drinking-water link has not been well established. In light of this lack of knowledge, the cost of installing removal technology may be excessive.

An argument for setting a standard is that the per capita costs are minimal and that the control mechanism is simple. The pathways of chloroform into man are well defined, and control technology can be applied easily at the treatment plant to minimize the risk of exposure for large segments of the population.

Both of these arguments must be considered carefully before a standard is established. However, one benefit of the standard-setting exercise is the information that it reveals. It makes the cost of achieving adequate drinking water supplies explicit. A combination of the Federal Water Pollution Control Act and the Safe Drinking Water Act provides an institutional mechanism for evaluating drinking water alternatives.

INSTITUTIONAL CONSIDERATIONS

The combination of the Safe Drinking Water Act and the Federal Water Pollution Control Act provides an ideal mechanism for making the costs of safe drinking water explicit to the public (Public Law 92–500). The ANPRM cites various portions of the Federal Water Pollution Control Act that have an impact on the quality of drinking water sources, including control of effluents from point sources under Sections 304, 307, and 311; nonpoint source controls and area-wide management under Section 208; and reporting requirements under Section 308. Proper use of PL 92–500 could prevent contamination of water sources, resulting in reduction in organic loadings in raw water, thereby assisting the water utility manager in maintaining satisfactory finished water quality.

Although strict control of pollution discharges in order to protect drinking water sources is difficult—for example, nonpoint sources are difficult to control—the interaction of these two laws (PL 92–500 and PL 93–523) provides a framework for informing the American public about the cost of maintaining adequate raw water quality. The public knows that it must incur the cost of controlling discharges at the source or providing a barrier at the water treatment plant. An institutional framework has been established which internalizes the external costs of pollution, making these costs explicit to the consumer or discharger. Therefore, evaluating the costs of the standards to be implemented by the Safe Drinking Water Act has greater implications than simply mechanically fulfilling the requirements of the act. It provides vital information which can be used by the public in making important choices as to whether control technology must be applied at the waste discharge or at the intake. Therefore, the Safe Drinking Water Act should not be viewed in isolat on, but in its proper relationship to the other pieces of legislation which make up the body of water laws in the United States.

A concrete example of the institutional implications of PL 93–523 is the use of regional solutions to water supply problems. Regionalization may take the form of a physically connected water supply, a regional management system, or an integrated regional utility which includes both water supply and wastewater systems. Much work still remains to be done in this important area.

SUMMARY AND CONCLUSIONS

Historically, water supply and water resources development have played a vital role in the development of civilization. In the water-rich, eastern United States, the application of English common law and its emphasis on riparian rights served as the early basis for water law. As the population expanded westward into arid lands and as population densities increased in the eastern states, a new concept of appropriative rights tempered with the "American rule of reasonable use" came into existence.

Eventually the federal government became active in passing water quality and water resource legislation. This legislative activity has increased significantly over the years, resulting in a complex framework of water-related legislation. The most recent of these laws is the Safe Drinking Water Act. Each law viewed in isolation may appear to be the work of special interest groups but, when viewed as a part of a growing body of laws, reflects an increasing awareness and concern on the part of the American public for the protection of the environment and preservation of natural resources.

The Safe Drinking Water Act establishes primary and secondary standards for drinking water supplies and provides for the protection of underground sources of water. It contains many complex and unusual provisions, including a requirement for public notification when a utility is in violation of the act and a citizen's suit provision. In combination with PL 92–500 it provides a framework for internalizing the external costs of pollution.

At the time of writing (December 1976), there have been no standards promulgated under the act, although there is great controversy over what standards and levels should be set. Much of this controversy is generated by the utilities and the water supply industry that will be regulated. Their reluctance to install expensive equipment to meet the act's provisions is understandable, but in examining their arguments one is reminded of similar arguments presented in the past against such now-accepted practices as the use of sand filtration and the banning of the common drinking water cup on interstate carriers.

For example, Ripley Nichols of MIT stated as late as 1884 that experiments performed by him and others had convinced him that filtration would not remove the color "generally affecting American supplies nor the disagreeable tastes and odors to which they are liable" (Fielding 1976, pp. 16–19). Although careful filtration could improve such supplies he doubted whether the results were worth the cost and warned communities not to embark on such a plan of "artificial" filtration unless prepared to spend a possible $2.50 per million gallons for operation alone. The elimination of the common drinking water cup on interstate carriers met strong opposition. The hypothesis was advanced that if the cups became unavailable for any reason, the crowd so deprived of drinking facilities would have its health seriously endangered and might even be forced to succumb to the obvious temptation of alcoholic beverages (Symons).

The writer is not suggesting that the arguments given against the provisions of the Safe Drinking Water Act are irrational, as the two arguments cited above appear to be. It is well to remember that these two arguments did not seem irrational when originally formulated.

No matter how one views the Safe Drinking Water Act and its implications, it is the writer's opinion that the drinking water issue is and will be under closer public scrutiny than in the past. Water utility managers will be faced with growing public interest in their activities; and defending a position that does not include installation of the best available technology for water treatment and distribution will be increasingly difficult. Drinking water standards can be viewed as a warranty between the producer and consumer that drinking water will be of a given quality. The waterworks industry should be aware of and should plan for this growing consumer interest. The writer's opinion is that this interest is genuine, healthy, and lasting, and should be encouraged.

REFERENCES

Ciriacy–Wantrup, S. V.; Hutchins, Wells A.; Martz, Clyde O.; Sho Sato; Stone, Albert W. 1967. *Water and Water Rights: A Treatise on the Laws of Waters and Allied Problems: Eastern, Western, Federal.* Vol. 1. Indianapolis: The Allen Smith Co.

Clark, Robert M.; Guttman, Daniel L.; Crawford, John L.; and Machisko, John A. 1976. "Appendix 1 of the Interim Treatment Guide for the Control of Chloroform and Other Trihalomethanes—The Cost of Removing Chloroform and Other Trihalomethanes from Drinking Water Supplies." Cincinnati, Ohio: U.S. Environmental Protection Agency, Office of Research and Development, Municipal Environmental Research Laboratory 45268.

Federal Register, 7-14-76. Vol. 41, no. 136, Drinking Water, 28991–29011.

Fielding, Liz 1976. "A Revolutionary Idea—Water for the People." *Water and Wastes Engineering*, July.

Gindler, Barton J. 1967. *Water and Water Rights: A Treatise on the Laws of Water and Allied Problems: Eastern, Western, Federal.* Vol. 3. Indianapolis: The Allen Smith Co.

Hines, N. Williams. "Public Regulation of Water Quality in the United States." Springfield, Virginia: U.S. Dept. of Commerce, Legal Study 18, prepared for National Water Commission, Department of Commerce, PB–208–309. Report no. NWC–L–72–036.

Laurance, William W. 1976. *Of Acceptable Risk.* Los Altos, California: William Kaufmann, Inc.

McDermott, James H. 1973. "Federal Drinking Water Standards—Past, Present, Future." *Journal of the Environmental Engineering Division*, ASCE, Vol. 99, no. EE 4, Proc. Paper 9924, August.

Page, Talbot; Harris, Robert H.; and Epstein, Samuel S. 1976. "Drinking Water and Cancer Mortality in Louisiana." *Science* 193.

Public Law 92–500, *Amendments to the Federal Water Pollution Control Act.* 92nd Congress. Washington, D.C.: GPO.

Public Law 93–523, Safe Drinking Water Act, 93rd Congress. Washington, D.C.: 16 December 1974.

Report on the Carcinogenesis Bioassay of Chloroform, Carcinogen Bioassay, and Program Resources Branch, Carcinogenesis Program Division of Cancer Cause and Prevention. Bethesda, Maryland: National Cancer Institute.

Symons, James M. 1976. "Interim Treatment Guide for the Control of Chloroform and Other Trihalomethanes." Water Supply Research Division, Municipal Environmental Research Laboratory, U.S. Environmental Protection Agency 45268, June.

Symons, James M. "Fluoridation of Water Supplies." Mimeographed. Cincinnati, Ohio: U.S. Environmental Protection Agency, Water Supply Research Division, Municipal Environmental Research Laboratory.

Symons, James M. et al. 1975. "National Organics Reconnaissance Survey for Halogenated Organics." *Journal of the American Water Works Association* 67, (11), November 1976.

PRESENT AND FUTURE DIRECTIONS FOR MUNICIPAL WATER SUPPLY AND WASTEWATER REUSE RESEARCH

FRANCIS T. MAYO, Director,
and
JOHN N. ENGLISH, Sanitary Engineer
Wastewater Research Division
Municipal Environmental Research Laboratory
U.S. Environmental Protection Agency
Cincinnati, Ohio

Major gaps exist in our knowledge of virtually all the areas of water supply and wastewater research which is being conducted by the Environmental Protection Agency. All too frequently, the decisions relating to municipal water systems must be made in an atmosphere of extreme and competing views. In making these decisions, some insist on complete scientific explanations before action is taken. Others, often operating under great pressure, are prepared to act without adequate understanding of the consequences of those actions.

In the face of growing demands for accelerated regulatory action, it is not easy to travel a middle road between those who require infallible knowledge and those who prefer to make use of opportunities. The difficulties are increased by the failure of current public laws to face many important aspects of reality and by the fact that the courts have imposed interpretations of these laws that may not have been anticipated by the lawmakers.

These issues are brought into sharp focus when we address ourselves to the problem of the integrity of our public water supplies in regard to human health. Our attitudes toward and knowledge about these health problems will have extremely important consequences for wastewater treatment requirements and for water quality standards. In addition, they may have a profound impact on the pace at which wastewater reuse will be accepted, especially for general municipal purposes.

It is in the context of such concerns that I want to discuss some of the research being done directly by, or under the coordinating role of the Municipal Environmental Research Laboratory of the U.S. Environmental Protection Agency. I will confine myself principally to the research programs concerning water supply and wastewater reuse.

WATER SUPPLY

For many years Americans paid very little attention to their drinking water. Recently, however, the public's interest in water supply has grown rapidly. This phenomenon is certainly more than the result of simple curiosity. There are indeed serious reasons for concern. The root cause of these concerns is the universal importance of water to man's very existence. It is interesting to note that such a basic fact was not given legislative recognition until the passage of the Safe Drinking Water Act (PL 93–523) in December 1974. The act has, by its very existence, contributed substantially to the public concern about what we drink.

It is ironic that much of the concern should be directed at chlorination. For almost 75 years chlorination has been used to protect the drinking water of hundreds of millions of people throughout the world. In fact, the chlorination of public water supplies has undoubtedly contributed to the increase in man's life expectancy and the decrease in infant mortality that is enjoyed in the developed countries of the world.

Not until very recently did we learn that this versatile chemical, chlorine, when introduced into public water supplies as a disinfectant, frequently reacts with organic materials in the water. These reactions create a variety of complex compounds, some of which, such as chloroform, are known to be carcinogenic in animals.

Such words as carcinogens and mutagens are used with increasing frequency in discussions of public water supplies. Sanitary engineers and public health officials are struggling with ten-syllable names for complex organic compounds—names that have in the past been largely limited to the vocabularies of industrial chemists. This is occurring against a growing background of conclusions by leading scientists and medical authorities that 60 to 90 percent of human cancers are environmentally induced.

The discovery of many organic compounds in the nation's drinking water and worries about their associated health implications led to enactment of the Safe Drinking Water Act. Research under the act is directed toward assuring the availability of dependable and safe supplies of drinking water. Attention is also given to health effects of contaminants in drinking water. This includes development of analytical methods to assess quality of drinking water and development of water treatment processes to remove or reduce undesirable contaminants for which current methods are not adequate.

One of the major goals of this research is the creation of valid criteria for drinking-water quality standards. These standards will, of course, have to be based on a scientific understanding of organic, inorganic, and microbiological contaminants. Another major goal is the evaluation, improvement, and development of an adequate control technology in order to attain these standards. This will involve both the adaptation of large-scale technology to small water systems and the development of new or special technologies.

The products which this research should eventually provide to municipal water supply systems include:

— Improved methods to identify and measure contaminants in drinking water and to identify sources of contaminants.

— Improved methods to identify and measure health effects of contaminants in drinking water.

— New or improved methods of treating raw water to prepare it for drinking. This involves improving the efficiency of water treatment and contaminant removal.

— Improved ways to provide dependable supplies of safe drinking water. This includes water purification and distribution improvements and methods to assess health-related hazards of drinking water.

— Improved ways to protect groundwater sources of public water supplies from contamination.

Current Research

Activities have already been inaugurated by the EPA in the areas of water treatment, system management, health effects, and measurement and identification techniques. Efforts are also under way to evaluate and demonstrate pilot-scale technologies to inactivate germs and to remove potentially toxic or aesthetically displeasing contaminants. These efforts are directed toward achieving compliance with both present and future drinking water quality standards. Technologies to remove organic contaminants and to develop alternatives to existing chlorination methods are receiving special attention. Improved methods of operation are also being studied for new and existing water supply facilities.

The primary emphasis in these research programs is the evaluation of potential health hazards from organics and the validity of possible general organic indicators such as carbon chloroform extraction. Also extremely important are efforts to evaluate the nature, concentration, and effects of inorganic and microbiological contaminants of drinking water. The work undertaken by the EPA Office of Research and Development will have to be carefully coordinated with the work of other federal agencies such as the National Cancer Institute.

Sensitive measurement and identification methods for low concentration levels of many toxic and carcinogenic substances must be developed. These methods require special concentration and separation techniques. Present methods for organics are capable of detecting only small amounts of total organic content, and research is being directed toward improving methods for identification of both the organic contaminants and their sources.

Development of virus detection methods and rapid instrumentation methods for detection of inorganic substances is receiving more attention. To carry through and complement current program objectives in fiscal year 1977, studies are being conducted on the determination of the health effects of organics, tin, manganese, cadmium, arsenic, selenium, barium, molybdenum, antimony, nitrates, and asbestos.

Planned Research

Efforts to develop measurement and identification methods will be continued and expanded. These efforts will focus on more practical techniques to identify, measure, and determine the sources of organic substances and viral agents. The techniques will be designed for use by state and local public health officials responsible for safeguarding public drinking water supplies.

More accurate health effects data for organic, inorganic, and microbiological contaminants of drinking water will be developed through short- and long-term toxicological studies and comparative epidemiological studies. The findings of these studies will be redirected as necessary when the National Academy of Sciences (NAS) completes its evaluation of the health effects of contaminated drinking water. The NAS study is required by PL 93–523.

Work will be continued on the removal and inactivation of cadmium, asbestos, nitrates, bacteria, viruses, and organic compounds. In addition, similar work will be undertaken for such substances as lead and radium. The EPA also intends to determine how to prevent water quality deterioration that may occur during the distribution of drinking water. Technology applicable to small water-supply systems will be emphasized.

A substantial research and development effort will be made to control organic contaminants in drinking water. The mechanisms of halogenated organics formation in normal disinfection practices will be determined and control methods will be developed. Alternatives to chlorine disinfection will be thoroughly studied in the near future. Among these alternatives are methods employing chlorine dioxide or a combination of ozone and ultraviolet light.

Increased effort is planned on methods to remove and dispose of organics. Studies will continue to provide criteria for waste-disposal site selection and for groundwater basin management.

WASTEWATER REUSE

The development of advanced waste-treatment technology capable of treating wastewater to a reusable commodity that is "too good to throw away" has attracted much attention, particularly from agencies responsible for maintaining adequate water supplies in water-short areas. However, the amount of water being reused is presently rather meager. Less than two percent of the available municipal wastewater is being reused on a planned basis. The lack of adequate health effects data on the residues in high-quality effluents has stymied any potential reuse situation that is associated with health questions, and the information on the feasibility of source substitution as a means of increasing planned reuse is sparse. Furthermore, the deficiencies of water-resource management concepts in regard to reuse are hampering its development even for the less controversial purposes that do not involve much apparent risk.

Research efforts are under way in EPA to project the need for reuse other than for potable purposes and to develop the institutional arrangements for bringing reclaimed water into our systems. In addition, a long-term health effects research program is being implemented which addresses potable reuse and which should have a considerable impact on the needs of communities in areas where source substitution cannot provide sufficient water to meet future domestic water supply needs.

Direct Potable Reuse as a Long-term Goal

Unless and until adequate health effects data are obtained on the residues in high-quality wastewater treatment effluents, most potential applications of wastewater reuse will be blocked.

The Water Pollution Control Federation (WPCF) and the American Water Works Association (AWWA) issued a joint resolution that urged the federal government to support a massive research effort to develop needed technology and evaluate potential health problems related to recycling of wastewater for domestic supplies. These organizations underscored the "lack of adequate scientific information about possible acute and long-term effects upon man's health from such reuse," and also noted that "the essential fail-safe technology to permit such direct reuse has not yet been demonstrated." The resolution recognizes the need for an "immediate and sustained multi-disciplinary, national effort to provide the scientific knowledge and technology relative to the reuse of water for drinking purposes in order to assure full protection of the public health."

A relatively new program has been initiated by the EPA Health Effects Research Laboratory in Cincinnati to deal with the health effects associated with the potable reuse of municipal wastewater. The projects being conducted within this program are based on the results of a workshop held in March 1975 to identify "Research Needs for the Potable Reuse of Municipal Wastewater." The objectives of the program are to determine the nature and concentrations of organic, inorganic, and microbiologic contaminants present in advanced waste treatment (AWT) plant effluents which may actually or potentially be used as a source of potable water supply (WPCF Adopts Water Reuse Policy 1973, p. 2404); to conduct long-term toxicological and epidemiological studies to determine the health effects of consuming such waters (*Journal American Water Works Association* 1973, p. 700); and to provide health effects criteria for the reuse of renovated wastewater to assure the safety of the product (U.S. EPA 1975). Active projects in this program include:

— analysis of organics in AWT effluents

— mutagenic testing of AWT organic concentrates

— biological evaluation (using mice) of toxic effects of organics present in AWT effluents

— chemistry and cytotoxicity studies of health

— effects of consumption of renovated water

— pyrogenic activity of carbon-filtered wastewaters

— effects of ozone on organics in wastewater.

The health effects research needed to establish confidence in potable reuse parallels the ongoing and planned research directed toward presently used water supplies. Since we are living in a world where millions of people are already using wastewater indirectly for potable purposes, the same questions must be answered for both direct and indirect reuse. What are the health effects of reusing wastewater either directly or indirectly? What technology is needed to remove potential health-hazardous constituents?

Health effects data for present domestic water supplies and properly treated wastewater used for potable purposes can be collected by applying the contaminant measurements and toxicity testing techniques al-

ready developed or currently being developed. A comparison of the two
sets of data should provide a useful basis for evaluation of reuse.

Source Substitution as a Near-term Goal

The volume of wastewater potentially available for planned reuse is significant; however, the quantity presently reused is small. The U.S. Water
Resources Council estimated that in 1970 municipalities used 9,850 billion gallons (bg) of water of which 7,670 bg or about 78 percent was
returned as wastewater. In 1971, only 135 bg of municipal wastewater
treatment plant effluents was being reused for planned purposes (Water
Policies for the Future 1973). This represents less than two percent of the
available waste flow (Schmidt et al. 1975, p. 2229). The remainder of the
wastewater is returned to receiving waters to provide the basis for much
unplanned reuse.

Because of the health-effects questions and the high costs associated
with treating wastewater to provide a safe potable quality water, it is
anticipated that the priorities for reuse will pattern themselves in such a
way that water of high quality will not be used for purposes that can
tolerate a lesser degree of purity. Thus, source substitution is a means of
conserving approved sources of potable water in water-short areas by
using poorer quality water for purposes that can readily adapt to it.

Source substitution is often proposed for industrial uses. However, the
viability of expanding industrial reuse of municipal wastewater depends
on the ability of industry to adapt its technology to use a lower-quality
water. Many industries use the available municipal potable water supply
and they often do not know if they can maintain product quality with a less
pure water. On the other hand, the cost of municipal water supplies will
increase because of the need for more sophisticated treatment technology
to remove recently identified health-hazardous materials associated with
many conventional surface supplies. Industries will consequently be looking for cheaper sources of water. If expansion of industrial reuse is to
be facilitated, studies must be undertaken to identify both institutional
arrangements and the water quality requirements of industry.

Reuse is potentially an effective tool for water quality management.
Where receiving waters are subject to stringent water quality criteria in
order to protect them from pollutants, the cost of wastewater treatment to
meet the stream standards may be greater than the combined cost of (1) a
lesser degree of treatment designed to meet an industrial or other use,
and (2) of transporting the effluent from the point of treatment to the site
of reuse.

DIRECTIONS FOR REUSE RESEARCH

The reuse program of the EPA Office of Research and Development is following two avenues of research. The first is directed toward the more near-term and less controversial reuse of wastewater for nonpotable purposes only. The second avenue leads toward potable reuse. This is necessarily a long-term program which will be affected by health research on presently used conventional surface supplies. Potential research projects identified with each of these two areas are:

Nonpotable Projects

— Identification of t! e need for reuse and development of the institutional arrangements for bringing reclaimed water into our systems

— Determination of industry's ability to adapt to various levels of water quality

— Evaluation of dual distribution systems and economic incentives to promote their use

— Compilation of water utility experiences with conservation programs such as installation of water meters, public education, and the use of water saving devices.

Potable (Direct–Indirect) Projects

— Epidemiological study of a community using water supplies containing significant quantities of wastewater

— Development of a data base on residues in effluents and their health effects

— Fractionation and identification of organics in AWT effluents

— Survey of inorganics in AWT effluents

— Testing of the toxicity of organic concentrates

— Survey to identify the proportion of wastewater at water supply abstraction points and to address waste-discharge/water-intake relationships

— Evaluation of AWT processes to remove toxic materials

— Evaluation of the effects of groundwater hydraulics and aquifer characteristics on recharged wastewater constitutents.

Industries, municipalities, and the general public will make the decision for reuse when the time is right for their particular situation. EPA is attempting to provide the necessary research information to allow each concerned water user to determine the proper place for reused wastewater in its water-resource management program.

REFERENCES

Journal American Water Works Association 1973, vol. 65.

Schmidt, C. J. et al. 1975. "Municipal Wastewater Reuse in the U.S." *Journal Water Pollution Control Fed.*, vol. 47.

U.S. EPA 1975. "Research Needs for the Potable Reuse of Municipal Wastewater." EPA Tech. Ser., EPA 600/9–75–007, December.

"Water Policies for the Future" 1973. Final Report of the National Water Commission, June.

"WPCF Adopts Water Reuse Policy" 1973. *Journal Water Pollution Control Fed.*, vol. 45.

AUGMENTING SUPPLY:
WASTEWATER REUSE

Within the hydrologic cycle nature is engaged in a process of continuous water reuse. Water is evaporated, transported and deposited on land, and finally returned to the sea—in the process making available to man highly purified water at minimum cost. Nature makes available, however, only a minuscule portion of the earth's waters, and in some areas man has captured virtually all of it. In the search for more water, it is now frequently proposed that man employ his technology to "short-circuit" the hydrologic cycle and utilize his own wastewater for supply purposes. In fact, it is often argued that wastewater is already being reused inadvertently, and this is certainly the case for many cities on the lower reaches of the nation's major river systems.

Reuse, both planned and inadvertent, has recently generated considerable interest—and considerable controversy. How safe is it? Will the public accept it? Is it economically feasible? The three papers of this section present widely divergent views on the role of reuse and the difficulties involved in its implementation.

Dan Okun speaks for a great many health officials and concerned citizens when he warns that the consequences to human health from reused wastewater are largely unknown and perhaps unknowable. He agrees with Francis Mayo, who in the previous chapter suggests that reuse should not be considered for potable purposes. With regard to human consumption of water, Okun maintains that the only prudent course is a continued reliance on the hydrologic cycle. However, because of increasing population and the limited amount of drinking-quality water available. reuse will be needed to meet demands for other uses of water. In many cases dual distribution systems may be required.

LeRoy Reuter joins Okun in emphasizing the distinction between reuse for potable and nonpotable purposes, but unlike Okun he is interested in developing reuse for potable water supply. From his involvement in the development of a practical potable reuse system for the U.S. Army, he has concluded that it is crucial to resolve health and safety questions connected with reuse. Until these health questions are answered, reuse will be at a considerable competitive disadvantage as a supply alternative because of uncertainties in the safety factors required for the design of the water treatment facilities.

147

Richard Heaton can be fairly described as an advocate of potable wastewater reuse. He is, of course, concerned with health implications, but he believes that the health problems associated with reuse are no more serious than those associated with many existing sources of supply. After summarizing the most important research activities concerning reuse currently being conducted in the U.S., he describes the process by which Denver, Colorado, reached the decision to develop a potable reuse system.

OPTIONS FOR PROTECTING THE QUALITY OF MUNICIPAL WATER SUPPLIES

DANIEL A. OKUN,
Kenan Professor of Environmental Engineering
University of North Carolina at Chapel Hill

A significant portion of the U.S. population, estimated at one-third, draws its water from polluted sources, a practice that we now fear may pose a threat to those obliged to ingest these waters over a lifetime. The health effects of using polluted sources are far from completely understood. Furthermore, direct wastewater reuse is becoming an increasingly attractive option for water supply in many areas. Reuse has serious implications for human health.

THE USE OF POLLUTED SOURCES FOR POTABLE WATER

The decisions to use large rivers for potable water supplies were made originally because such supplies were available at low cost, the rivers serving as natural aqueducts. Dr. John Snow's classical epidemiological studies in the mid-nineteenth century, identifying the Thames as the source of a cholera epidemic, followed by the development of the germ theory of disease, led to the first questioning of this well-established practice. However, both the filtration of water and more particularly its disinfection with chlorine, techniques developed at the beginning of the twentieth century, made engineers sanguine about the hazards of such convenient supplies. Many large U.S. cities, among them Philadelphia, Cincinnati, and New Orleans, took the expedient course, drawing water from nearby rivers that drained vast areas upstream. In fact, whenever New York City engineers have considered the need for new sources of water in addition to their upstream mountain supplies, the Hudson River has been urged upon them.

With the number of upland and underground protected sources limited, and becoming more costly to develop, the pressure to use river sources that are inevitably polluted has been growing. This phenomenon is certainly not limited to the U.S. In Britain, the now-defunct Water Resources Board proposed a national strategy that used the rivers as

149

aqueducts with supplies to be drawn from their lower reaches (Water Resources Board 1973).

The synthetic chemical revolution following World War II, the growing sophistication in analytical techniques, and populations that survive infectious diseases only to succumb to environmentally-induced chronic diseases, all point to the need for an examination of river water strategy on the part of those who manage our water resources.

Where water sources are polluted, a breakdown in treatment may serve to infect large numbers of users. While bacterial diseases may no longer constitute a major problem in this country, the enteric viruses are another story. Only a few virus particles need to be ingested for infection to result. Most of those who become infected will not become visibly ill, but the infections cannot be considered innocuous as they may spread further through other routes. Breakdowns are not likely to occur in the large well-managed systems, but the evidence is clear that the smaller systems offer little security against failure.

More important than infections, however, are the health threats posed by the lifelong ingestion of even low levels of the synthetic organic chemicals inevitably present in all waters drawn downstream from extensive industrialized areas. Many of these chemicals, either alone or in concert with others, have been demonstrated to be carcinogenic, mutagenic, and/or teratogenic. More than 15 years ago, W. C. Hueper of the National Cancer Institute presaged our current concerns (1960).

> It is obvious that with the rapidly increasing urbanization and industrialization of the country ... the danger of cancer hazards from the consumption of contaminated drinking water will grow considerably within the foreseeable future.

Actually, it was the finding of organic chemicals in Mississippi River water and the epidemiological study conducted in New Orleans by the Environmental Defense Fund and Resources for the Future (Page and Harris 1974) that triggered the TV special, "Drinking Water May Be Dangerous to Your Health" in November 1974 and led to passage of the Safe Drinking Water Act one month later.

The significance of the long-term ingestion of low levels of contaminants in water is difficult to ascertain because their effects are insidious and often screened by other factors having similar effects. This is not the place to debate the matter, as it is being extensively examined elsewhere. Certainly it will be many years before a final determination can be made, if it ever can be, as to the health significance of these chemicals in drinking water. In the meantime, just as Dr. Snow ordered the handle removed from the Broad Street pump to end a cholera epidemic in Soho before anything was known about the germ theory of disease, we too might be prudent in planning our water resources developments before we have all the knowledge we need. Decisions made today on water sources will affect our descendants for generations into the future.

Three options are available to us:

1. *Eliminate contaminants at the source.* While this was the goal of PL 92–500, it was not realistic in 1972 and is even less so today, and EPA administrators have acknowledged this. New legislation has already slowed and will continue to slow the development of new chemicals, but talk of their elimination from the aquatic environment is a deception on the public. According to *Science,* some 2 million recognized chemical compounds exist today, and nearly 250,000 new ones are formulated annually. EPA estimates that 1,000 new chemicals enter the market each year (Toxic Substances 1976, pp. 40–41). Preventing these chemicals from reaching the major rivers of the nation is just not feasible.

2. *Allowing that some chemicals will find their way into surface waters, we might monitor and remove them in wastewater and water supply treatment.* The technology for monitoring and treatment is in its infancy for some chemicals and nonexistent for many others. Obviously the developing of monitoring techniques will always lag behind the development of the chemicals themselves. Even if monitoring and treatment were at all feasible for the larger water enterprises, and only very few systems have the resources for using even the technology available, myriad small systems would be helpless.

3. *The final option is to avoid using polluted sources for potable purposes.* Protected sources, even where they now serve, are not likely to be adequate to meet future demands if they continue to be used indiscriminately for all purposes. If polluted rivers or reclaimed wastewaters can be used for nonpotable purposes, then the protected supplies can be conserved for their highest use—drinking. This would require the installation of dual systems, the extent of such systems depending upon availability of protected supplies in the region. At the least, or in the beginning, the polluted sources or reclaimed wastewaters can be used for large industrial supplies and for urban irrigation. If this is not sufficient, the nonpotable supply can be extended to toilet flushing in residences. Just such a development has taken place in the industrial area of Singapore.

There are, of course, objections to dual systems. When they hear the term "dual supply," public health people immediately respond with "cross connection." In any such system the nonpotable supply would be treated and disinfected and would resemble in quality the water that cities such as Cincinnati and New Orleans are now providing. Therefore, occasional inadvertent ingestion would not constitute a serious hazard. The potable supply would be distinguished from the nonpotable both in the assurance of its freedom from synthetic chemicals and in its more aesthetic appeal.

Many papers have been written about dual supplies and I will not go into the subject here other than to offer it as an increasingly attractive option that should be considered among other options for new water developments and, if it can prove itself on a comparison of costs, adopted. Even slightly higher costs might be justified by the assurance of a water supply free of the contaminants that would inevitably be present in water provided in some other way.

To those who would delve more deeply into the subject, I would suggest the proceedings of a recent seminar on dual distribution systems held by the American Water Works Association (1976), and papers by Haney and Hamann (1965, pp. 1073–1098), Deb and Ives (1974), Dove (1974), and Jackson (1973), the last an investigation into using the polluted Trent River in England for industrial water supply.

WATER REUSE

It is important to distinguish carefully between reuse for *nonpotable* and *potable* purposes. The potential for nonpotable reuse is far greater than that for potable reuse, if for no other reason than the demands for nonpotable uses far exceed potable requirements. Also, the public health hazards are far less significant in nonpotable uses.

It is important to note that direct nonpotable reuse is already being widely practiced, beginning with Bethlehem Steel's use of Baltimore's wastewaters, and now far more extensively in the arid west (Okun 1973, pp. 617–22). The only instance where direct reuse for potable purposes has been planned and executed is at Windhoek, Namibia (until recently, South-West Africa). Other options having been found preferable, potable reuse is no longer practiced. To my knowledge, in the United States, only in Denver is serious consideration being given to direct potable reuse.

As already pointed out, we have a great many instances of indirect reuse for potable purposes, the consequences of which we know very little. It seems to me that our efforts should be directed at studying and perhaps reducing indirect potable reuse before attempting to inflict direct reuse for potable purposes on a population that cannot know its health significance because even the professionals in the field do not know the hazards involved. To list the failure of public acceptance of potable reuse as a constraint to development of this approach is misleading at the very least. We might do better to encourage public questioning of the practice of indirect reuse. Public acceptance of reuse for nonpotable purposes is high, as indicated in California State Department of Health studies, and should not prove to be an impediment to such reuse (Bruvold and Ward 1972, pp. 1690–96).

Lastly, proponents of direct reuse often cite their product as meeting "Drinking Water Standards." Two points need to be made about the current (1962) PHS Drinking Water Standards: (1) the standards of chemical and bacteriological quality were based upon using the best available source, not wastewater; and (2) the standards are widely recognized as being entirely inadequate to protect the public health if water is drawn from a polluted source, as the standards do not mention viruses or any specific organic chemicals. Even when new standards are adopted, they are bound to reflect only our limited knowledge of the health significance of known chemicals, with little capacity to protect against chemicals not now detectable. As is well stated in these standards, the first, and best, line of defense against health hazards is a protected source.

CONCLUSIONS

As we face problems of potable water quality resulting from increasing urbanization and industrialization, the dual system is one of the options that should be considered for municipal water supply. Direct reuse of wastewater might very well be feasible for the nonpotable system. The potable system should be supplied, wherever possible, from a protected source. Dual systems offer promise of protecting the public against the lifelong ingestion of viruses and chemical-laden waters.

REFERENCES

Bruvold, W. H. and Ward, P. C. 1972. "Using Reclaimed Wastewater—Public Opinion." *Journal Water Pollution Control Federation* 44.

Deb, A. K. and Ives, K. J. 1974. *Dual Water Supply Systems.* Report submitted to Science Research Council, United Kingdom.

Dove, Lloyd A. 1974. *Total Wastewater Recycling and Zero Discharge in St. Petersburg, Florida.* Paper presented at the 47th Annual Conference, Water Pollution Control Federation, Denver, Colorado. October.

Haney, Paul D. and Hamann, Carl L. 1965. "Dual Water Systems," *Journal American Water Works Association* 57.

Hueper, W. C. 1960. "Cancer Hazards from Natural and Artificial Water Pollutants," *Proceedings, Conference on the Physiological Aspects of Water Quality.*
Washington, D.C.

Jackson, Keith 1973. *Dual Supply System.* Trent Research Programme, vol. 9,
Water Resources Board, Great Britain.

Okun, Daniel A. 1973. "Planning for Water Reuse." *Journal American Water
Works Association* 65.

Page, T. and Harris, R. H. 1974. "The Implications of Cancer-Causing Substances
in Mississippi River Water." Washington, D.C.: Environmental Defense Fund.

Proceedings, Seminar and Dual Distribution Systems, 1976. New Orleans,
Louisiana: American Water Works Association, in press.

"Toxic Substances: Five-Year Struggle for Landmark Bill May Soon Be Over."
Science 194, October 1976.

Water Resources Board (Great Britain) 1973. *Water Resources in England and
Wales,* 2 vols., HMSO.

HEALTH CONSIDERATIONS IN
WASTEWATER REUSE

LEROY H. REUTER, LT. COL. MSC,
Chief, Environmental Protection Research Division
U.S. Army Medical Bioengineering Research
and Development Laboratory
Fort Detrick, Maryland

I choose to speak of health "considerations" and not health "hazards" in regard to wastewater reuse because the health effects associated with water from any source are very poorly understood. Whether water for a supply system is produced from treated effluent or from a river, adequate scientific data about the health effects of all sorts of contaminants is not available at this time. Much theory about health "hazards" is thus necessarily based on untested assumptions, and current drinking water standards are consequently a source of concern to many.

WATER QUALITY STANDARDS

It is toward the questions concerning the standards for drinking water that most research on wastewater reuse is directed, and a few words about existing standards for drinking water are in order. Specifications for viruses and organics are very inadequate. Both our inability to detect viruses and organics at low levels of concentration and the absence of dose–response data for human consumption stand in the way of improving those specifications. For instance, coliform organisms are often used as indicators, but they are not good indicators of viruses in water that has been chemically disinfected. Measurements of such things as chemical oxygen demand and total organic carbon are used as gross indicators of water quality, but they give little clue about waterborne health hazards. Generally, the lower these numbers, the better the water quality is considered to be.

While the inadequacy of current drinking water standards is understood by many public health officials, it is not at this time a matter of great concern to the public at large. This situation becomes radically altered, however, when wastewater reuse is proposed as an alternative for public water supply. At this juncture, the questions about the adequacy of standards can become political issues.

155

Research on wastewater reuse has already had the effect of focusing the interest of public officials on drinking water standards. In the future, continued reuse research will undoubtedly help answer some of the current questions and perhaps raise new ones. Nonetheless, the standards regarding potable water are only one aspect of the health considerations associated with reuse.

NONPOTABLE REUSE

It is important to distinguish between water which is to be used for drinking and water intended for all other uses. As a matter of fact, less than one percent of the water used in the United States today needs to be of drinking water quality. However, the municipal systems, which produce most of the country's water, are designed and operated to deliver water of sufficient quality to meet the standards required by this minor use.

This will not necessarily continue to be the case. And even if it is, the majority of wastewater reuse applications in the next 50 years will not include direct human ingestion of the renovated water. The principal purposes for which renovated wastewater will be used in the foreseeable future include:

— Agricultural irrigation and land treatment

— Industrial processes not involving food or drugs

— Creation of recreational lakes

— Groundwater recharge

— Nonpotable public utility uses such as firefighting and greenbelt irrigation

— Limited domestic use.

The potential for eventual or inadvertent human contact and/or ingestion is present in all of these uses. Thus, all have health considerations associated with their implementation.

It is important to differentiate between user quality *requirements* and user quality *concerns*. The former do not change as a function of the water source, while the latter may vary greatly as a function of the source. Thus the user requirements for reused water for any purpose will be identical to those for water from more traditional sources; but the user concerns about reused water are likely to be increased significantly.

Health concerns to humans from reused water can be reduced to two classes—microorganisms and chemicals. Some research has been directed toward health effects associated with noningestion exposures from both of these. However, most evaluations must be made by transferring data from research done for other purposes.

Some of the possible routes of human exposure to microorganisms and chemicals associated with the various nonpotable modes of reuse previously listed include aerosols, food from both plants and animals, skin and eye contact from recreation, industrial processes, land treatment, and contact for hygienic purposes.

Biological warfare studies have given us some understanding of the infectivity of aerosolized microorganisms. Little is known, however, about viruses in aerosols, since the methodology to detect and identify viruses was not well advanced during the days of biological warfare research. Food studies directed toward both microorganisms and chemicals have been conducted, but knowledge of the effects of organic chemicals in foods is sketchy.

Most data on skin and eye problems resulting from exposure to microorganisms must be transferred from studies conducted on swimmers. Information on skin and eye problems resulting from exposure to chemicals is based chiefly on occupational health studies. Use of renovated waters to fill recreational lakes will continue to have limited applications because of the costs involved, but should not be delayed by the lack of accepted health standards.

Reuse within industry, except for food processing and pharmaceutical applications, now can be fully exploited, with a low probability of increasing the health hazard. Industrial reuse presents relatively few health concerns, and controlling the treatment of the influent wastewater allows an additional opportunity for reducing these concerns. If the addition of organic chemicals is controlled by the nature of the water usage, the reuse treatment train can be simplified. The major factor delaying the expansion of wastewater reuse in industry is not health concerns but rather the difficulty of producing and delivering water to the user at a competitive price and meeting quality specifications required for the industrial operations.

Land treatment offers a near-term reuse application of potentially significant magnitude. In the U.S. about one-half of the states already have regulations or guidelines for the design and operation of wastewater land treatment systems. Many of these regulations are intended to prevent hazards to human health and to the environment from the incomplete renovation of the wastewater before application and from the distribution of contaminants during the application process, such as the generation of aerosols from spray irrigation machinery. The requirements set by different states vary widely, and there is no uniform federal policy toward land treatment with renovated wastewater. This confusion stems primarily from gaps in our knowledge of the dose–response relationships for many organisms and chemicals.

The research needs concerning the health effects of land application of wastewater are achievable within a couple of years. Crucial to the public and professional understanding and acceptance of these reuse techniques is the completion of several key research efforts dealing with both microbial and chemical hazards. These efforts include identifying appropriate indicators of wastewater microbial levels; determining the human dose–response relationship for wastewater microbial aerosols; defining the potential for translocation of microbial or chemical contaminants to surface and groundwaters; and evaluating the usability of crops and domestic animals raised at land treatment sites.

Many of the requirements for research on potential chemical hazards should be transferable from ongoing or planned efforts on sludge land treatment. On the other hand, studies of potential hazards due to pathogenic micoorganisms must be specific to wastewater because of the great differences in the microbial quality of wastewaters and sludges.

As mentioned earlier, studies on organic contaminants are generally lacking.

RISK

Reuse systems can be designed and operated today that will present no greater apparent risk to humans than currently used "conventional" wastewater and water treatment systems. Clearly, an analysis of risk which compares wastewater reuse with other alternatives must include the summation of all risks over the entire population exposed. As there are health and environmental risks associated with currently practiced wastewater and water treatment methods, comparing the risks of reuse only to those of water treatment is an unfair penalty to reuse and an incomplete risk analysis. Indeed, the situation may be that the risk from either a proposed wastewater reuse system or from an existing conventional system for water and waste treatment is greater than the public will accept; but the risk from the existing system is tolerated because it has not been quantified and confirmed.

The health hazards that are of concern in designing both reuse and conventional treatment systems are generally divided into three categories: acute, subacute, and chronic. The acute and subacute hazards are relatively easy to identify and there is little debate that they are as controllable for reuse systems as they are for other wastewater and water treatment systems when the systems are operating at their design potential. Chronic hazards from both organic and inorganic chemicals are more difficult to identify. Research on chronic hazards is complex and costly, and the possibility of synergistic effects cannot be overlooked.

Consideration of human health hazards must necessarily have an impact on the design, management, and operation of any system proposed for reuse. Conversely, the design, management, and operation of a reuse system will inevitably have an impact on possible health hazards. Wastewater reuse systems have certain inherent advantages over single-pass systems:

— The water source may be more clearly defined and characterized and thus control of contamination more easily eliminated at the source.

— The specific uses of the water produced may be limited and certain uses may be excluded.

— There may be a willingness to pay treatment costs considerably higher than the costs of conventional systems.

The gaps in our knowledge concerning the health effects of reuse are significant, but they do not preclude a limited, constrained application of the nonpotable reuse modes at this time. Due to the limitations of the data base, however, the design and operation of reuse systems cannot be optimized, and this fact has obvious significance for the economic competitiveness of reuse as opposed to other sources of supply.

MUST

One of the most intensive current research efforts in wastewater reuse is being conducted by the U.S. Army Medical Department as part of a program to develop equipment for field hospitals. The field hospital equipment system is called MUST: Medical Unit, Self-contained Transportable. The MUST hospital will contain a module for the direct recycling of wastewater for reuse. This module, called the Water Processing Element (WPE), is important because of the exacting design specifications for its performance.

The WPE has two principal operating modes (see table 1). Mode 1, the wastewater for both nonpotable and potable reuse. The WPE must function under combat conditions, and it must be operable by a minimally trained high school graduate of average intelligence, working under stress.

Table 1

OPERATIONAL MODES
OF THE MUST WATER PROCESSING ELEMENT

Operational Mode	Function
1	Treatment and recycle of nonsanitary MUST hospital wastewaters
2	Treatment and discharge to the environment of nonsanitary MUST hospital wastewaters
	Treatment of natural fresh and brackish waters for potable and nonpotable use in a MUST hospital

Since the WPE is a direct reuse system, it must be designed to cope with several problems that are not involved in indirect systems. These problems include relatively little dilution water, reduced time between production and use, and the buildup of certain contaminants due to the multiple passage of water. Those disadvantages make it necessary to place increased emphasis on system control and real-time monitoring. Furthermore, each process must be designed to meet strict requirements under the full range of expected field conditions.

The WPE has two principal operating modes (see table 1). Model 1, the integrated mode, has a single function: to transform nonsanitary wastewater streams from a MUST hospital to "drinking water quality." The nonsanitary wastewater includes flows from showers, kitchen, laboratory, X-ray room, operating room, and laundry. Excluded are wastes from toilets.

For the present, water produced under Mode 1 will be used for nonpotable purposes only. The goal is that eventually this water will actually be of a quality acceptable for potable supply. Mode 1 allows 85 percent recovery of net influent water at a flow rate of approximately 4,200 gpd.

In Mode 2 operation, the WPE has two functions. One set of unit processes, the Water Treatment Unit (WTU), treats the nonsanitary wastewater from the MUST hospital for discharge to the environment. Simultaneously, another set of unit processes, the Water Purification Unit (WPU), treats natural fresh or brackish water for potable use. Under Mode 2 operation, the WTU will produce at least 3,900 gpd of treated wastewater, with at least 95 percent influent discharged. The WPU will produce at least 3,500 gpd of potable water with no more than 10 percent loss of influent. Special considerations will be made for natural waters high in dissolved solids and silica.

To achieve these goals, studies have been conducted on a one-quarter scale integrated system. A full-scale pilot facility is currently being designed and fabricated. The pilot plant will undergo extensive evaluation in the U.S. Army Medical Bioengineering Research's development laboratories at Fort Detrick, Maryland. This testing will start in February 1977 and will continue for approximately 18 months.

The unit processes that will be employed in the reuse mode include equalization, ultrafiltration by the tubular ABCOR HFD membrane, reverse osmosis by DuPont B-10 modules in a three-stage configuration, followed by UV-activated ozone oxidation in a multistage reactor, with chlorination of the product water.

The functional requirements of the WPE have changed little since the late 1960s, but the instrumentation design goal for satisfying them has.

The current instrumentation concept relies upon technology developed since 1973. A microprocessor will coordinate data acquisition, data analysis, monitoring, and control functions from a 30–60 sensor network. All unit processes of the WPE will be integrated by feedback, feedforward, and time clock loops manipulated by the microprocessor. Fault detection, fault isolation, and maintenance aids will be provided on the following priority basis: operator safety, mechanical integrity, mission satisfaction.

The man–machine interface will be designed in such a manner as to make the WPE as easily operable as a large truck. The bulk of routine control functions and many minor decision functions will be performed by the microprocessor. The operator will handle setup, startup, shutdown, disestablishment, movement, and first-echelon maintenance. It is anticipated that situations will arise in which one operator will have responsibility for several WPEs. The man–machine interface will recognize such constraints.

Capital cost of the control and monitoring subsystem of the WPE is anticipated to lie between $75,000 and $100,000. It is anticipated that this same subsystem, or one similar to it, would be capable of satisfying the control and monitoring requirements for any larger direct recycle system.

ACCEPTANCE OF REUSE

Although the costs involved in the design and operation of the WPE obviously are high, they are justified by the extraordinary conditions and requirements of an Army field hospital. Where these conditions do not prevail, as in a municipality which is trying to expand its water supply, such expenditures would be hard to justify. In order to gain acceptance, reuse must have a clear cost advantage over its competition because of the burden of unfamiliarity and uncertainty that it carries.

Three groups—the public, the consulting engineer, and the regulatory agencies—stand in the way of fuller reuse implementation. Each of these groups opposes reuse on different grounds.

The public accepts the risks associated with the present water quality produced by their utilities largely because there is no evidence apparent to them that the water is a source of adverse health effects. Nonetheless, the best water quality that can be produced is not being produced, and at least some adverse health effects are no doubt attributable to municipal water systems. A water supply could meet all EPA drinking standards and still present a health risk. As long as public ignorance of this situation continues, reuse is likely to meet with continued opposition from people who think they are concerned about health hazards.

Consulting engineers design systems they are familiar with, and this is understandable because their reputation is riding on the resulting design. As yet some of the technology necessary for reuse systems has not been transferred from the research community to the consulting engineer. Furthermore, a good data base on performance does not exist for many of the processes. Finally, control and monitoring systems may be the least understood of all important components in a reuse system.

Regulatory agencies take the position that a community should utilize the best quality source available. If reuse is proposed, the community must provide proof that the resulting water quality will be as good as, or better than, a single-pass system. The burden of proof is thus on the proponent—a difficult barrier for any single system to overcome. Several states require environmental impact statements for reuse systems. These can provide the basis for lengthy court cases if citizens take exception to the reuse proposal—not an attractive prospect for any utility.

RESEARCH NEEDS

To enable reuse system design and operation to be optimized and thereby to become more cost competitive, a better understanding of water-related health hazards is required. In the face of a very sketchy data base, large safety factors are presently being used in the design of reuse systems. As the data base is expanded, those safety factors can be reduced. More extensive toxicological research may indicate that an adverse effect can be expected at a lower contaminant concentration than was previously believed, but such findings may frequently be offset by the need to apply a much smaller safety factor.

I cannot be optimistic about the likelihood of extensive health-effects research being conducted on reuse systems in the foreseeable future, unless there is a water shortage of crisis proportions affecting a major population center. I will be working hard, however, to make my prediction wrong.

Reuse systems that employ the "overkill" concept in their design standards will be the first locations available for study in the U.S. Of primary concern to these projects will be the control of adverse chronic effects—that is, of effects that appear only after a long and continuous exposure. To measure these effects will require costly long-term research. If epidemiological studies conducted on the exposed population indicate no increased hazard, the only conclusion that can be drawn is that the water produced caused no discernible increase in adverse health effects—but these results would not in themselves provide sufficient information to relax the system design requirements. Therefore, in addition, dose-response data at the effect level, as well as at the no-effect level, must be generated.

In the meantime, proposed reuse systems will be at a disadvantage for two reasons. First, they will have the political disadvantage of being forced to prove that reuse represents no greater health hazard than conventional water supply and waste treatment systems. Second, they will have the economic disadvantage of having to compete on the basis of a reuse system that is significantly overdesigned. These factors will not preclude reuse, but they will restrict its implementation.

BIBLIOGRAPHY

Aschauer, M. N., and Chian, E. S. K. 1976. "A Practical Use of Modelling and Optimization for Hyperfiltration Plant Design." Paper to be submitted to *Desalination* for publication.

———, 1976. "Optimization of a Two-Stage Tubular Module Hyperfiltration Plant for Sea Water Desalination." Paper to be submitted to *J. AIChE* for publication.

Bahr, G. F.; Boccia, J. A.; and Shoemaker, R. H. 1975. "Analysis of Cytotoxic Reactions Produced by MUST-Water Constituents." Ann. Progr. Rept. for 30 Sept. 74–30 Sept. 75 (RCS–MEDDH–288iRI), Armed Forces Inst. Pathology, Washington, D.C., December.

Bausum, H. T.; Schaub, S. A.; Small, M. J.; Highfill, J. W.; and Sorber, C. A. 1976. "Bacterial Aerosols Resulting from Spray Irrigation with Wastewater." USAMBRDL Technical Report 7602, AD A028359, June.

Bryce, C. A.; Heist, J. A.; Leon, R.; Daley, R. J.; and Holyer Black, R. D. 1973. Final Report, "MUST Waste Water Treatment System" to U.S. Army Res. Development Command, Contract No. DADA–17–71–C–1090. Washington, D.C.: AiResearch Manufacturing Co. of Arizona, 15 July.

Chian, E. S. K., and Aschauer, M. N. 1975. "Evaluation of New Reverse Osmosis Membranes for the Separation of Toxic Compounds from Wastewater." Third Ann. Summary Rept. U.S. Army Med. Res. Develop. Command, Washington, D.C., Contract No. DADA17–73–C–3025, Univ. Illinois Tech. Rept. UILU–ENG–75–2028, Urbana, Illinois, October.

————, 1975. "Effect of Freezing Soybean Whey upon the Performance of Ultrafiltration Process." AIChE. Sym. Series 144, Water—1974 I. *Ind. Wast. Treat.*, pp. 163–69.

Chian, E. S. K.; Bruce, W. N.; and Fang, H. H. P. 1975. "Removal of Pesticides by Reverse Osmosis." *Environ. Sci. Technol.*, 9, 52–59.

Chian, E. S. K.; Cheng, S. S.; DeWalle, F. B.; and Kuo, P. P. K. 1976. "Removal of Organics in Sewage and Secondary Effluents by Reverse Osmosis." Paper submitted for presentation at the 8th Int. Water Pollution Res. Conf., Sydney, Australia, October.

Chian, E. S. K., and Fang, H. H. P. 1975. "Constrained Optimization of Cellulose Acetate Membrane Using Two-Level Fractorial Design." *J. Appl. Polymer Sci.* 19, 251–63.

————, 1974. "Evaluation of New Reverse Osmosis Membranes for Separation of Toxic Compounds from Water." *AIChE Sym. Series 136, Water—1973*, pp. 497–507.

————, 1975. "Removing Toxicity from Tower Blowdown." ibid., pp. 40–43.

Chian, E. S. K.; Fang, H. H. P.; DeWalle, F. B.; and Smith, J. W. 1975. "Physical-Chemical Treatment of Hospital Waste Waters for Potential Reuse." Paper presented at the 30th Ann. Purdue Waste Conf., Purdue Univ., Lafayette, Ind., May.

Christian, R. T.; Cody, T. E.; Clark, C. S.; Lingg, R.; and Cleary, E. J. 1973. "Development of a Biological Chemical Test for the Potability of Water." *AIChE Symp. Ser.*, 70 (136), 15–21.

Christian, R. T.; Clark, C. S.; Cody, T. E.; Lingg, R.; Saltzman, B.; and Cleary, E. J. 1973. Report no. 4, "The Development of a Test for the Potability of Water Treated by a Direct Reuse System." Contract No. DADA17–73–C–3013 for the U.S. Army Med. Res. Develop. Command, Washington, D.C., University of Cincinnati, Ohio, 30 September.

Christian, R. T.; Clark, C.S.; Cody, T. E.; Witherup, S.; Gartside, P. S.; Elia, V. J.; Eller, P. M.; Lingg, R.; Copper, G. P.; Cleary, E. J.; and Kinman, R. N. 1975. Rept. no. 8, "The Development of a Test for the Potability of Water Treated by a Direct Reuse System." Contract No. DADA17–73–C–3013 for the U.S. Army Med. Res. Develop. Command, Washington, D.C., Univ. Cincinnati, Ohio, June.

Christian, R. T.; Cody, T. E.; Lingg, R.; and Clark, C. S. 1973. "The Development of a Test for the Potability of Direct Reuse Water." *Proc. First Ann. AIChE Southwestern Ohio Conf. Energy Environ.*, Oxford, Ohio, 25–26 October.

Clark, C. S.; Eller, P. M.; Lingg, R. D.; Anderson, J.; Pesci, E.; and Cleary, E. J. 1974. "Bench-Scale Treatment and Chemical Analysis in the Development of a Potability Test for Hospital Reuse Water." Paper presented at 1974 Intersociety Conf. Environ. System, Seattle, Washington, 31 July.

Cowen, W. F., and Cooper, W. J. 1975. "Analysis of Volatile Organic Compounds in Walden Research MUST-Integrated Test Samples and in a Laboratory Waste Reverse Osmosis Permeate." Memorandum for record, Environ. Prot. Res. Div. (SGRD–UBG), U.S. Army Bioeng. R&D Lab., Fort Detrick, MD, Dec.

Cowen, W. F.; Cooper, W. J., and Highfill, J. W. 1975. "Evacuated Gas Sampling Valve for Quantitative Head Space Analysis of Volatile Organic Compounds in Water by Gas Chromatography." Anal. Chem. 47 (14) 2483–85, December.

Dept. Army, Office of the Surgeon General 1973. "Report of Decisions Reached at Formal In-Process Review (IPR)." Washington, D.C. (SGRD–SDM–M) 26 Feb.

———, 1973. "Revised Approved Qualitative Material Requirement (WMR) for a Medical Unit, Self-contained, Transportable (MUST)," amended to include changes approved through In-Process Review of 8 May 1973, Annex B (Water and Waste Management Sub-System), Washington, D.C., June.

Dept. Army, U.S. Army Environ. Hygiene Agency, 1971. "Water Quality Engineering Special Study No. 99–003–71; Evaluation of the Water Processing Element, Medical Unit, Self-contained, Transportable (MUST)." Sept. 1970– Feb. 1971, Edgewood Arsenal, Md., June.

Dept. Army, U.S. Army Med. Res. Develop. Command 1973. Memorandum for the Commander: "Recommended Course of Action for Research on MUST Waste Water Management." Washington, D.C. (SGRD–EDE), 8 June.

Ehrlich, K., First Quart. Rept. 1975. "Development of a Biological Detector for Toxic Components in Drinking Water." Contract No. DAMD17–76–C–6005, to USAMBRDL, Ft. Detrick, Md. (SGRD–UBG); Gulf South Res. Inst., New Orleans, 10 October.

Ehrlich, K., Second Quart. Rept. 1976. "Development of a Biological Detector for Toxic Components in Drinking Water." Contract No. DAMD17–76–C–6005, to USAMBRDL (SGRD–UBG), Ft. Detrick, Md.; Gulf South Res. Inst., New Orleans, La., 13 Jan.

Environ. Prot. Agency 1975. "Interim Primary Drinking Water Standards." Federal Register 40 (51) Part II, Friday, 14 March.

Fang, H. H. P., and Chian, E. S. K. 1976. "Reverse Osmosis Separation of Polar Organic Compounds in Aqueous Solution." Paper accepted for publication in Environ. Sci. Technol.

Gollan, A. Z.; McNulty, K. J.; Goldsmith, R. L.; Kleper, M. H.; and Grant, D. C. 1976. "Evaluation of Membrane Separation Process, Carbon Adsorption, and Ozonation for Treatment of MUST Hospital Wastes." Preliminary draft final rept. U.S. Army Med. Res. Develop. Command, Contract No. DAMD17–74– C–4066, (Fort Detrick, Md. 21701), Walden Res. Div. Abcor, Inc., Cambridge, Massachusetts, January.

Grieves, R. B., and Bhattacharyya, D. 1975. "Membrane Ultrafiltration to Treat Non-Sanitary Military Wastes." Ann. Rept. U.S. Army Med. Res. Develop. Command; Contract No. DADA–17–72–C–2050, Univ. Kentucky, Lexington, March.

———, 1975. "Criterion of Ion Separation by Reverse Osmosis." J. Appl. Polymer Sci., 19, 2889–2895.

———, 1975. "Removal of Alcohols, Amines, and Aliphatic Acids in Aqueous Solution by NS-100 Membrane." J. Appl. Polymer Sci., 19, 1347–1358.

————, 1975. "Removal of Dissolved Solids by Reverse Osmosis." Paper presented at the AIChE 68th Ann. Mtg. Los Angeles, November.

————, 1975. "Reverse Osmosis May Help Blowdown Reuse." *Cooling Towers, CEP Tech.* Manual, AIChE, pp. 11–15.

————, 1975. "Optimization of NS-100 Membrane for Reverse Osmosis." *J. Appl. Polymer Sci.* 20, Jan.

Jarman, W. F.; Thorton, T. A.; Wold, T. M.; Dunstan, J.; Laughlin, R. C.; Palmer, J. E.; and Smith, R. 1971. "Engineering Test of Water and Waste Management System, Medical Unit, Self-contained, Transportable—Final Report." RDTE Proj. No. 3A643324D828, USATECOM Proj. No. 7–ES–205–000–014/016. U.S. Army Gen. Equip. Test Activity, Fort Lee, Va., June.

Johnson, D. E., et al. 1976. "Evaluation of the Health Effects Associated with the Application of Wastewater to Land." Annual Report—Phase I, Southwest Research Institute, San Antonio, Texas, December.

Klein, S. A., et al. 1974. "An Evaluation of the Accumulation, Translocation, and Degradation of Pesticides at Land Wastewater Disposal Sites." University of California, Berkeley, Final Report, Nov.

Lambert, W. P., and Reuter, L. H. 1976. "Wastewater Reuse within an Army Field Hospital." *Proceedings of the Third National Conference on Complete Water Reuse:* Symbiosis as a Means of Abatement for Multi-Media Pollution, June 27–30, 1976, Cincinnati, Ohio, pp. 447–56.

Lloyd, J. P.; Hines, R. T.; Tarkenton, W. V.; Shave, H. A.; Palmer, J. E., Jr.; Foley, J.; and Benfield, J. 1969. "Integrated Engineering and Service Test of Medical Unit, Self-contained, Transportable (MUST) Water and Waste Management System-Test Plan." RDTE Proj. No. 3A632214D828, USATECOM Proj. Activity, Fort Lee, Va., April.

Mix, T. W., and Scharen, H. 1975. "Development of Techniques for Detection of Low Molecular Weight Contaminants in Product Water from Water Purification of Water Reuse System." Draft final report, Contract no. DADA17–72–C–2169, U.S. Army Med. Res. Develop. Command, December.

Sagik, B. P., et al. 1976. "The Survival of Human Enteric Viruses in Holding Ponds." Annual Report, University of Texas at San Antonio, 19 July.

Schaub, S. A.; Meier, E. P.; Kolmer, J. R.; and Sorber, C. A. 1975. "Land Application of Wastewater: The Fate of Viruses, Bacteria and Heavy Metals at a Rapid Infiltration Site." USAMBRDL Technical Report 7504, AD A011263 May.

See, G. G.; Kacholia, K. K.; and Wynveen, R. A. 1975. "Control and Monitor Instrumentation for MUST Water Processing Element." Final report for U.S. Army Med. Res. Develop. Command, Washington, D.C., Contract No. DADA17–73–C–3163, Life Systems, Inc., Cleveland, Ohio, June.

Sorber, C. A.; Schaub, S. A.; and Guter, K. J. 1972. "Problem Definition Study: Evaluation of Health and Hygiene Aspects of Land Disposal Sites." University of California, Berkeley, Final Report, November.

Witherup, S., 1975. "The Toxicity and Irritancy of Ultrafiltrates of Nonsanitary Military Wastes." First quart. rept., Contract No. DAMD17–76–C–6006 to U.S. Med. Res. Develop. Command, Washington, D.C.; Kettering Lab., Dept. Environ. Health, Univ. Cincinnati, Ohio, 28 October.

POTABLE REUSE: THE U.S. EXPERIENCE

RICHARD D. HEATON,
Reuse Project Director
American Water Works Association Research Foundation
Denver, Colorado

Potable reuse is the renovation of sewage effluent to a water product suitable for human consumption and the recycling of that water into a supply system. Wastewater can, of course, also be reused for nonpotable purposes, and this is already being done in industry, agriculture, and recreation.

As interest in renovated wastewater grows, more and more communities and organizations are investigating its potential. The uses to which reused water should be put will, of course, vary with local conditions; any community which is considering reuse will have to evaluate fully the problems and possibilities of its own situation.

Potable reuse can be accomplished in any of three ways:

1. *Direct potable reuse* is the reintroduction of highly treated sewage effluent from the treatment plant directly back into the existing water distribution system. This is the classical "pipe-to-pipe" definition of reuse.

2. *Planned indirect reuse* involves the purposeful discharge of highly treated wastewater upstream from a water supply intake.

3. *Groundwater recharge* involves either the injection of effluent into an aquifer which is the source of potable supply or the "spreading" of effluent on the ground to allow it to filter down to the aquifer.

In each of these methods, renovated wastewater eventually reaches the home water tap.

In the following pages I would like to present a broad if necessarily superficial picture of activities related to reuse in the United States. First I will describe briefly the role of the American Water Works Association Research Foundation. Then I will summarize the most interesting projects on both the East and West coasts. Finally I want to describe in somewhat more depth the experiences of Denver, Colorado, in planning for direct potable reuse.

THE AWWA RESEARCH FOUNDATION

Potable reuse as a supply alternative involves a particularly complex set of problems. The American Water Works Association Research Foundation became aware that sufficient interest existed among several water utilities and federal agencies to justify the formation of an information clearing-house and coordination program for activities directed toward potable reuse alone. Thus, the foundation since July of 1976 has assumed respon-sibility for collecting this information and for keeping its supporting agen-cies abreast of rapidly changing reuse technology.

At the present time, the foundation is receiving financial support in this effort from ten utilities and federal agencies on a year-to-year renewable contract basis, and several other groups are contemplating membership in the program. Information is currently being provided on a range of topics including advanced wastewater treatment research, process reliability and redundancy, sequencing, instrumentation, monitoring, automation, health effects and epidemiological studies, public acceptability of reuse, planning strategies, development of standards, socioeconomic studies, federal legislation, funding capabilities, and reuse efforts in foreign coun-tries.

Apart from providing valuable information to the participating agen-cies, the foundation also intends to provide a mechanism to improve effective interaction among those people doing research on potable reuse. In addition, much of the overlapping and redundant research that occurs in the field can be eliminated, and those areas which have been neglected can be identified. Initial efforts have been in the form of newsletters and in-depth reports as well as meetings to discuss openly all common inter-ests and needs.

WEST COAST RESEARCH

Much of the research directed toward water reuse in the West has been conducted in California. Most of the utilities which are interested in water reuse and conservation are members of an organization called the Califor-nia Association of Reclamation Entities of Water, or WATERCARE. Among these utilities are Lake Tahoe, Santee, Santa Clara, Water Fac-tory 21, Irvine Ranch, and Las Virgenes. Several of them already have subpotable reuse systems, but all have a definite interest in potable reuse.

Orange County. In 1939, by special legislation, the Orange County Water District was created and charged with the responsibility for the overall management of the Santa Ana River groundwater basin. The district differs from a true water utility in that its chief business is the recharging of the aquifer, after which a number of small water pumping companies pay for the privilege of tapping the groundwater and distributing it to the communities in the region.

Orange County is located on the semiarid coastal plains southeast of Los Angeles. Although precipitation amounts to only 13 inches per year, the county contains a population of nearly 1.6 million and is one of the fastest-growing areas of the country. Colorado River and Northern California waters were brought in to recharge the steadily dwindling groundwater source, but in time they too proved to be inadequate.

The seriousness of the problem was increased by rapid saltwater intrusion up to four miles inland in some places. A system of injection wells was established, and it was calculated that 20,000 to 30,000 acre-feet of water were needed each year for a reliable fresh water curtain.

The Water Factory 21 was conceived in response to both needs. The original concept involved the desalinization of seawater which would then be blended with advanced treatment effluent for direct injection into the coastal barrier system and into the aquifer which provided water for potable supply systems. Construction began in 1971 on a 15 mgd advanced wastewater treatment plant. At the same time and on the same site the Office of Saline Water began building a 3 mgd VTE/MSF distillation plant. Unfortunately, federal funding for the desalinization plant was terminated in the spring of 1976.

Some injection of the treated wastewater was begun in September of 1976. However, it was not possible to utilize the plant to full capacity because of the lack of adequate blending water. The district, therefore, contracted with Universal Oil Products at the cost of $2.5 million to construct a 5 mgd desalinization facility using reverse osmosis technology. When completed in early 1977, this plant will be the largest of its kind in the world.

One of the most interesting aspects of Water Factory 21 is its energy consumption. Instrumentation for the entire plant has been keyed to all unit processes so that data can be gathered in terms of kilowatt-hours per acre-foot of reclaimed water. A comparison of these figures with those of other water projects in the state shows that the energy consumed in providing supply from reused water is less than that consumed by other potential sources. Thus reused wastewater may well become the most important source of supply for Orange County.

The Irvine Ranch Water District is also in Orange County. The district is now faced with a recent decision by the Regional Water Quality Control Board to disallow ocean discharge of sewage effluent. Thus, some sort of recycling and reuse is mandatory. Effluent is already being used for agriculture after only a filtration and disinfection process. To be completed with 18 months, however, is a new 15 mgd advanced wastewater treatment plant for the purpose of providing irrigation water in a dual distribution system to the entire community. Some of the pipes have already been laid to provide water to school grounds, parks, street landscaping, and the front yards of many homes.

Los Angeles.   The Department of Water and Power of the City of Los Angeles is responsible for providing a safe and adequate water supply for over 3 million people. Limited freshwater resources have forced the department, in conjunction with wastewater and flood control agencies, to investigate water recycling and reuse. The department currently has three major projects under consideration (see figure 1).

The Glendale plant is a recently completed facility for relief of an overload sewer to the main Hyperion plant. Although secondary effluent is presently discharged to the Los Angeles River, with some incidental infiltration to the groundwater basin, pipelines have already been laid to Griffith Park and nearby industries, with a view to future reuse.

At Sepulveda an advanced wastewater treatment plant with a capacity of 40 mgd is currently in the preliminary design stage. It is to be strictly a wastewater reclamation facility. Originally it was proposed to construct the plant near the existing Headworks Spreading Ground in order to use the highly treated effluent for aquifer recharge. The state health department would not allow this and ruled that the water would have to be discharged into the Los Angeles River. Although the river is basically a large concrete-lined channel, some sections downstream from the proposed Sepulveda site do not have a lining. Thus, some wastewater will infiltrate and enter the aquifer in any case. The project is awaiting federal funding consideration.

The third project in Los Angeles is perhaps the most dramatic. This is the plan to construct a 50 cfs facility at Hyperion for the injection of advanced treatment effluents into the system of coastal barriers against seawater intrusion. At present imported fresh water is used for this process. It has been demonstrated that more than 50 percent of the injected water eventually reaches the protected inland aquifers, so any effluents would ultimately reach the potable water supply system. Currently the costs of constructing and operating the Hyperion plant are not competitive with the cost of imported water, and the start of the project has been delayed.

Los Angeles County.   The sanitation districts of Los Angeles County are now operating three major reclamation plants. The best known among them is the 12 mgd facility at Whittier Narrows, where secondary effluent

FIGURE 1
CITY OF LOS ANGELES WASTEWATER SYSTEM

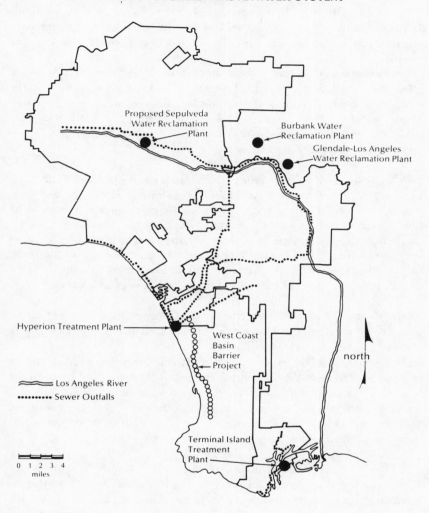

has for the past eight years been used for spreading to recharge the 450-acre Rio Hondo basin aquifers. Several studies have shown no deterioration in groundwater quality over this period.

The 15 mgd treatment plant at San Jose Creek is the newest facility in the county. Here again, secondary effluent can be used for recharge purposes when sufficient blending water is available. The plant is capable of running on a steady-state basis, withdrawing a constant flow from the nearby trunk sewer and returning all solids for further treatment down the line.

Dual media filters are being added to both the Whittier Narrows and the San Jose Creek plants. Carbon treatment will be added to the county's plant at Pomona because of growing concern over viruses and downstream recreational use.

Los Angeles County has perhaps more individuals involved in work on reuse than any other utility in the country and has a $1 million yearly research budget. Currently there are plans for yet another major reuse study entitled the Montebello–Forebay Project. Health effects, epidemiology, and organic analysis will be addressed directly in order to meet stringent quality standards.

Malibu. The Tapia wastewater reclamation plant is operated by the Las Virgenes Water District near Malibu, California. Here, as at Irvine Ranch, ocean discharge is not allowed, so the effluent is used for irrigation. An interesting aspect of this project has been some auxiliary research on hydroponics or aquaculture. Very healthy tomato plants and cucumbers are being grown in secondary effluent in greenhouses on the plant site. Studies have shown that trace metal uptake occurs to a small extent in the stem and leaves of plants, but never in the vegetables themselves.

Santa Clara. At the southern end of San Francisco Bay, saltwater intrusion will be combatted with a system similar to that employed by Water Factory 21. Highly treated effluent will be injected into a series of wells some distance from the shore and then extracted through a second series of wells located near the shoreline. The extracted water will be used for several subpotable purposes, but the potable aquifer will be affected. Extensive water quality studies are being conducted at nearby Stanford University. Reclaimed water costs will approach $100/acre-foot as compared to $110/acre-foot for other sources.

San Diego. Several experiments using reverse osmosis technology are being conducted in the San Diego area. The city itself has just completed a major planning report calling for several reclamation activities. Its Mission Valley research pilot plant has for the last eight years demonstrated the successful treatment of raw sewage by reverse osmosis. Virus tests have been conducted with good results and the small operation produces an excellent water. The original goal of the plant was to initiate several small on-site reuse systems where the water could be taken from a sewer near an industry, treated, used, and then returned to the sewer.

The Santee project located inland from San Diego is still an international showpiece for visitors, but, because of financial limitations, little research is being done. A new trunk sewer nearby has made the plant itself unnecessary for the area-wide sewage treatment needs, but 1 mgd is still produced for use in the recreational lakes downstream.

At the present time secondary effluent is passed through several oxidation ponds, then allowed to infiltrate through 400 feet of soil before recovery and pumpage into a series of recreational lakes. No viruses have ever been recovered in the reclaimed water. Public response to water recreation is still favorable, with fishing and boating allowed. However, even though the safety of swimming was demonstrated, the swimming pool is now filled with city water.

At this time much of the advanced treatment equipment at the Santee plant is standing idle, but the City of San Diego is formulating plans for a national operator-training center there.

The number of projects under way in California which involve wastewater reuse is high, and the preceeding list describes only a few. Legislative mandates require that the state water-planning agencies examine reuse thoroughly as an alternative source of supply before attempting to develop further sources of raw water.

In 1974 a "Blue Ribbon" panel of experts was created to consider carefully the health impacts of reuse and to suggest a long-term research program. After two years of study, the panel has formulated recommendations calling for:

1. Characterization of contaminants in reclaimed wastewater

2. Improved removal techniques for organics

3. Assessment of toxicological risks

4. Disinfection studies for virus hazards

5. Epidemiological studies of exposed populations

6. Study of the behavior of pollutants in soils

7. Research on monitoring techniques.

To work in conjunction with the panel a 60-member Reuse Task Force was established by the state water resources control board to implement reuse in California and to see that a fair share of the appropriate $1-billion public works money goes to reuse. Special funding consideration will be given to selected demonstration projects intended to resolve health questions.

On the other hand, before the final recommendations of the above two groups were reported, the state health department proposed stringent regulations for groundwater recharge with reclaimed effluents. Essentially the proposed regulations require extremely expensive treatment processes, involving activated carbon and reverse osmosis, before spreading on the ground. In addition, a minimum of one year of detention time in the ground is necessary in conjunction with full-scale research in geohydrology and continuous biological monitoring.

At public hearings held in June 1976, 27 out of 29 utilities stated that they were aggressively opposed to the proposed regulations. They pointed out that some of the proposed concentration levels of pollutants, such as the 2 mg/l limit for chemical oxygen demand, were considerably lower than the levels to be found in several existing supply sources. As a result of this opposition, the enactment of the regulations has been postponed pending further review.

EAST COAST RESEARCH

In the eastern part of the U.S., water reclamation efforts are concentrated in the Washington, D.C., area. Several of the projects are sponsored by the federal government, and thus, unlike most of the work in California, they are intended to be more experimental in nature or to serve as prototypes for projects elsewhere in the country.

Blue Plains Plant.   On the site of Washington, D.C.'s huge sewage treatment plant at Blue Plains, the federal government has operated since 1967 a small pilot plant for advanced wastewater treatment research. This plant is now managed by the Environmental Protection Agency (EPA) as an experimental station.

At present a 35 gpm treatment sequence has been producing an extremely high quality effluent for over a year. Over 107 parameters have been measured, including viruses, pathogenic bacteria, metals, radioactivity, pesticides, and trace organics. During this period no existing drinking water standard has been exceeded in respect to any of these measured parameters. One hundred and twenty thousand gallons of the product water is being concentrated in order to be fed to laboratory animals for a one-month period to test for organic and inorganic uptake.

After years of faithful service the Blue Plains Pilot Plant will soon be closed. The EPA will probably build another $2.5-million facility in Cincinnati, closer to their other research labs.

Fairfax County.   A major project for indirect reuse is being constructed by the Upper Occoquan Sewage Authority in Fairfax County, Virginia. A 10 mgd advanced treatment plant, to be completed in the spring of 1978, will replace several small, inadequate facilities. The treated effluent from the new plant will be discharged into the Occoquan Reservoir, which serves as the water supply source for 500,000 people in northern Virginia.

In 1971, the state water control board issued what was termed the "Occoquan Policy," which mandated a fail-safe design for the treatment sequence, including complete component redundancy. The following stringent standards were required for allowable discharge levels:

Biological Oxygen Demand	1mg/l
Chemical Oxygen Demand	10 mg/l
Suspended Solids	0
Unoxidized Nitrogen	1 mg/l
Phosphorus	0.1 mg/l
Coliform Bacteria	2/100 ml

The total cost of the project is calculated to be $79 million. This is extraordinarily high, but necessary in order to meet the design requirements.

Montgomery County.   The story of the proposed advanced wastewater treatment plant in Montgomery County, Maryland, is perhaps one of the most frustrating in the history of sanitary engineering. A 60 mgd plant was to be built north of Washington, D.C. It was to receive and process county-wide sewage flows and dispose a safe effluent above the D.C. water intakes on the Potomac. Some of the effluent would have been used for industrial purposes in the nearby Dickerson electric power plant, with the organic sludges providing a supplementary fuel source.

After six years of site selection, preliminary design studies, environmental impact assessment, formal design, public forums, and several reevaluations by the county, the plant remains on the drawing boards. Questions concerning public health, total project costs, and growth stimulation ultimately led to the withdrawal of financial support by the EPA in the spring of 1976.

As the Washington area is in severe need of additional wastewater treatment capacity, it seems fair to ask why the Montgomery plant has been defeated even as the neighboring Occoquan plant is nearing completion.

Washington, D.C.   Provision of water supply to the District of Columbia is the responsibility of the U.S. Army Corps of Engineers. The national capital is facing potentially serious problems of water shortage, and the Corps is evaluating several alternatives to increase the available supply. One of them is reuse.

In March of 1974, PL 93–251 authorized the corps to construct, operate, and evaluate a pilot project on the Potomac Estuary. What has been nicknamed the "Six Million Dollar Plant" will treat both highly polluted estuary water taken from near Blue Plains and secondary effluent to determine which is the better water source. The National Academy of Sciences is reviewing the project and will report to Congress on the scientific aspects of the program.

MIUS. The Multiple Integrated Utility System (MIUS) is a project being undertaken by the U.S. Department of Housing and Urban Development (HUD). Essentially, the project aims to provide heating, cooling, electric power, water, and wastewater service from a centralized utility unit to new communities of 2,500 people. Other federal agencies participating in the study include ERDA, NASA, HEW, EPA, FEA, and the Department of Defense, with the National Bureau of Standards acting as technical adviser. The efficient use of energy is one of the primary goals of the study, and one component of the system will be the recycling of wastewater for community watering needs. A demonstration unit will be constructed near St. Charles, Maryland, southeast of Washington, D.C., within the next few years.

A major role in developing the potential of reuse will be played by the U.S. Office of Water Resources and Technology (OWRT). The office has developed a multistep national reuse needs program. Among the most important areas of activity will be:

1. Evaluation of national needs

2. Evaluation of existing technologies

3. Research and development projects

4. Evaluation of the planning and management aspects of reuse.

The OWRT itself will perform some of the research on the project. Other items will be let out on a contractual basis. The office has budgeted $1.7 million for the project in fiscal year 1977 and has a funding capability of $25 million over the next five years.

DENVER'S REUSE EFFORTS

Denver, Colorado, is the site of one of the largest and most carefully conceived projects for wastewater reuse in the United States. Denver is also one of the few places that is actively planning a direct "pipe-to-pipe" reuse system. Thus, it is instructive to examine the Denver project in some detail.

Denver was founded at the confluence of two small rivers which provided an adequate water supply in what was generally a semiarid region. However, the rapid growth of agriculture, cattle ranching, and mining soon strained the limits of supply from available water resources, and water scarcity has been a dominant factor in the growth of the city for nearly a century.

Today the Denver Water Department is politically and financially independent of the city and is governed by a separate board of water commissioners. All the revenues from water sales go into the water department treasury and not to the city. No tax monies are used for support.

The utility serves close to one million people with a service area of 300 square miles. In 1974, 72.0 billion gallons of water were distributed to customers. This equals a yearly average consumption of 220 gallons per capita per day, one of the highest in the country. Denver is continuing to grow very rapidly, and even conservative forecasts of future demands far exceed the yield from current sources of supply.

In response to this demand, the water department has committed itself to a logical and multifaceted approach to develop additional supplies. However, the word "develop" can mean many things in the West. It can mean either more raw water acquisition or water conservation. It can also mean weather modification to increase snowfall and runoff; or it may mean watershed management to optimize the available supply through proper forest-cutting or vegetation patterns; its meaning may include canal linings or evaporation control. Finally, it may mean reclamation of the city's own wastewater.

For the past ten years Denver has been evaluating the potential of reuse. A variety of alternatives have been explored. Reuse for irrigated agriculture was considered theoretically viable, but in the Denver region it is simply prohibited by certain water rights decrees. Groundwater recharge is precluded by the absence of the appropriate underlying geology, and in addition there are serious questions of ownership and control of any injected water. Reuse for industrial purposes only was found to be economically unfeasible on a number of grounds. An extensive study of the possibility of a dual-pipe system for the new suburbs was also found to be economically unfeasible.

After an analysis of all reuse alternatives, the decision was taken to move toward potable reuse for the city's existing supply system. Once this decision was made, two modes of operation became available— direct or indirect. The possibility exists in Denver to let secondary effluent flow downstream a few miles before being picked up at the reclamation plant. This, according to many, allow's nature's magic mile of stream to dilute or purify the sewage. Perhaps it is also more esthetically pleasing to see water being withdrawn from a river rather than from an outfall.

However, in Denver many problems exist with the indirect mode of operation. For some months of the year with low stream flow, sewage effluent is the basis of the South Platte River. There is practically zero dilution. During the rest of the year the quality of the water is highly questionable due to storm runoff, industrial discharges, and frequent accidental spills from upstream sewage plants. Direct reuse, where the sewage outfall is connected to the reclamation plant intake and this plant's product taken directly to the distribution system, appeared safer than indirect methods.

The line of reasoning which led to this decision applies only to the Denver situation, which is certainly not typical. It should be emphasized that direct potable reuse is not by any means automatically the best alternative available to other cities faced with a potential supply shortage.

With the decision to turn to potable reuse for supply augmentation comes, of course, the question of public acceptability. An original Denver premise was that no program could succeed without the approval of an informed public.

FIGURE 2
PROCESS FLOW DIAGRAM – PROPOSED DENVER PLANT

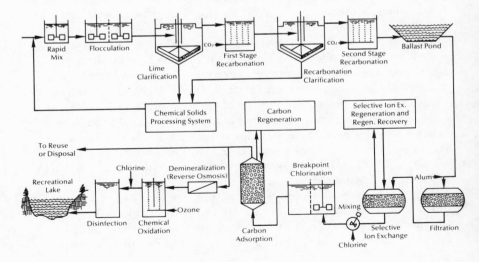

Several public attitudinal studies have been conducted. The results have shown a high degree of willingness among the general population to consume reused water. The more people know about potable reuse, the more positive their response. However, they are only willing to accept reused water if it is equivalent in quality to the best available natural source. Clearly, to achieve this level of quality is a formidable task.

Ultimately Denver hopes to have the capacity to reclaim up to 100 mgd of effluent. The first step in this process will be the construction of a small demonstration plant. Preliminary design work has been completed on a 1 mgd facility which will cost approximately $8 million to build and about $.5 million per year to operate (see figure 2). During the first years of operation, the water from the plant will be used for health-effects testing. Only when the water produced has been found totally safe for human consumption will Denver proceed to expand its reuse program.

CONCLUSION

Time does not permit discussion of several other reuse projects being undertaken in this country or of the research being conducted in foreign countries such as the Netherlands, Israel, and South Africa. However, in spite of growing activity worldwide, there are a number of tasks concerning reuse that remain to be completed.

The most important of these tasks concerns the health effects of the ingestion of all sorts of chemicals and organisms. Threshold limits for waterborne diseases and illnesses need to be established, and this will undoubtedly require millions of research dollars.

Furthermore, a full-scale demonstration of the feasibility of potable reuse is needed. No one has yet produced, on a consistent basis and under exacting conditions, a water that would be considered drinkable over a long period of time.

Finally, it must be recognized that water supply and wastewater reuse are problems of a national scale and concern. Increased and continued federal support will be necessary to solve these problems.

Many detractors of potable reuse say that it can never be done, that it is impossible to isolate and understand every potentially deleterious compound in wastewater. To those individuals it must be said that reuse is already here. We're drinking those contaminants, unfortunately, because of the unplanned or covert or incidental or unintentional presence of wastewaters in our current supplies. Therefore, the health questions which must be answered concerning reuse are in reality identical to those which must be answered for water supply in general.

BIBLIOGRAPHY

Five-volume water reuse bibliography published by Office of Water Research and Technology and available from National Technical Information Service (NTIS), U.S. Department of Commerce, 5285 Port Royal Road, Springfield, Virginia 22161:

> Vol. 1—PB 221 998/LL
> Vol. 2—PB 221 999/LL
> Vol. 3—PB 241 171/LL
> Vol. 4—PB 241 172/LL
> Vol. 5—PB 255 818/LL

Two water reuse bibliographies available from Water Resources Center, Texas Tech. University, P.O. Box 4630, Lubbock, Texas 79409:

Pettit, Gary M., and Whetstone, George A. "Reuse of Effluent—An Annotated Bibliography." 1965–1972, WRC Report #73–3.

Whetstone, George A. "Reuse of Effluents in the Future." Annotated bibliography, 1942–65, Report #8, Texas Water Development Board.

World Health Organization, International Reference Centre for Community Water Supply, P.O. Box 140, Leidschendam, The Netherlands: Technical Paper #7, September 1975, "Health Effects Relating to Direct and Indirect Re-use of Wastewater for Human Consumption."

EPA 1975 Report, "Research Needs for the Potable Reuse of Municipal Wastewater." Available from NTIS as PB 249 138/9WP.

EPA October 1976 Report 600/1–76–033, "Renovated Wastewater as a Supplementary Source for Municipal Water Supply: An Economic Evaluation."

Water Resources and Marine Sciences Center, Cornell University, Ithaca, New York: Technical Report #78, "Some Data and Methods for Analyzing Metropolitan Wastewater Renovation and Reuse Systems."

EPA Water Planning Division Report, April, 1975. "Cost-Effectiveness Analysis of Municipal Wastewater Reuse." Available from NTIS as PB 252 932/9WP.

U.S. Army Engineers, Institute for Water Resources, Kingman Building, Fort Belvoir, Virginia 22060: "An Evaluation of Water Reuse for Municipal Supply." Available from NTIS as AD A 005–053.

EPA Report, May 1975. "Demonstrated Technology and Research Needs for Reuse of Municipal Wastewater." Available from NTIS as EPA–670/2–75–038.

REDUCING DEMAND: WATER CONSERVATION

With the exception of dangerous drugs and possibly firearms, any attempt to reduce the demand for a product is viewed in America with extreme suspicion. In a country of seemingly boundless resources, ever-growing demands have come to be looked upon as the prime indicator of economic health. Nonetheless, our resources, including our water resources, are limited and simple mathematical extrapolation indicates that we are approaching those limits. In some regions we are already attempting to allocate more water than is actually available. In others we are rapidly mining groundwater supplies which have accumulated over hundreds and thousands of years.

Water differs from most of our other resources, however, in that it is not ultimately "depletable." Rather, like solar radiation, a certain amount of water will always be available, and technology can vastly increase the portion of this amount which can be diverted to human use. The technology to transport water over great distances is well known; the technology to recycle human wastes is rapidly being developed. The major difficulty with these technologies is the costs associated with them. These costs will continue to rise, and as they do, less expensive alternatives will inevitably become more attractive. Many of these alternatives involve water conservation.

The following selections explore water conservation from three distinct points of view. Murray McPherson assesses national trends and reviews recent studies of conservation before concentrating his attention on the possibilities of, and the impediments to, conservation in the household. Ernie Flack provides a systematic classification and evaluation of all the methods available to communities which are interested in exploring water conservation. William Hudson discusses the continuous vigilance that is necessary to maintain an efficient distribution system and ensure that a minimum of water is wasted.

The idea of resource conservation is not new to the United States, but it has been accepted only in an incremental fashion. Ever since the turn of the century, we have accepted the need to conserve forests and areas of great natural beauty. Later, droughts in the Central Plains and soil erosion in the South and East taught us the importance of soil conservation to agriculture. Only quite recently have we recognized the need to conserve our remaining fossil fuels. Water is one of our most valuable resources, and we will eventually have to learn that it too must be conserved.

CONSERVATION IN HOUSEHOLD WATER USE

MURRAY B. McPHERSON,
Director
ASCE Urban Water Resources Research Program †
Marblehead, Massachusetts

The increasing variability of the world's climate, coupled with increasing urbanization and population growth, strongly suggest that it is going to be much more difficult to continue to augment water supplies in the future than it has been in the past. In addition, the obvious linkage between the sources of our water supply and the waters that receive our effluents has finally been widely recognized. These and other considerations have led to a quite recent acceptance of conservation measures as alternatives to open-ended enlargement of water supply facilities.

I would like first to explore some of the major reasons for this acceptance of conservation and to attempt to describe some of the most important considerations for future planning of water resources. Then I will turn to one of the most challenging possibilities—conservation in household water use. I will review quality, quantity, and economic aspects of household water use, with an emphasis on their implications for conservation. A large number of references is provided as a guide to those requiring further information on these topics.

FORECASTS AND TRENDS

The U.S. Water Resources Council in its report (1968, pp. 4–1, 4–1–3) expected major national withdrawal uses collectively to quadruple, with a doubling of their consumptive portion, by the year 2020. These projections place total withdrawals for all fresh water uses in the year 2020 at approximately two-thirds of the average annual runoff of the cotermi-

†This paper contains considerable material from a recent ASCE Program Technical Memorandum (McPherson 1976). Preparation of that report and this paper was supported via a contract between the Office of Water Research and Technology, U.S. Department of the Interior, and ASCE, as authorized under the Water Resources Research Act of 1964, Public Law 88–379, as amended. The objectives, activities and products of the ASCE Urban Water Resources Research Program through 1974 have been summarized elsewhere (McPherson and Mangan 1975, pp. 847–55).

nous United States. At the time these projections were made, total fresh water uses were equal to about one-fifth the total natural runoff. On the basis of such a massive increase in the demands upon the nation's water resources, this writer concluded (1972) that it appeared quite safe to predict that water resources conservation measures would be practiced much more extensively in the future. He further noted (1972) that about one-tenth of the total national withdrawals in 1965 was for municipal supplies, and the amount of water used for municipal purposes was expected by the council to treble by the year 2020. Further, the council expected that that portion of national municipal withdrawals "consumed" (lawn irrigation, distribution system leakage, and so forth) would also rise significantly.

Projections of greatly increased water use are by no means confined to the United States. A recent United Nations publication (1976) focuses on the need for national and regional water demand projections as a basis for long-range planning and policy formulation. Total worldwide withdrawals for domestic, industrial, and agricultural uses are expected to more than double between 1970 and 2000. The portion for domestic use will nearly quadruple, and this suggests a growing competition between urban and agricultural water use. It has been concluded that there will be an increased need for greater farming efficiencies and improved husbandry of urban water resources, perhaps by more extensive reuse in certain regions of a number of nations (UNESCO 1974, p. 23).

In the expectation that the climate of our crop-growing areas will become more variable than it has been in the recent past, we are advised to brace ourselves, over the long haul, for the prospect of numerous poor harvests ("Weather Turns World Topsy-Turvy," 1976, pp. 48–50). On a global scale, "while there is not enough evidence to conclude that the world's climate is deteriorating, it is clear that climate has become more variable" (ibid.). The resultant increased uncertainty on the reliability of water supplies will surely exacerbate the already anticipated conflicts among and within various classes of water users. In what may be an indication of these climatic trends, parts of Western Europe are now facing a severe drought "that meterologists say is the worst in at least 500 years" ("Europe, Survival Tactics in a Disastrous Drought," 1976, p. 46). In Britain, the National Water Council has taken rather drastic steps to conserve supplies and has gone to public advertisements in a "Save Water Now" campaign (ibid.).

Such emergency campaigns to save water have, of course, always been available to water system managers. No water supply project can be designed for an "ultimate" projected drought, which means that a risk of service curtailment under unusual circumstances must be accepted. In the final analysis, the balance of yield–security against use–curtailment is generally resolved in the political arena and is a decision process that every public water supply agency must go through (McPherson 1971). Thus, the practice of conservation during the rarely encountered, but quite unpredictable, occurrence of shortages is an inherent feature of all water supplies and occurs in a reactive mode. However, the type of conservation we are discussing here is in more the predictive mode, involving long-term practices intended to mitigate expected shortages and/or to ameliorate competition over scarce supplies.

Within the United States the advent of persistent water shortages severe enough to bring about serious consideration of water conservation will vary widely among regions. Observations made by Abel Wolman (1963) are surely relevant today.

> On the whole, the East receives two-thirds of the nation's rainfall, and the West the remaining third.... At present, the limited undeveloped, uncontaminated water resources of the arid West are almost at an end.... On the other hand, probably half of the States could afford to double their water withdrawal, and the cost involved would be relatively low. Still, the problem is essentially a regional one (pp. 1255, 1258).

Clearly, one of the most important steps to be taken by any community faced with either a water shortage or rising costs is the preparation of an adequate forecast of demand. Considerations in forecasting future water demands and requirements have been surveyed in a compendium dealing with risk and uncertainty in metropolitan water resource systems (Mc-Bean and Loucks 1974).

The attitudes of those responsible for water management have been a serious impediment in attempts to institute conservation practices in this country. The prevailing view in the waterworks field until very recently was that the public should be provided with as much water as it wanted, at a level of service it desired, provided it was willing to pay for it. Despite the fact that about four-fifths of municipal water is in the hands of units of local government (Wolman 1976, pp. A13–A18), an image of utility self-sufficiency has been fostered by the "water industry."

Municipal water managers also persisted in regarding municipal water supply as being paramount to, and independent from, the water pollution issue, apparently in an attempt to preserve a comparative immunity from federal regulation and interference. The Water Pollution Control Act Amendments of 1972 and, particularly, the Safe Drinking Water Act of 1974 have resulted in a perceptible shift in viewpoint. While the American Water Works Association (AWWA) long championed joint management and accounting for water and wastewater services, it has only recently been articulating a total resources management perspective.

The integrated approaches that are now required to manage urban water resources will probably involve increased reliance on simulation modeling. A comprehensive review of future urban water resource modeling needs, including consideration of waterworks modeling, is now available (Water Resources Engineers 1976). One of the conclusions reached by this study was that much more work could be justified in simulation and economic modeling analysis of urban water use.

A METROPOLITAN PERSPECTIVE

Figure 1 (McPherson 1975) is a graphical representation of water quantities in a hypothetical urban area of one million inhabitants. National averages have been used to calculate the magnitude of the various components. These magnitudes are thus individually typical, but their combination in figure 1 is not. Nonetheless, two important facts are illustrated: the bulk of the supplied water originates outside urban areas; and well over half of all the water handled one way or another is in private hands. This means that there is typically only a partial overlap in local government water supply source planning and metropolitan general planning, and that the usual approach of focusing on public water supply can overlook a much larger user group. The situation for water pollution control is similar, as over half the volume of discharges to receiving waters are from private corporation lands, and the region impacted by water pollution often extends well beyond the metropolis of origin.

Cooling water withdrawals of thermoelectric power plants are essentially all self-supplied. While such withdrawals in urban areas have not been segregated from national totals (Tucker, Milan, and Burt 1972), they are quite possibly on the order of three times the nonthermoelectric industrial withdrawals of figure 1.

Figure 2 (McPherson 1976) depicts a breakdown of that portion of figure 1 termed "public water supply withdrawals." Figure 2 is drawn to scale and is again based upon a composite of national annual averages that resulted from a reconciliation of estimates for individual components made by various experts. Thus, the distribution of component amounts for any given community will vary from those shown. For example, there are cases where industrial use is minuscule and cases where it predominates. Because of difficulties in quantity accounting generally, there is considerable uncertainty about the extent of "unaccounted-for" water and "infiltration and inflow." This is the result of the necessity to arrive at amounts for these two elements by determining the residuals or leftovers remaining after the magnitudes of all other elements had been taken into account. Incomplete system quantity measurements and errors in regis-

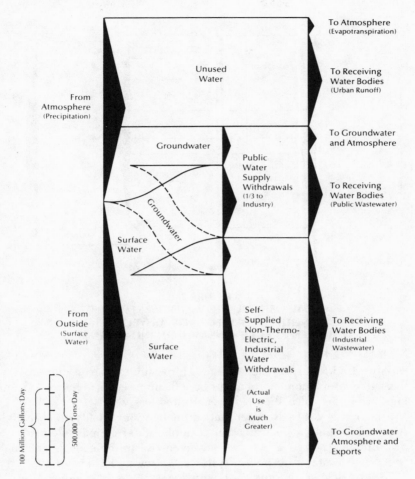

FIGURE 1
ANNUAL AVERAGE WATER QUANTITY BALANCE FOR A
HYPOTHETICAL URBAN AREA OF ONE MILLION INHABITANTS

tration of measuring devices also contribute to the accounting uncertainties. Finally, difficulties in calculation arise from the fact that water and wastewater jurisdictions often differ in size.

In spite of these qualifications, the illustrations provide an important reference in any discussion of household water conservation. First, it can be seen that, on the average, the amount of public water supply withdrawals is a relatively small fraction of total metropolitan withdrawals. Second, domestic use represents a modest fraction of total public water

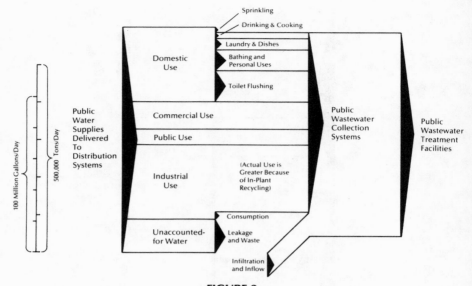

FIGURE 2
COMPOSITE PUBLIC WATER/WASTEWATER
INPUT-OUTPUT BALANCE FOR A HYPOTHETICAL
URBAN AREA OF ONE MILLION INHABITANTS

supply withdrawals, on the average. Third, any savings in domestic use through conservation efforts might be difficult to confirm because of ambiguities in the calculation of "unaccounted-for" water.

From figure 2 it is also clear that "drinking water quality" is absolutely required for only a small fraction of public water supplies delivered to distribution systems, a fact that has given rise to the concept of "dual" community water distribution systems (Haney and Hamann 1965, pp. 1073–98). Revived interest in dual water systems is evidenced by the conduct of a special seminar on dual water systems at the annual conference of the AWWA in June 1976. This seminar was justified on the basis of both dwindling water resources and new national water pollution abatement goals.

It is the writer's opinion that the possibilities for nationwide conservation, in the near-term, are greater for reduction in leakage and waste than for household conservation. This is primarily because the former is almost solely in the hands of the waterworks themselves, and the latter depends on the political acceptability of social and/or economic incentives that would be necessary to gain public cooperation. Nonetheless, over the long term, there are considerable potential savings in household use, and they will be achieved only through the development of new policies and

techniques. Obviously, pursuit of one objective does not preclude simultaneous pursuit of the other.

While a decision to adopt policies directed toward conservation could
conceivably be reached voluntarily, it is more likely to be a response to
exogenous considerations. Thus, the issue of water conservation has already arisen in water-short areas and where jurisdictional disputes over
the resource have been encountered. The "energy crises" may make the
public at large more amenable to adoption of a conservation ethic, in a
fallout or spillover sense, but who can say what direction public attitudes
will take over the next decade in response to economic and social forces
that are only now beginning to exert themselves? It is evident that conservation is coming and that some regions will confront it sooner than
others. The only uncertainty is when it will become a crucial issue in any
one place.

Conservation for municipalities can take several forms. It is not solely a
matter of reducing the total quantity of water withdrawn and distributed.
For instance, reductions in peak rates of water use offer potential savings
from reduced energy consumption and from the deferment of enlarge-
ments to existing waterworks facilities. The remainder of this paper is
concerned with all aspects of water conservation within the household,
with an emphasis on research that has been undertaken. Parenthetically,
I would like to note that the AWWA Research Committee on Distribution
Systems has made a number of recommendations on needed research,
including the subject of conservation (AWWA Research Committee
1974a, pp. 385-90; 1974b, pp. 507-509).

CONSERVATION OF DOMESTIC WATER

The East Bay Municipal District, headquartered in Oakland, California,
considers water conservation to be a "logical, necessary, and wholly
proper part of [its] overall water management plan to guarantee adequate
supplies for the future (Lattie 1976, pp. 11-13). The district has designed
a public education program to increase appreciation of water as a resource, establish a clear concept of conservation, and give customers
specific means for conserving water in their own homes or businesses.
According to the district, "Water conservation in some form is here to
stay—it's a fact of life today; tomorrow it must be a way of life" (ibid.).

In a similar vein, a consulting engineer who is a specialist in water
supply development asserts, "If we are to avert disaster in our water
supply industry, demand will have to be dampened and conservation will
have to become routine in our lives and business pursuits" (Romano 1976,
pp. 50-54). He notes that the AWWA has estimated that a family of

four can save almost $50 per year on water, sewer, and power costs by installing water-saving devices at shower heads and faucets. These devices have a total cost of less than $8 in place (ibid.), and there is a growing number of such water conservation devices on the market (Sharpe 1976, pp. 7–9).

According to a spokesman for the Washington Suburban Sanitary Commission (WSSC), "built-in" water conservation for new residential developments has been facilitated in its suburban Maryland service area by modifying the plumbing code to require water-conservative plumbing appliances for new and replacement installations (McLeod 1976, p. P&R 17). WSSC's Virginia neighbor, the Fairfax County Water Authority, has instituted a special summer-use pricing plan that is being watched with great interest by many waterworks across the nation.

Water conservation has often been emphasized as one of the advantages of wastewater reuse in urban areas (Water Resources Scientific Information Center 1975; Dworkin 1975, pp. 607–15). Whereas reuse of reclaimed wastewater for domestic purposes is still controversial, recycling for industrial uses is not. Furthermore, the requirements of PL 92–500 for wastewater treatment in the 1980s are expected to result in such stringent controls on the disposal of effluents into receiving waters that recycling via groundwater recharge and augmentation of industrial supplies may become much more cost-effective than one-time use.

As local shortages and conflicts over the enlargement of facilities continue to grow, more serious attention to reuse can be expected, but this attention is now only beginning to emerge.

QUALITY ASPECTS OF HOUSEHOLD WATER USE

The cost of treating water for municipal use has been rising steadily. Almost certainly, increased requirements for monitoring and treatment will accelerate this trend. Consequently, it may be useful to summarize the costs to households that are associated with poor water quality.

Household appliances and personal items that have been in contact with water supplied municipally or from private sources have been found to be subject to physical damages from chemical and other constituents of the water. These damages have been estimated at an average national cost of about $1.75 billion per year (1970), or $8.60 per person per year, in an assessment (Tihansky 1973) that has been summarized in technical periodicals (Tihansky 1974b, pp. 145–54; 1974a, pp. 905–18).

While many have held that "Economic benefit analyses of pollution control are necessary to insure that future water quality standards improve or enhance social welfare" (Tihansky 1974a, pp. 905–18), far less attention has been paid to the benefits than to the costs (Abel and Tihansky 1974, pp. 276–81). It has also been suggested that the costs imposed on homes and industries by total dissolved solids and hardness concentrations in water need to be investigated more completely (Sonnen 1973, pp. 1849–64). Further, because the damages already identified represent perhaps only a small portion of the total damages, significant benefits remain to be quantified. The accurate quantification of all benefits would have a marked effect on levels of investment in future water resource protection (Sonnen 1975, pp. 451–53).

Even detailed evaluations by water distribution district of the impacts of mineral content on both industry and domestic users (Lawrence 1975, pp. 517–33) may be inadvertently overlooking other important factors. For example, it is suspected that constitutents closely correlated with hardness of drinking water are linked to cardiovascular and other disease. Canadian research indicates that magnesium appears to be the element most probably responsible for the correlation between cardiovascular mortality and water hardness (Neri et al. 1975, pp. 403–409), but this tentative conclusion may be applicable only to Ontario (Anerson 1976, pp. P&R 21, 41).

Results of a Gallup Poll (1973, pp. 513–19) conducted for the American Water Works Association indicated that a majority of respondents were opposed to drinking recycled wastewater and viewed pollution as a contemporary threat to the safety of drinking water. PL 93–523, the Safe Drinking Water Act of 1974, was passed in the midst of controversial reports of contaminants and carcinogens in drinking water in several cities. The implied greater costs for more thorough water treatment increase the need for a better determination of epidemiological factors. Current water production costs are well documented (Montanari and Mattern 1975, pp. 251–54), but costs of incremental changes in treatment may not be easy to calculate. Research on community attitudes toward the adoption of more extensive reuse is being continued on several fronts (Kasperson, R. E. et al. 1974).

About one-third of the U.S. population is served by on-site wastewater disposal systems such as septic tanks. In order to meet new pollution abatement goals, treatment units utilizing intermittent sand filtration of household effluents have been investigated as an alternative to subsurface disposal (Sauer, Boyle, and Otis 1976, pp. 789–803).

QUANTITY ASPECTS OF HOUSEHOLD WATER USE

The Gallup Poll cited previously also included indications that Americans were considerably concerned about the possibility of not having enough water for their future needs. At present, residential water use probably represents close to a third of total municipal system production (Howe and Vaughan 1972, pp. 118–21). Researchers have argued that reducing household water use

> is an attractive and practical way of aiding the fight against water and waste problems. Waste prevention is one method of pollution control that will not become obsolete as new treatment technology is developed. No matter what the method of treatment either for large installations or for individual homes, handling and treatment of the waste will be more efficient and less expensive when it is concentrated in a smaller volume (Bailey et al. 1975).

Findings of a comprehensive study of potentials for reduction of water through-put in households have been summarized elsewhere (General Dynamics Corp. 1969; Bailey and Wallman 1971, pp. 68–70). Almost half of in-house water use is for flushing toilets; an approximately equal amount is used for bathing, personal uses, laundry, and dishes; the remainder of about one-tenth is used for drinking and cooking. There are obvious possibilities for using that portion of water free from fecal contamination a second time for the flushing of toilets. A first demonstration of this possibility showed that household water usage could be reduced about one-fourth by such recycling (General Dynamics Corp. 1974; Bostian 1974, pp. 24–25). On the average, this might mean a community use reduction of less than one-tenth, but the potential would be highest in predominantly residential communities.

A study by Resources for the Future (1971) for the U.S. National Water Commission concluded on the basis of evidence then available that while water reuse within households was technically feasible, it was deemed impracticable at that time because of high costs and excessive requirements for homeowner operation and maintenance. On the other hand, the study also concluded that water-saving devices could save one-third of in-home use, although an economic incentive for adoption of such devices did not exist.

Major economic and social changes have occurred in the past few years. Some of them were anticipated in another study done by the National Academy of Sciences (1971) for the U.S. National Water Commission. The study attempted to predict relations between potential technological advances and their impact on water requirements, including urban supplies and related waste disposal. Since this study appeared, prudent management of all resources has come into sharpened focus. Therefore, a brief review of some of the more recent investigations appears to be in order.

Renewed interest in alternative schemes for more efficient use and disposal of household water is reflected in attempts to quantify the various water quality characteristics of such major use components as bath/ shower, laundry, and toilet (Ligman, Hutzler, and Boyle 1974, pp. 201– 13; Bennett and Linstedt 1975). Use of waterless and sewerless toilets in locations remote from sewer services or where wastewater disposal is particularly difficult appears to be growing rapidly ("Waterless System Treats Domestic Waste," 1975; "A Rush to Sell Sewerless Toilets," 1975). Pressure sewer systems using individual home pump-grinder units (Carcich, Hetling, and Farrell 1974, pp. 25–40) are increasingly accepted in locations where conventional gravity systems are infeasible or very costly. Even the use of home water treatment units is on the rise (Fielding 1975, p. 12). A preliminary investigation has been made of possibilities for augmenting neighborhood water supplies with stormwater collected on individual residential lots (Beers 1973). A study of sprinkling/watering use led to the conclusions that residents applied more water than needed to maintain their landscape plantings and that landscape design criteria could be adopted that would result in water savings while preserving esthetic attractiveness (Cotter and Croft 1974).

Proposals that solid wastes from households be conveyed via wastewater sewers and that wastewater and refuse be treated jointly have been made for a number of years. However, one recent study indicates a cost superiority of such systems over conventional vehicular collection only under favorable circumstances (Kuhner and Meier 1976, pp. 769–88).

Where poor sewer construction and illicit connections to the wastewater sewer system are prevalent, flows of stormwater and groundwater infiltrated into sewer systems may considerably exceed domestic flows (Geyer and Lentz 1966, pp. 1138–48). Results from a survey of communities in the U.S. and Canada (American Public Works Association 1970) indicated that such infiltration and inflow problems are widespread. More stringent federal pollution abatement requirements (PL 92–500) and related increased investment in wastewater treatment facilities have necessitated consideration of ways to diminish these extraneous sewer flows in order to reduce the capacities of new or enlarged treatment plants (Cesareo and Field 1975, pp. 775–85). It has been calculated that almost $5.3 billion will have to be spent to correct inflow and infiltration problems nationally (ibid.). Diminishing extraneous flows would also increase the effective carrying capacity of wastewater sewers, which in some cases would offset the growth in wastewater loads. Under certain circumstances, auxiliary capacity could be added by installing flow-smoothing basins at key locations in a system, as an alternative to the provision of relief sewers (ibid.).

Projections of water demands are needed for water system operations, not just for planning and design; and the most acute need in operations is for automatic control. These needs extend from hourly to seasonal demand variations. Some of the latest advances in automatic control research have been summarized recently (Bree et al. 1976).

ECONOMIC ASPECTS OF HOUSEHOLD WATER USE

The preceding discussions of the quality and quantity aspects of household water use have touched on issues that affect the value and price of water. Unfortunately, many economic calculations concerning water use are rather difficult to make. For instance, investigations of relationships between price and demand (Howe and Linaweaver 1967, pp. 13–32; Howe 1968, p. 497–501; Scarato 1969, pp. 929–36; Hanke and Boland 1971, pp. 677–81; Gysi and Loucks 1971, pp. 1371–82; Hanke 1975, pp. 215–19; Goolsby 1975, pp. 220–24; Hogarty and Mackay 1975, pp. 791–94) and metering and demand (Hanke and Flack 1968, pp. 1359–66; Hanke 1970, pp. 1253–61; Feldman 1975, pp. 490–94) have been handicapped by the limited amount of representative detailed demand data available in usable form. Only limited national data are available on the percentage of unaccounted-for water (Howe 1971, pp. 284–86) because of the difficulties in separating this component. While there are some data on the amount of water used for fighting fires (Cote and Goodman 1970, pp. 407–11) firefighting usually constitutes only a small part of the unmetered demand in a community.

Universal metering is required to collect reliable water-use data for any system. Furthermore, metering provides a firm basis for water-use accounting on which rational pricing structures with proper cost allocation can be built. Waste and leakage can also be better detected and reduced in metered communities, but leak and waste surveys are also needed. At present, many systems are not completely metered, and in others meter readings are not totaled. As already stated, it is not clear to what extent metering affects demand; but a study of residential water use indicated that a charge based on metering does not have much effect on reducing per capita water use, in comparison to a flat-rate charge for multihousehold buildings (Linaweaver, Geyer, and Wolff 1967a, pp. 267–82; 1967b). However, an extension of this study indicated that residential metering has the greatest effect in single-family buildings where the use for lawn sprinkling is large (Howe and Linaweaver 1967, pp. 13–32).

An important point to be remembered in calculating the benefits from conservation is its simultaneous impact on both supply and wastewater systems. Domestic wastewater volumes are approximately equal to domestic water-use volumes, and any savings in water use will reduce facility requirements for both types of service (Mulvihill and Dracup 1974, pp. 170–75).

CONCLUSION

In the face of steadily rising demands and a fixed level of potential supply, it appears inevitable that, in the future, some forms of water conservation will be more extensively practiced than at present. Some conservation programs have already been instituted by waterworks facing severe water shortages—but these have usually been on a short-term or emergency basis. A growing number of utilities, however, is beginning to accept the need for a more careful, long-term evaluation of water conservation policies.

Conservation in household use can take many forms, including innovative rate structures, in-house water-saving devices, and recycling for some uses. Currently, our inability or failure to calculate the potentials for conservation may be severely limiting its implementation. For instance, we know relatively little about the impact of public education campaigns directed toward water-saving practices. That these campaigns will produce significant reductions in use over the long term is open to question. There are, of course, various incentives which may reinforce these campaigns, but their effects are also poorly understood.

In addition, there is a dearth of reliable data on the actual usage of water in municipal systems. Consequently, the volume of water saved by a conservation policy is extremely difficult to calculate. It is also apparent that the traditional methods used to calculate the economic benefits to a utility from reduced consumption are seriously deficient. Even a relatively small reduction in use could represent a great savings through reduced or delayed expenditure for system expansion.

Research in all these areas should not be difficult or expensive in terms of possible benefits, and accurate information on these subjects could lead to great potential savings to waterworks across the country.

REFERENCES

"A Rush to Sell Sewerless Toilets." *Business Week*, November 3.

Abel, Fred H., and Tihansky, Dennis P. 1974. "Methods and Problems of Estimating Water Quality Benefits." *Journal American Water Works Association*, vol. 66. no. 5, May.

American Public Works Association 1970. *Control of Infiltration and Inflow into Sewer Systems*. Water Pollution Control Research Series 11022 EFF 12/70. Washington, D.C.: GPO, December.

Anderson, P. W. 1976. "Water Hardness and Heart Disease." In "Counterpoint," *Journal American Water Works Association*, vol. 68, no. 7, July.

AWWA Research Committee on Distribution Systems 1974a. "Water-Distribution Research and Applied Development Needs." *Journal American Water Works Association*, vol. 66, no. 6, June.

————, 1974*b*. "Priorities in Distribution Research and Applied Development Needs." *Journal American Water Works Association*, vol. 66, no. 9, September.

Bailey, James R. et al. 1975. "Water Flow Reductions from Households." *Water & Sewage Works*, Reference Number, pp. R–57 to R–66, April 30.

Bailey, J., and Wallman, H. 1971. "Flow Reduction of Waste Water from Households." *Water & Sewage Works*, vol. 118, no. 3, March.

Beers, Gary D. 1973. "Management of Storm Water Runoff in Suburban Environments." Cincinnati: Engineering-Science, Inc., November (available from NTIS as PB 228 010).

Bennett, E. R., and Linstedt, K. D. 1975. "Individual Home Wastewater Characterization and Treatment." Fort Collins, Colorado: Colorado Environmental Resources Center, Completion Report Series no. 66, July (available from NTIS as PB 245 259).

Bostian, Harry E. 1974. "Water Conservation by the User." *APWA Reporter*, vol. 41, no. 3, July.

Bree, D. W., Jr.; Budanaers, D. H.; Horgan, D. N., Jr.; and Markel, L. C. 1972. "Improved Methodology for Design and Operation of Water Distribution Systems." Palo Alto, California: Systems Control, Inc., June.

Carcich, Italo G.; Hetling, Leo J.; and Farrell, R. Paul 1974. "Pressure Sewer Demonstration." *Journal of Environmental Engineering Division*, ASCE Proc., vol. 100, no. EE1, February.

Cesareo, David J., and Field, Richard 1975. "Infiltration–Inflow Analysis." *Journal of Environmental Engineering Division*, ASCE Proc., vol. 101, no. EE5, October.

Click, C. N., and Mixon, F. O. 1974. "Flow Smoothing in Sanitary Sewers." *Journal of the Water Pollution Control Federation*, vol. 46, no. 3, March.

Cote, Donald R., and Goodman, Alvin S. 1970. "Cost of Providing Water for Fire Protection." *Journal American Water Works Association*, vol. 62, no. 7, July.

Cotter, D. J., and Croft, D. B. 1974. "Water Application Practices and Landscape Attributes Associated with Residential Water Consumption." Las Cruces, New Mexico: New Mexico Water Resources Research Institute, Report no. 049, November (available from NTIS as PB 244 724).

Dworkin, Daniel M. 1975. "Water Reuse: A Flexible and Efficient Management Alternative for Municipal Water Supply." *Water Resources Research*, vol. 11, no. 5, October.

"Europe, Survival Tactics in a Disastrous Drought." 1976. *Business Week*, September 13.

Feldman, Stephen L. 1975. "Peak-Load Pricing Through Demand Metering." *Journal American Water Works Association*, vol. 67, no. 9, September.

Fielding, Liz 1975. "There's No Place Like Home." *Water and Wastes Engineering*, vol. 12, no. 12.

Gallup Poll 1973. "Water Quality and Public Opinion." *Journal American Water Works Association*, vol. 65, no. 8, August.

General Dynamics Corporation, Electric Boat Division 1974. *Demonstration of Waste Flow Reduction from Households*. Environmental Technology Series

EPA–670/2–74–071. Washington, D.C.: GPO, September (available from NTIS as PB 236 904).

———, 1969. *A Study of Flow Reduction and Treatment of Waste Water from Households*. Water Pollution Control Research Series 11050FKE 12/69. Washington, D.C.: GPO, December.

Geyer, J. C., and Lentz, J. J. 1966. "An Evaluation of the Problems of Sanitary Sewer System Design." *Journal of the Water Pollution Control Federation*, vol. 38, no. 7, July.

Goolsby, William, 1975. "Optimal Pricing and Investment in Community Water Supply." *Journal American Water Works Association*, vol. 67, no. 5, May.

Gysi, Marshall, and Loucks, Daniel P. 1971. "Some Long-Run Effects of Water-Pricing Policies." *Water Resources Research*, vol. 7, no. 6, December.

Haney, Paul, and Hamann, Carl L. 1965. "Dual Water Systems." *Journal American Water Works Association*, vol. 57, no. 9, September.

Hanke, Steve 1975. "Water Rates: An Assessment of Current Issues." *Journal American Water Works Association*, vol. 67, no. 5. May.

———, "Demand for Water Under Dynamic Conditions." *Water Resources Research*, vol. 6, no. 12, December.

Hanke, Steve H., and Boland, John J. 1971. "Water Requirements or Water Demands?" *Journal American Water Works Association*, vol. 63, no. 11, November.

Hogarty, Thomas F., and Mackay, Robert J. 1975. "The Impact of Large Temporary Rate Changes on Residential Water Use." *Water Resources Research* vol. 11, no. 6, December.

Howe, Charles W. 1971. "Savings Recommendations with Regard to Water-System Losses." *Journal American Water Works Association*, vol. 63, no. 5, May.

———, 1968. "Water Pricing in Residential Areas." *Journal American Water Works Association*, vol. 60, no. 5, May.

Howe, Charles W., and Linaweaver, F. P. 1967. "The Impact of Price on Residential Water Demand and Its Relation to System Design and Price Structure." *Water Resources Research*, vol. 3, no. 1, first quarter, 1967.

Howe, Charles W., and Vaughan, William J. 1972. "In-House Water Savings." *Journal American Water Works Association*, vol. 64, no. 2, February.

Kasperson, R. E.; Baumann, D.; Dworkin, D.; McCauley, D.; and Reynolds, J. 1974. "Community Adoption of Water Reuse Systems in the United States." Worcester, Massachusetts: Clark University (available from NTIS as PB 234 030).

Kuhner, Jochen, and Meier, Peter M. 1976. "Hydraulic Collection and Disposal of Refuse." *Journal Environmental Engineering Division*, ASCE Proc. vol. 102, no. EE4, August.

Lattie, James E. 1976. "Water Conservation Promotion." *Willing Water*. American Water Works Association, vol. 20, no. 1, January.

Lawrence, Charles H. 1975. "Estimating Indirect Cost of Urban Water Use." *Journal Environmental Engineering Division*, ASCE Proc., vol. 101, no. EE3, June.

Ligman, Kenneth; Hutzler, Neil; and Boyle, William C. 1974. "Household Wastewater Characterization." *Journal Environmental Engineering Division,* ASCE Proc., vol. 100, no. EE1, February.

Linaweaver, F. P., Jr.; Geyer, J. C.; and Wolff, J. B. 1967a. "Summary Report on the Residential Water Use Research Project." *Journal American Water Works Association,* vol. 59, no. 3, March.

———, 1967b. *A Study of Residential Water Use.* Final report to FHA/HUD, Washington, D.C.

McBean, Edward A., and Loucks, Daniel P. 1974. "Planning and Analyzing of Metropolitan Water Resource Systems." Water Resources and Marine Sciences Center Technical Report no. 84. Ithaca: Cornell University, June (available from NTIS as PB 235 257).

McLeod, Robert J. 1976. "Water Conservation . . . Good." In "Viewpoint,"*Journal American Water Works Association,* vol. 68, no. 6, June.

McPherson, M. B., 1976. "Household Water Use." ASCE UWRR Program Technical Memorandum no. 28, ASCE. New York, New York: January (available from NTIS as PB 250 879).

———, 1975. *Regional Earth Science Information in Local Water Management.* New York, N.Y.: ASCE, July.

———, 1972. "Hydrological Effects of Urbanization in the United States." ASCE UWRR Research Program Technical Memorandum no. 17. New York, N.Y.: ASCE, June (available from NTIS as PB 212 579).

———, 1971. "Management Problems in Metropolitan Water Resource Operations." ASCE UWRR Program Technical Memorandum no. 14. New York, N.Y.: ASCE, September (available from NTIS as PB 206 087).

McPherson, M. B., and Mangan, F. G., Jr. 1975. "ASCE Urban Water Resources Research Program." *Journal Hydraulic Division,* ASCE Proc., vol. 101, no. HY7, July.

Montanari, F. W., and Mattern, David E. 1975. "True Cost of Conventional Water." *Journal American Water Works Association,* vol. 67, no. 5, May.

Mulvihill, Michael E., and Dracup, John A. 1974. "Optimal Timing and Sizing of a Conjunctive Urban Water Supply and Waste Water System With Nonlinear Programming." *Water Resources Research,* vol. 10, no. 2, April.

National Academy of Sciences, Committee on Technologies and Water 1971. "Potential Technological Advances and Their Impact on Anticipated Water Requirements." Washington, D.C.: GPO, June (available from NTIS as PB 204 053).

Neri, L. C. et al. 1975. "Health Aspects of Hard and Soft Waters." *Journal American Water Works Association,* vol. 67, no. 8, August.

Resources for the Future, Inc. 1971. "Future Water Demands: The Impacts of Technological Change, Public Policies, and Changing Market Conditions on the Water Use Patterns of Selected Sectors of the United States Economy, 1970–1990." Washington, D.C.: GPO, March (available from NTIS as PB 197 877).

Romano, James A. 1976. "Where Will We Find the Water?" *Water and Wastes Engineering,* vol. 13, no. 7, July.

Sauer, D. L.; Boyle, W. C.; and Otis, R. J. 1976. "Intermittent Sand Filtration of Household Wastewater." *Journal of Environmental Engineering Division*, ASCE Proc., vol. 102, no. EE4, August.

Scarato, Russell F. 1969. "Time–Capacity Expansion of Urban Water Systems." *Water Resources Research*, vol. 5, no. 5, October (see also discussion by M. Gysi, in vol. 5, no. 3, pp. 993–95, June 1970).

Sharpe, William E. 1976. "Water Conservation Devices." *Willing Water*. AWWA, vol. 20, no. 2, February.

Sonnen, Michael B. 1975. Discussion of "Damage Assessment of Household Water Quality." *Journal Environmental Engineering Division*, ASCE Proc., vol. 101, no. EE3, June.

————, 1973. "Quality-Related Costs of Regional Water Users." *Journal Hydraulic Division*, ASCE Proc., vol. 99, no. HY10, October.

Tihansky, Dennis P. 1974a. "Damage Assessment of Household Water Quality." *Journal Environmental Engineering Division*, ASCE Proc., vol. 100, no. EE4, August.

————, 1974b. "Economic Damage From Residential Use of Mineralized Water Supply." *Water Resources Research*, vol. 10, no. 2, April.

————, 1973. *Economic Damages to Household Items from Water Supply Use*. Socioeconomic Environmental Series EPA–600/5–73–001, (no. EP1.23:600/5–73–001), Washington, D.C.: GPO, July.

Tucker, L. S.; Millan, J.; and Burt, W. W. 1972. "Metropolitan Industrial Water Use." New York, N.Y.: ASCE Urban Water Resources Research Program Technical Memorandum no. 16, May (available from NTIS as PB 212 578).

Unesco 1974. *Hydrological Effects of Urbanization*. Studies and Reports in Hydrology 18. Paris: The Unesco Press.

United Nations 1976. *The Demand for Water: Procedures and Methodologies for Projecting Water Demands in the Context of Regional and National Planning* (available from UNIPUB, Box 433, Murray Hill Station, New York, N.Y. 10016).

United States Water Resources Council 1968. *The Nation's Water Resources*. Washington, D.C.: GPO.

Water Resources Engineers 1976. *Future Direction of Urban Water Models*. Environmental Protection Technology Series EPA–600/2–76–058. Washington, D.C.: GPO, February (available from NTIS as PB 249 049).

Water Resources Scientific Information Center, OWRT, 1975. *Water Reuse, A Bibliography*, vols. 3 and 4. Washington, D.C.: GPO, March.

"Waterless System Treats Domestic Waste" 1975. *Water and Wastes Engineering*, vol. 12, no. 1, January.

"Weather Turns World Economics Topsy–Turvy" 1976. *Business Week*, August 2.

Wolman, Abel 1976. "200 Years of Water Service." *Journal American Water Works Association*, vol. 68, no. 8, August.

————, 1963. "Status of Water Resources Use, Control and Planning in the United States." *Journal American Water Works Association*, vol. 55, no. 10, October.

MANAGEMENT ALTERNATIVES FOR
REDUCING DEMAND

J. ERNEST FLACK,
Professor, Department of
Civil, Environmental, and Architectural Engineering
University of Colorado

Water utilities have historically considered their function to be the provision of all the water a customer wanted. This attitude is gradually being replaced by a conservation ethic. Instead of stressing the supply side of the supply–demand equation, increased emphasis is being placed on methods of reducing demand. It is known that a significant portion of the costs of a water utility system are the result of providing the capacity needed to meet peak demands (Lobb 1975, p. 246). Numerous methods of reducing these peak demands have been proposed (Milne 1976; Bailey 1969). Some of these methods are also useful in reducing total average demands (Program Solicitation 75–42, 1976).

In this paper we attempt to make a critical assessment of alternative means of reducing demand, discussing them in terms of their feasibility, net benefits, and interrelationships. Arranged against these *means* of accomplishing demand management are a series of socioeconomic–political factors that have to do with the *decision* to adopt one or a combination of these means. The availability of the means to conserve water in no way assures a forthcoming decision to implement conservation.

THE ROLE OF CONSERVATION

It is not likely that implementation of water conservation practices will automatically accompany the discovery of new procedures of reducing water usage. Rather, known procedures will be applied in order to determine exactly how much they reduce demands. Then, the cost of implementation will be compared with the benefits resulting from the demand reduction. A review of the literature reveals large variations in the economic values attributed to water-saving methods (Sharpe and Fletcher 1975; Chan et al. 1976; Howe et al. 1971). Errors in quantification of water savings may be widespread, and claims about the amount of water saved through proposed water conservation programs appear to be overstated in many cases (McPherson 1976, p. 1; Final and Comprehensive Report 1974, p. 10). That this is also the judgment of many water utility managers probably explains why so little water conservation is practiced in this country. Managers are skeptical that suggested demand-reducing programs will actually result in the water savings envisioned or that the economic savings will be as large as forecast (Sharpe and Fletcher 1976, pp. 12–13).

In general, the same benefits accrue to a utility from a reduction in either peak or average demands. The most important among these benefits are:

— Reduced costs of operation and maintenance

— Postponement of system expansion

— Extension of the planning horizon for new water supply acquisition and for construction of water treatment, distribution, and waste treatment facilities

— Increased ability to conform to a steady-state or no-growth situation

— Conservation and improved utilization of other resources such as materials, fuel, and energy.

The peak demands in municipal water systems are typically associated with fire flow requirements, industrial use, and residential use. This paper is primarily concerned with residential water use because it is the dominant factor in determining peak loads in most systems. Residential lawn sprinkling and air conditioning can impose large demands on water utility systems. Although other high rates of usage over short periods are associated with hotels, apartments, mobile home parks, schools, laundromats, and service stations; in the aggregate, residential peak demands are usually more important than the other uses because of the large number of units for which peak demands tend to coincide. In terms of overall system demand, only large apartment complexes or numerous hotels or mobile home parks could approach the total effect on peak demand of private residences. It is, of course, necessary to analyze the peak demand in a particular utility to determine which classes of customers are most important in determining that particular system's peak demand. Schools and laundromats, while they have extreme peak demands, are not usually large or numerous enough to affect system design in a metropolitan area.

Four general methods of reducing demands can be identified: structural, operational, economic, and social. Each of them and their combinations need to be evaluated by a water utility interested in implementing a water conservation program.

STRUCTURAL METHODS

Physical devices or processes provide structural methods which result in peak flow reductions. Most of the burden of installation and operation of the devices rests with the utility. In the case of customer leakage reduction, however, a cooperative program would be necessary. The most important structural methods are:

1. *Mechanical or hydraulic flow regulators.* These consist of restrictions or controls on the system which limit the delivery capacity. The net effect of these controls is to reduce the pressure in the system, thus negating any increase in demand that would otherwise result. The water savings that result are a function of the pressure reduction that occurs. Moses suggests that a low pressure system would deliver about 5 gpm less than a typical system and 10 gpm less than a high pressure system (Moses 1975, p. 118). The Washington Suburban Sanitary Commission estimates a 33 percent reduction in water usage as a result of pressure regulation (Metcalf and Elby 1976).

2. *Metering.* The metering of a water customer who was previously on a flat rate has two effects. The first is psychological and is manifested by a sudden reduction in water usage upon installation of the meter, followed by a recovery which is nearly as abrupt, to a higher water use rate. This new rate of usage is not as high as the former usage under a flat rate. A second, and long-term, effect can be attributed to price. The reduction that may be attributed to the psychological effect alone is not well understood, and the available information applies largely to residential customers (Hanke 1970, pp. 1883–86).

Although the effect of metering depends on conditions such as price, climate, income, lot size, family size, and so forth, a conservative estimate is that a reduction in water usage of approximately 30 percent will result from metering a flat-rate residential water system (Brauer et al.).

3. *Leakage reduction.* Reduction of system leakage can be related to peak demands in two ways. One is by reduction of average use; the other is by reduction in peak period leakage. A tendency for large leakage rates to coincide with peak demands seems to characterize some systems, but this relationship needs additional verification. It has been shown that even at very modest costs of water, it pays to repair large leaks (Howe 1971, pp. 284–85).

4. *Recycling systems.* Reuse, successive use, and recycling of water in residences, commercial, and industrial establishments can help to reduce system demands. Even excluding requirements for potable water, recy-

cled or gray waters can be put to many uses. Industrial applications of recycling or successive use are now widespread. The costs, effectiveness and hazards (primarily through inadvertent cross-connections with a potable water supply) need to be assessed for a range of applications of recycle systems, from individual homes and businesses to entire utility systems (Flack 1973, pp. 69–99). According to Cohen and Wallman (1974), recycling of gray waters within households for toilet and lawn use could result in water savings of 26 percent. For a new subdivision DeLapp (1973, p. iv) estimated that a dual system using gray water would be cost-effective at treated water prices of 60¢ per 1,000 gallons.

5. *Water-saving devices.* These include low-water-use appliances such as toilets, dishwashers, and clothes-washers, as well as controlled-flow faucets and shower heads and nonwater waste handling facilities. They have application to households, industrial plants, commercial establishments, schools, hospitals, and private and public buildings.

Water-saving devices operate to reduce both average and peak usage. Many of these devices have been described in the literature and their costs and benefits and their interrelationships with other components of system usage have been estimated (Watson 1975, pp. 12–13; Bailey 1969; Sharpe 1975). Double counting of the savings resulting from the devices, especially in combination with price increases and assumed human behavioral patterns, probably results in overestimation of their effects.

According to the Washington Suburban Sanitary Commission (Final and Comprehensive Report 1973), if properly installed and maintained, reduced-flush toilets could save 12 to 20 percent of the water previously used, and flow-limiting shower heads could save an additional 12 percent. Aerators have been estimated to save as much as 50 percent of the use from faucets (Bailey 1969, p. 55). In a comprehensive study, Howe and Vaughan calculated the water savings for various household appliances singly and in combination (Howe and Vaughan, pp. 118–22). In a similar study, Sharpe arrived at quite different values (1975, pp. 4–9). A comparison of the findings of Howe and Sharpe is presented in table 1.

6. *Clear storage.* A certain amount of storage must be provided to meet directly the peak demand on a system. Clear storage for an entire system is generally centrally located and is held in reserve to meet peak demands upon the system over a period of time, say a work week. Clear storage may also be located at or near the peak demand location and scaled to meet short-period peak demands of less than a day. As a conservation device, on-site storage of this type would require a large number of installations with associated problems of location, protection, reliability, cleaning, and so forth, and is not likely to be cost-effective until peak water costs become very high.

Table 1

**REDUCTION IN USAGE FROM
HOUSEHOLD WATER-SAVING
DEVICES**

Item	Percent Reduction	
	Howe	Sharpe
Toilet	'41 to 56	up to 30
Shower	20 to 34	50 to 70
Laundry	20 to 27	—
Faucet	—	50
TOTAL	32	up to 70

7. *Customer leakage reduction*. The goal of individual customer leakage reduction is to reduce or eliminate plumbing leaks and water wastage at the place of use (Hanke 1959, p. 157). This is a structural method whose costs are typically covered by the individual water user. In the case of industrial, commercial, or other large water users, this method can include control of water-using processes such as cleaning, cooling, food preparation, and so forth.

OPERATIONAL METHODS

Within the day-to-day operation of a water system there are possibilities to reduce demand which do not involve the installation or maintenance of devices to control water usage:

1. *System pressure reduction*. The reduction of the total pressure in a system will reduce the delivery capability of a system during peak demand periods. In most water utilities pressures drop significantly during times of peak demand. As an operational method to reduce demand the pressure is lowered before the peak demand period to discourage maximum demand on the system. The lower limit for pressure is usually considered to be the curbside pressure necessary at fire hydrants to ensure fire flows. This method has the same effect on water demand as the flow regulators previously described under structural methods.

2. *Restrictions on deliveries*. Limiting the volume of water delivered to certain classes of customers as peak demands occur is a more selective operational method to reduce demand. In implementing this method, it

would be necessary to anticipate the peak demand periods and notify the customers of impending restriction. Customers so affected would logically be the largest users, including industries, commercial users, and wholesale customers of treated water who, in turn, retail the water in their own systems.

3. *Elimination of unauthorized uses.* Unaccounted-for water may be attributable to system leaks, public uses, illegal connections, bypassed meters, and so forth. Detection of these uses can be important. Reduction of these uses would usually reduce both peak demand and average usage. The costs of locating and controlling unauthorized uses must be determined for each individual utility. Both the time and the amount of use for public purposes, such as street flushing, park and median strip watering, and ghetto hydrant use, need to be controlled. System losses of less than 10 percent are considered to be excellent and values from 10 to 20 percent are reasonable (Keller 1976, pp. 159–62). Because of the low price of water in most utilities, bypassing of meters is probably not prevalent but may become so with increased water prices.

4. *Restrictions and prohibitions.* Regulations can be promulgated which prohibit certain activities entirely or restrict them to certain times. A wide range of possible actions may be taken. Among them are:

1. Restriction of lawn and garden irrigation to specified hours or days. This method requires policing action for enforcement, and while it will work during droughts, there are serious questions about compliance with restrictions over long periods, say years.
2. Filling of swimming pools can be prohibited during peak demand periods, and other uses such as fountains can be prohibited.
3. Curtailment of total use. This is generally considered unacceptable except in times of crises when either storage is entirely depleted or the means of conveyance is lost.

ECONOMIC METHODS

Until recently, the generation of adequate revenue was the primary concern of water utilities, and economic policy was simply a matter of selling more water in order to increase the revenue. However, a wide range of economic policies is available which provide incentives to save water or reduce waste and which do not necessarily lead to inadequate revenues:

1. *Rate structures.* Changing from the traditional declining block rate to a uniform rate per volume of water delivered, or to an increasing block rate (inverse pricing) where additional increments cost more than previous increments of use, may significantly reduce consumption. In a study

of the Denver water system, Roussos found that a savings of 4 percent could be realized through use of inverse pricing (1976, p. 90).

2. *Seasonal or peak demand pricing.* The imposition of a higher price per unit of water demanded during periods of peak demand for all customers, whether or not they contribute directly to the peak, is relatively new to water utility practice. The magnitude of the peak price and effect on demand must be determined from a careful analysis of the particular utility. Hanke and Davis, in a study for the Washington Suburban Sanitary Commission (1971, p. 559) devised a seasonal price structure which was estimated to save 2.6 percent of water (Hanke and Davis 1971, p. 559). Using the same general model, Roussos found that in the Denver water system an actual increase in water usage would result. By modifying the peak and off-peak seasonal prices he was able to devise a pricing scheme that would result in a 5 to 10 percent reduction in water demand compared to present usage (1976, p. 46), depending on the assumed value of elasticity of demand with price.

In assessing the effect of various price structures, one major difficulty is the lack of good data on price elasticities. The usual data source is the Howe-Linaweaver study (1967, pp. 24–26), but more recent analysis of operating systems has indicated considerable variance, in some categories of use, from these values (Burns et al. 1975, pp. 3–10).

3. *System development charges.* An indirect effect on peak demand will result from controlling system growth. Such a policy not only ensures that the costs of bringing additional users onto a system are recovered; it also discourages the installation of oversized service lines and meters. Zoning and building codes can have a similar effect.

4. *Reduced rates.* Incentives for conservation and reduced usage may include payments or, more often, reduced charges for those customers who (1) reduce leakage and wastes, (2) irrigate during off-peak hours, and (3) install water-saving devices. Tax credits can also be explored to accomplish the same end.

5. *Demand metering.* A meter may be installed which records the rate of use and charges more per unit the greater the demand. In order to increase customer response, the meter can include a signal (for example, a light coming on in a conspicuous place) when demand exceeds some predetermined rate. An alternate approach would be the installation of a meter that controls the flow to a specified maximum and does not permit the peak rate to exceed this maximum.

6. *Penalties.* Fines may be imposed on customers who waste water. This approach is not necessarily limited to outside uses such as lawn

irrigation and car washing. It requires policing, issuance of summonses, and collection of fines, or the installation of a penalizing meter which limits the rate of flow to a customer.

SOCIAL METHODS

Noneconomic methods which tend to encourage customers to reduce demands can be described as social methods. They are usually relatively indirect, long-term methods, and their success is difficult to assess:

1. *Public education in water conservation.* In-house conservation is important, not only in that it saves water, but also because it establishes a conservation ethic which carries over to uses such as lawn sprinkling which significantly affect peak demand. Using less water and timing uses to avoid peak demand periods can be stressed through public information and education. Means include radio and television announcements, newspaper releases, films, and public school programs (Brigham 1976, pp. 665–68).

2. *Horticultural practices.* An additional but little used social means has to do with changes in horticultural practices by residential and other users. For instance, in those utilities where peak demands are caused by lawn sprinkling, such demands can be significantly reduced by encouraging the use of less water-demanding species of plants and grasses (Water Conservation in California 1975, p. 23). An efficient sprinkling system in itself can reduce residential overwatering by as much as 50 percent (Uno 1975).

While it can be demonstrated that horticultural changes can result in water savings, wide acceptance of these changes requires a high degree of public response. There is some evidence that residential owners who have high water-using lawns and vegetation also have a tendency to over-irrigate (Cotter and Croft 1974). Implementation of water-saving means through building and plumbing codes has largely been confined to the installation of water-saving devices and the proper sizing of water meters. Similar kinds of controls could be extended to horticultural practices and lawn sizes.

EVALUATION OF ALTERNATIVES

Evaluation of the alternative methods of reducing water demands can be done from the point of view of (a) engineering feasibility, (b) economic feasibility, (c) sociopolitical consequences, and (d) social well-being, for each of the alternative methods—structural, operational, economic, and social.

Engineering feasibility can be evaluated in terms of availability of energy and materials, the reliability of the system in use, and the necessary incentives, if any, to make a method generally available.

Economic feasibility involves the evaluation of the costs of implementing a method and evaluating the net benefits on both a short- and a long-term basis. Economic calculations must include both construction and maintenance costs and long-term effects, such as postponement of system expansion.

Evaluation of sociopolitical consequences includes environmental concerns, political acceptance, determination of how costs are to be recovered, and any possible associated health hazards.

Evaluation of social well-being involves the public acceptability of alternative methods, short- and long-term changes in social attitudes, possible invasions of privacy and infringment on personal property rights, acceptance of the need for conservation, and evaluation of changes in life styles that may be associated with adoption of any of the alternative methods.

The alternative methods which singly or as a group show high levels of feasibility as measured by the criteria just mentioned can be given priorities, and their recommendation can then be justified. That any one, or a few, of the alternatives will be best for all utilities seems unlikely, and a decision matrix of feasibility versus acceptability by type and location of utility could be adopted. For instance, utilities of a certain size and type geographically located in the Southwest will almost certainly have a different set of feasible alternatives than utilities of a different size and type located in the Northeast.

CONCLUSION

A large number of means of reducing urban demand have been proposed. Whether or not any or all of them are feasible for implementation in a particular utility is a question which must be answered by the decision makers and managers of that utility. It seems apparent that many of the structural alternatives are sufficiently attractive from an economic standpoint to warrant investigation. Inexpensive water-saving devices such as dams, washers, and flow restrictors are recommended because they help develop a conservation ethic among water users. The installation of more costly low-water-use plumbing fixtures is not economically justified at this time for retrofitting existing buildings, but such fixtures could be incorporated into new construction. Similar conclusions can be drawn with regard to metering and dual systems, at least, at low water prices.

Other water conservation means such as horticultural changes, innovative pricing policies, and credits and incentives depend for their justification on customer responses after implementation. The responses are largely unknown and predictions of the amount of water saved by implementation of any of these techniques or procedures is problematic and needs to be tested in various regions among utilities of different sizes.

REFERENCES

Bailey, J. R. et al. 1969. "A Study of Flow Reduction and Treatment of Waste Water from Households." NTIS PB 197–599, General Dynamics Corp. p. 55.

Brauer et al. "A Study of Water Use and Its Conservation in Northern Colorado." Term Project CE 539–Econ 691, Fall Semester, University of Colorado.

Brigham, Arthur P. 1976. "A Public Education Campaign to Conserve Water." *Journal American Water Works Association*, vol. 69, no. 12, December.

Burns et al. 1975. "The Effect of Price on Residential Water Demand—A Comparative Use Study." Project Report CE 539–Econ 691, fall semester, University of Colorado.

Chan, M. L. et al. 1976. "Household Water Conservation and Wastewater Flow Reduction." Mimeographed. Cambridge, Mass.: Energy Resources Co., Inc.

Cohen, S. and Wallman, H. 1974. "Demonstration of Water Flow Reduction for Households." EPA 670/2–74–071, General Dynamics Corp., September.

Cotter, D. J. and Croft, D. B., 1974. "Water Application Practices and Landscape Attributes Associated with Residential Water Consumption." Water Resources Research Institute, New Mexico State University, WRRI Report no. 049, November.

DeLapp, John R. 1973. "Water Reuse with a Dual Distribution System," M.S. thesis, University of Colorado.

Final and Comprehensive Report 1974. Washington Suburban Sanitary Commission's Water Conservation/Wastewater Reduction... Program, November 22.

———, 1973. Washington Suburban Sanitary Commission Final and Comprehensive Report for the Cabin John Drainage Basin, Water-Saving Customer Education, and Appliance Test Program. Washington, D.C.

Flack, J. Ernest 1973. "Consultant's Report on Resources." In *Public Water Supply Treatment and Technology*, American Water Works Association Research Foundation.

Hanke, Steve H. 1970. "Some Behavioral Characteristics Associated with Residential Water Price Changes." *Water Resources Research*, vol. 6, no. 5, October.

———, 1959. "The Demand for Water under Dynamic Conditions." Ph.D. dissertation, University of Colorado.

Hanke, Steve H. and Davis, Robert K. 1971. "Demand Management through Responsive Pricing." *Journal American Water Works Association*, vol. 63, no. 9, September.

Howe, Charles W. 1971. "Savings Recommendations with Regard to Water System Losses." *Journal American Water Works Association*, vol. 63, no. 5, May.

Howe, C. W. et al. 1971. "Future Water Demands—The Impacts of Technological Change, Public Policies and Changing Market Conditions on the Water Use Patterns of Selected Sectors of the U.S. Economy, 1970–90." Resources for the Future, Inc., NTIS, NWC, EES, 71–001, March.

Howe, Charles W. and Linaweaver, F. P. Jr. 1967. "The Impact of Price on Residential Water Demand and Its Relation to System Design and Price Structure." *Water Resources Research*, vol. 3, no. 1, 1st quarter.

Howe, Charles W. and Vaughan, William J. "In-House Water Savings." *Journal American Water Works Association*, vol. 64, no. 2.

Keller, Charles W. 1976. "Analysis of Unaccounted-for Water." *Journal American Water Works Association*, vol. 68, March.

Lobb, Howard J. 1975. "Demand–Rate Economics." *Journal American Water Works Association* 67, May.

McPherson, Murray B. 1976. "Household Water Use." ASCE Urban Water Resources Research Program, Tech. Mem. #28, January.

Metcalf and Eddy, Inc. 1976. "Water Savings," for Santa Clara Valley Water District. San Jose, California. May.

Milne, Murray. 1976. *Residential Water Conservation*. Report no. 35. Davis, California: California Water Resources Center, University of California, March.

Moses, H. L. 1975. "Research on Water Saving Devices at Virginia Polytechnic Institute and State University." In *Proceedings, Conference on Water Conservation and Sewage Flow Reduction with Water-Saving Devices*. Information Report 74, Institute for Research on Land and Water Resources, Pennsylvania State University, July.

Program Solicitation No. 75–42, 1976. "Methods of Reducing Peak Water Demands." National Science Foundation/RANN, May.

Roussos, George J. 1976. "An Assessment of Alternative Rate-Making Policies for the Denver Water System." M.S. thesis, University of Colorado.

Sharpe, William E. 1975. "Water Conservation." Special Circular 184, Institute for Research on Land and Water Resources, Pennsylvania State University.

Sharpe, William E. and Fletcher, Peter W. 1976. "Conservation Will Be a Management Tool in Future Water Use Planning." *Willing Water*, vol. 20, no. 10, October.

———, eds. 1975. *Proceedings, Conference on Water Conservation and Sewage Flow Reduction with Water-Saving Devices*. Information Report 74, Institute for Research on Land and Water Resources, Pennsylvania State University, July.

Uno, Gordon 1975. "Be Water Wise, Water Conservation: It's Up to You." Denver, Colorado: Denver Water Department, December.

INCREASING WATER SYSTEM EFFICIENCY

WILLIAM D. HUDSON
President, Pitometers Associates
Chicago, Illinois

Many articles have been written on the future use of water. Some of these articles predict very high per capita use of water and what seems to be fantastic amounts of water for use in industry and irrigation in future years. It is logical, therefore, with population expanding at an ever-increasing rate, that the water available be used wisely.

Experience shows that as long as the supply of water in an area is abundant and the cost of manufacturing into a usable product is not expensive, the per capita use of water will be high. In such areas, normally little effort is made to conserve water and there is probably little justification for doing so. However, as the areas within the cities and the suburban areas become more solidly built upon, three principal changes take place which affect the supply and the demand for water:

1. Less ground area is available to retain the runoff and to absorb the water into the underground supply.

2. The pollution of both underground and surface supplies becomes more serious.

3. The per capita use of water becomes higher as the population increases.

These conditions eventually cause most small well and surface supplies to become inadequate, making it necessary to obtain a new supply, usually at a much higher cost. These conditions also make it necessary for water utilities to examine methods for increasing system efficiency.

The criteria used by most water utilities to determine distribution-system operating efficiency is the percentage of accounted-for water, that is, the ratio of the amount of water sold as compared to the amount of water produced or purchased. This is commonly referred to as the metered ratio (Beckwith 1958).

The metered ratio can vary considerably, and what may be considered good performance in accounting for water in one system may not be good performance in another system. If the water supplied to the distribution system is metered and all water supplied to the consumers, including free

211

water, is metered, the metered ratio of the water supplied to the distribution system to water registered on all meters in the system is an exact record of the accounted-for water. This ratio may be as high as 90 percent in a system (1) in which meters are maintained to register as accurately as possible; (2) which is free from underground leakage; (3) where a high percentage of the water is sold through industrial meters; and (4) where the number of services per mile of main is high.

In the case of a city with high industrial water consumption, a metered ratio of 90 percent may still represent inefficient operation with much avoidable leakage and waste, while in the case of a similar city with little industrial use, a ratio of 85 to 90 percent might indicate efficient operation. If the metered ratio is less than 85 percent, intensive leak detection, to determine the cause of the unaccounted-for water, is usually justified.

In evaluating a metered ratio, all user groups should be taken into account, along with the miles of main in the system. Of course, to account accurately for the water used in a city it is essential that all domestic, commercial, industrial, and fire services be metered. It is also necessary to meter all public buildings, swimming pools, fountains, golf courses, and other services, even though the water may be supplied without charge. The meters determine the revenue, and upon their accuracy depends the amount of revenue the water utility will receive. In an unmetered water system there is no accurate way to determine distribution system losses; however, reasonably accurate estimates can be based on factors such as per capita consumption.

In my opinion, every water distribution system should be operated as a public utility providing the best service possible, in an economical manner and without subsidies. To do this, it is necessary to sell as much water as possible at adequate rates. If the metered ratio indicates excessive distribution system losses, a program should be set up to control and eliminate these losses, where possible. It should be recognized, however, that although distribution system losses are recurrent and cannot be eliminated, they can be controlled.

The program for controlling distribution system losses and increasing system efficiency is described in the following sections. Such maintenance is necessary to generate adequate revenues and to ensure reliable service.

ACCURACY TESTS OF MASTER METERS

The master meters, which measure the water supplied to the entire distribution system, may either over- or under-register. Any error in measurement by a master meter will be directly reflected in apparent distribution system losses. It is not unusual to find that an increase in unaccounted-for water is a direct result of an inaccurate master meter (Hudson 1966, p. 867).

Of the several types of master meters, each has somewhat different capabilities and installation requirements. In planning an installation, ample straight pipe ahead of the meter should be provided to ensure maximum uniformity of flow and consequent accuracy of registration. Provision should be made for testing the master meter at least once a year (ibid.).

ACCURACY TESTS OF INDUSTRIAL AND COMMERCIAL METERS

In many cities the industrial and commercial meters produce a large percentage of the revenue for the water utility. The frequency with which industrial meters should be tested depends on the amount of use through them. It is our opinion that meters supplying large users of water should be tested at least once a year; more often, if the revenue is large.

It is important that the proper size and type of meter be installed. A meter that is too small may cause an excessive drop in pressure and wear out in a short period of time, while a meter that is too large may not be registering low flows. Underregistration is often found to be a major factor in solving the distribution system water-loss problem.

To ensure accurate registration, the meters must be properly installed. Provision should be made for testing the meters in place, preferably without interruption to service. The addition of a test plug on the large meters, making it possible to test the meters in place by use of a comparative test meter, is a major convenience.

ROTATION OF DOMESTIC METERS

Domestic meters are the principal revenue producers in many of the suburban cities and are equally important in cities where there is large revenue from industrial and commercial meters (Hudson 1964, p. 143). The domestic meters are also the most neglected part of the water system in many cities and villages. Unfortunately, a domestic meter will run for many years before it completely stops, and for most of the years it operates it will be underregistering and losing revenue for the water utility. As soon as a new meter is installed and begins to operate, its internal parts begin to wear. As these parts wear, the meter begins to underregister on the low flows. As the wearing process continues, the greater the underregistration. The rate at which the wear takes place depends on the properties of the water (ibid.).

The amount of water used in a water system at low rates of flow is larger than many water managers realize. In order to determine the amount of water used at various rates of flow through domestic meters, the results of five studies on this subject were examined (Kuranz 1942, p. 1175; Horandt 1939; *Economics of Water Meter Testing and Repair*, 1942; Graeser 1958, p. 925; Hardy 1958, p. 932.). From the results of four of the studies, the following average figures were obtained for the percentage of water used as various rates of flow through domestic meters:

Table 1

PERCENTAGE OF TOTAL FLOW THROUGH DOMESTIC METERS AT VARIOUS RATES

Rate of Flow (gpm)	Water Used (percentage of total)
0—1/4	13
1/4—1/2	3.4
1/2—1	6.8
1—2	13.3
2—4	43
More than 4	20.5

These data show that 23.2 percent of the water is used at flows of one gallon per minute or less. This is the range where domestic meters first start to underregister, especially at a flow rate of approximately ¼ gpm.

Some years ago the author's firm conducted a study in order to determine the amount of water lost through underregistration of domestic meters (Committee Report 1957, p. 1587). The meter test data available to us was approximately three percent of the total number of meters in the system. Nevertheless, the test data were sufficient to show a definite pattern of underregistration by age groups of the meters. These meters were in a system where the water is not corrosive and sand and grit is not a problem. Therefore, the results show the maximum that might be expected from a meter.

The results show that at least 20 percent of the meters with more than 8 or 10 years service will not register flows below ¾ gpm. Since 23.2 percent of the domestic water is used at this rate or lower, five percent of the system's revenue is lost. It is evident that, even under the best possible conditions, domestic meters should not be left in service more than 8 to 10 years before rebuilding. In systems where the water is more corrosive or contains sand and grit, this period should be shorter.

It is now possible to utilize computerized billing techniques that not only record total consumption but also designate unusual readings. These

Table 2

UNDERREGISTRATION OF METERS ACCORDING TO AGE†

Age of Meters (years)	Meters Inaccurate (percentage)	Minimum Registrable Flow (gpm)
0—9	5	3/4
9—19	20	3/4
19—29	50	1 1/4
More than 29	84	1 1/2

†Averages based on four separate studies.

systems are particularly useful for detecting meters that have ceased to function.

DETECTION OF UNAUTHORIZED USE

The unauthorized use of water may be a source of unaccounted-for water. The unauthorized use of water is usually accidental rather than deliberate. The most likely cause is unmetered fire lines in a building. The best way to avoid unauthorized use from fire lines is to install meters on them. If the fire and domestic services are separate, a detection-type meter on the fire line will indicate any use. If domestic and fire services are combined, a meter suitable for this type of service should be used.

The deliberate taking of water by circumventing meters or by tapping a main without authority is difficult to detect.

ESTIMATES OF USE FROM HYDRANTS

Although it is not unusual for cities to meter all industrial, commercial, residential, and public uses, very few cities attempt to make an accounting of the water used for fires, street flushing, sewer flushing, and other incidental uses. In fact, metering of these uses is often not feasible, but quite accurate estimates of the volumes used can be made. For firefighting, the amount used can be estimated on the number and size of hose streams, as well as on pressure and length of time used. Accurate records can be kept of water used by street-flushing trucks and streetsweepers merely by keeping track of the loads of water used. Water used for sewer flushing can also be estimated.

These incidental uses are not continuous, and despite the large quantities consumed during short periods, the daily average throughout the year is small, and the effect on the percentage of unaccounted-for water is comparatively unimportant. The American Water Works Association committee report on "Unaccounted-for Water" recommends that a figure of no more than one percent of total system water be assumed for these purposes. This figure has been verified by detailed studies in several cities.

ALLOWANCE FOR UNAVOIDABLE LEAKAGE

Unavoidable leakage refers to underground leaks which exist in every system and which would cost more to locate and repair than to tolerate. Throughout the years many formulas have been proposed to arrive at a fair figure to cover this item. Some methods are based on the inches of joints, others on the number of connections to the main, and others on both. Kuichling (cited in Case 1950) has stated:

> A discharge of one drop per second from each joint, five drops from each hydrant and stop valve, and three drops from each service pipe, including tap and unit cock, represents a fair measure of the average undiscoverable leakage in a well constructed distribution system. . . .
> On this basis and with the assumption that on the average there are 504 pipe joints, 12 hydrants, 10 stop valves and 100 service pipes per mile of distribution pipe, the leakage will amount to 2,742 gpd. per mile, or in round figures, say, from 2,500 to 3,000 gpd. per mile.

These figures are based on 12-ft lengths of pipe and small lots. In the newer sections of cities, the 18-ft length of pipe, with the improved type of joints, are used and there are fewer services per mile of main. In these areas, the allowable leakage per mile of main should probably not exceed 1,500 to 2,500 gpd per mile of main.

UNDERGROUND LEAKAGE

Underground leakage is frequently the principal cause of a high rate of unaccounted-for water. Although it is a problem confronting every water utility, it is much more serious in some areas than in others. Underground leakage cannot be eliminated, but it can be controlled. Such leakage follows no definite pattern and there are as many causes as there are types of leaks. To keep underground leakage to a minimum requires constant attention and a plan of water conservation.

In many cities throughout the United States and Canada the author's firm is employed on an annual basis to control and locate underground leakage. In these cities the method used involves dividing the distribution system into districts of from 10 to 20 miles of main. These districts are remeasured at regular intervals and any change in the night rate of flow into the districts is detected. If there is an increase in the night rate that cannot be accounted for, further measurements are made at night to determine the distribution of the night rate and to locate any leaks that may have developed.

The interesting result of these measurements is the emergence of categories. A given city will have areas where leakage will recur very quickly and where it will be necessary to make frequent, detailed investigations in order to keep the underground loss at a minimum. Yet, in the same city, some areas will not develop enough leakage to warrant detailed investigations more often than every 8–10 years. If we assume that workmanship and materials in the various areas of a city are nearly the same, it would appear that, in some areas, underground leakage is caused principally by the relative presence or absence of soil movement or corrosive soil conditions. These factors probably explain why some cities have more problems with leakage than others.

Materials and workmanship, however, can also be factors in underground leakage. Improper bracing of bends and special fittings, as well as improper bedding of the pipe, and rigid construction through valve vaults and manholes, all contribute to underground leakage. In recent years mechanical and compression joints have come into widespread use for pipe, and the use of copper for service lines is general throughout the water industry. These materials appear to be superior to the older types, for leakage is detected less frequently. Of course, this seeming improvement may be due to the short length of time the new materials have been used, but steps do appear to have been made toward reducing leakage.

Every water utility should be equipped with leak detection instruments so that periodic checks can be made on the valves, hydrants, and services to locate obvious underground leaks. It must be remembered that underground leakage is a recurrent problem requiring constant vigilance.

The June 1970 AWWA Journal contains a "Survey Form for Evaluating Water Utility Operations" (Cole 1970, p. 354). The use of this form should help in evaluating and determining distribution system losses.

CONCLUSIONS

If, after a reasonable check for the most obvious causes of the problem, the percentage of unaccounted-for water is still high, a complete audit should be made of the distribution system. This audit should be made by a professional firm specializing in the field of water distribution and having accurate instrumentation to perform all required tests, including efficiency tests of the pumping equipment (Beckwith 1958).

Distribution system losses are a luxury that no water utility can afford. Water passing unregistered through meters is revenue lost at retail prices. Water lost through underground leakage not only wastes energy and valuable chemicals which are in short supply but also wastes purification plant capacity, pumpage capacity, and main capacity.

Increasing system efficiency through controlling distribution system losses is economically feasible. Normally, the decrease in the cost of production and pumping resulting from the location and repair of leaks, and the increase in revenue as a result of repair of defective meters, will pay for the cost of the survey in a few months.

REFERENCES

Beckwith, H. E. 1958. "Pump Efficiencies of Centrifugal Pumps." *Water and Sewage Magazine*, March.

Case, E. D. 1950. "Water Waste Surveys and Unaccounted-for Water." *Journal American Water Works Association*, vol. 42, March.

Cole, E. Shaw 1970. Survey Form for Evaluating Water Utility Operations. *Journal American Water Works Association*, vol. 62, June.

Committee Report 1957. "Revenue-producing Versus Unaccounted-for Water." *Journal American Water Works Association*, vol. 49, December.

Economics of Water Meter Testing and Repair. 1942. New York: Neptune Meter Company.

Graeser, H. J. 1958. "Distribution Losses and Meter Repair Practices—Detecting Lost Water at Dallas." *Journal American Water Works Association*, vol. 50, July.

Gros, W. F. H. 1976. "Wasting Energy? Use This Simple Method to Check Pump Efficiencies." Unpublished, presented at National Conference American Water Works Association, June.

Hardy, R. W. 1958. "Distribution Losses and Meter Repair Practices—Meter Repairing at Fort Worth." *Journal American Water Works Association*, vol. 50, July.

Horandt, H. 1939. "An Outline of Water Meter Practice." New York: Neptune Meter Company.

———, 1964. "Reduction of Unaccounted-for Water." *Journal American Water Works Association*, vol. 56, February.

Hudson, W. D. 1966. "Field Testing of Large Meters." *Journal American Water Works Association*, vol. 58, July.

Kuranz, A. P. 1942. "Meter Maintenance Practice." *Journal American Water Works Association*, vol. 34, January.

PRICING POLICIES:
THEORY AND PRACTICE

Pricing policies for all water-related services have come under increasing scrutiny. In part this is due to a growing interest among water system managers about new methods to increase their revenues and to an interest among water users about the reasons for their increased water bills. In addition, however, there is a growing awareness of the social and environmental implications of water rate structures.

It is within this latter context that the following two papers by Steve Hanke and by Martin Lang are best understood. While some aspects of the interrelationships of water prices and demand are discussed earlier in this volume, the emphasis here is upon the broader social context in which economic policy is made. Both authors are concerned less with economic theory than with the difficulties involved in its implementation. Nonetheless, the great difference between their points of view is instructive.

Hanke is concerned primarily with the social efficiency of alternative rate structures, and he ascribes some of the blame for the present inequitable situation to economists. He makes a thoughtful analysis of the socially undesirable effects of the various rate structures currently used in the United States and points out that the problem of achieving an equitable price for water can be resolved only by the application of marginal cost analysis, in order to eliminate subsidies among consumer groups. He charges that economists have largely failed to demonstrate how this should be done. He then proceeds, by way of a case study of Adelaide, Australia, to describe in detail how marginal pricing policies should be applied.

With Martin Lang we find ourselves decidedly outside the realm of economic theory. He emphasizes instead the noneconomic forces that are often the critical factors in determining the price structure in large metropolitan areas. He too employs a case study to illustrate his position, but rather than projecting a theoretical analysis of how things ought to be, he presents an existing situation—water supply in New York City. Besides describing the many noneconomic factors that influence water rates in New York, he points out that water rates in New York have no direct relation to the cost of water system maintenance and that relatively few customers are even in a position to know that they are paying for water. Clearly, it would be possible to maintain that economic theory has only marginal relevance to New York's current pricing policies.

PRICING AS A CONSERVATION TOOL: AN ECONOMIST'S DREAM COME TRUE?

STEVE H. HANKE,
Professor of Applied Economics
The Johns Hopkins University

In an article which appeared in 1975 (Hanke 1975), it was noted that the rate-making function had become an active area of concern for most utilities. Because of increasing costs and intervention by environmentalists, it was predicted that this function would become more important in the future. It appears that this prediction was correct. A second prediction was that the utilities' notions as to what constitutes a good water–wastewater rate policy would begin to conform to those of economists. This second prediction appears to have been inaccurate. The policy prescriptions drawn from economic analysis have been misinterpreted and in some cases used as a shield for rate-making policies that are uneconomic.

My purpose now is to clarify the differences between current rate-making policies, proposed policies, and those policies derived from economic analysis. If this objective is accomplished, there should be (1) a clearer picture of the conclusions that can be drawn from economic analysis; (2) less of a tendency to use economics as a shield for uneconomic rate-making policies; and (3) perhaps a degree of convergence between the opinions of the managers of water utilities and the opinions of economists.

THE RATE-MAKING PROCESS

Over 10,000 utilities in the United States render periodic bills for water and/or wastewater service. The rate-making process for these utilities typically begins with a determination of revenue requirements or a revenue target. There are two general methods of making this determination: the utility basis and the appropriation basis.

When the revenue target is determined on a utility basis, the desired total revenue is ideally set equal to the full opportunity cost of the operation of the utility. In the case of government-owned utilities, the full opportunity cost includes the operating cost, the costs of investment and replacement of capital, and a charge equivalent to the local taxes that would have been paid had the utility not been publicly owned. In this way the users of the utility's services fully compensate the taxpayers for all costs of providing the services. In the case of investor-owned utilities, the full opportunity cost of operation includes the above items plus a "fair" return on the stockholder's investment, that is, the minimum return which still ensures sufficient capital availability. It can be argued that publicly owned utilities should also provide a "fair" return on any capital contributions by the taxpayers or on internally generated capital, but there is little experience with such an approach.

The appropriations basis for determining revenue requirements is more common, but it is used only by publicly owned utilities. With the appropriations basis, only those sums specifically budgeted and appropriated to accounts identified as utility-related are considered as utility costs. The revenue target is the sum of all such accounts. The appropriation basis may or may not include most operating and capital costs of utility's operation, depending upon the adequacy of the system of appropriation accounts. Not included would be payments in lieu of local taxes and the cost of many services which may be provided to the utility by other government agencies, such as legal services, purchasing services, and so forth. In many jurisdictions, the appropriations basis is applied on a cash basis rather than an accrual basis. Some government-owned utilities use a "tax account" in the appropriations process. In such cases, utility services are used as a tax base, and funds collected from those who purchase the utility's services are used for purposes unrelated to the utility.

After the revenue requirements (costs) are computed by one of these methods, they are allocated to customer classes. Numerous methods exist for accomplishing this task (Doran, Hoppe, Koger, and Lindsay 1973), all methods being equally arbitrary from an economic point of view.

The next step in the rate-making process is consideration of the elements which might compose a water and wastewater utility rate structure. These elements may be grouped under the following categories:

1. Commodity charges, which include any method of charging on the basis of the quantity of water used

2. Periodic fixed charges, which may consist of service charges levied in addition to commodity charges, or flat-rate charges levied where commodity charges are not used

3. Other charges, such as connection charges, benefit assessments, and *ad valorem* taxes.

A recent survey of rate-making practices provides some data on the frequency with which these various rate structure elements are used in the United States (Helt and Chambers 1976). The survey covered 115 rate structures used by 72 different utilities. Of these rate structures, all employed commodity changes, and 30 percent used periodic service charges in addition to commodity charges. Eighty-three percent of the rate structures contained decreasing-block-type commodity charges, where the charge per unit falls with increasing quantities of water used. However, in only 26 percent of these decreasing-block cases did the decreasing-block charges result in rate changes within the range of normal residential consumption. In the remaining 74 percent of the declining-block cases, the lower rates are available primarily to the larger commercial and industrial users. No information was presented on the frequency or basis of other charges.

The average costs of water service (excluding wastewater charges) reported in the Helt and Chambers survey (1976) ranged from $4.41 per 1,000 gallons downward to $0.10 per 1,000 gallons, a ratio of 44 to 1. Even within a single utility, average costs to different customers varied by a ratio as large as 38 to 1. By way of contrast, 17 percent of the rate structures were unblocked or level rates. In these cases the average cost, excluding the effect of a service charge or minimum charge, remains the same for all customers, regardless of use. Minimum charges, which provide for a fixed minimum bill to all customers, were included in 89 percent of the rate structures surveyed.

Several recent developments were not noted in the 1976 survey of rate structures. These include the introduction of seasonal rates, which normally involve a higher commodity charge in the summer season, and increasing-block rates, in which the price per unit increases with the amount of water used per billing period. Both types of rate structures are particularly noteworthy, since they are now being considered by many utilities.

Two water utilities in the Washington Metropolitan Area have adopted seasonal rate structures. In 1975, the Fairfax County Water Authority adopted a form of seasonal pricing. The basic rate design is unblocked and contains a quarterly service charge, equal to $3.00 for a typical residential user. The nominal price of water and wastewater service is $1.55 per 1,000 gallons of water used, with $0.95 allocated to wastewater service and $0.60 to water. Actual charges, however, are based on the winter quarter use for each customer. Wastewater charges computed on winter-quarter residential water use remain constant for the following three quarters, on the assumption that additional water used during the summer is not returned to the sewer. The actual water used during each of the three remaining quarters is compared to the winter use. All water used in excess of 1.3 times the winter quarter use (provided such excess is at least 6,000 gallons) is subject to a surcharge of $2.00 per 1,000 gallons.

Even more recently the Washington Suburban Sanitary Commission, in suburban Maryland, adopted a summer–winter differential. This structure went into effect July 1, 1976. The commission has long employed unblocked rate schedules, using neither a minimum bill nor a service charge. The new charge for water and wastewater service is set at $1.60 per 1,000 gallons of water used during October through May, and at $1.92 per 1,000 gallons June through September. Authorization for this change is currently limited to the period ending June 30, 1977.

Several utilities, located primarily west of the 100th meridian, have adopted an increasing-block structure. This approach is used in Tucson, Arizona, Carson City, Nevada, and Mesquite, Nevada. For example, the monthly tariff applying to all customers in Mesquite is $5.00 for the first 5,000 gallons, $0.40 per 1,000 gallons for the next 15,000 gallons, and $0.50 per 1,000 for all use in excess of 20,000 gallons.

EVALUATIVE CRITERIA

Various criteria may be used to evaluate the appropriateness of elements in a rate structure and the level at which the elements are set. The following criteria appear to be most often employed:

1. *Economic Efficiency*—Do the resulting rates promote the efficient allocation of society's resources (Hanke 1976)?

2. *Income Redistribution*—Do the resulting rates cause redistributions of income (involuntary subsidies) to occur between groups or classes of customers, and what is the nature of these redistributions (Boland and Hanke 1976)?

3. *Revenue Sufficiency*—Do the resulting rates produce the desired revenue (Howson 1966)?

4. *Rate Stability and Acceptance*—Are the resulting rates stable for expected fluctuations in customer demand; are they adequately understood by customers; do they produce public acceptance and support (Baxter 1960)?

5. *Rate Similarity*—Are the resulting rates similar to those used in neighboring communities (Faust 1959)?

6. *Water Conservation*—Do the rates encourage the conservation of water (Guarino 1976)?

The analyses in this paper are rather limited in scope and do not address many issues in the rate-making process. For example, it does not address questions related to the computation of revenue requirements and the allocation of these requirements to customer classes. The central issue in current rate-making debates is the design of rate structures; and this is the focus of the following analyses. The criteria utilized to evaluate rate structures include those just listed, with emphasis on economic efficiency and income redistribution.

MARGINAL COST PRICING

The great British economist Alfred Marshall was the first to develop a sophisticated approach for the analysis of utility pricing and rate structure policies. Marshall (1920) advocated the use of marginal or incremental analysis as a means of analyzing the economic efficiency of various pricing policies. Policy changes were judged by Marshall and generations of economists that followed as desirable if their incremental (marginal) benefits exceeded their incremental (marginal) costs. The most important criterion was economic efficiency, and efficiency was maximized when incremental benefits (consumers' surplus plus total revenues) were equal to incremental costs. This occurs when a product's price, which measures its marginal benefits, is equated to the product's marginal cost. For example, if the price of water per megaliter exceeds the cost of the last megaliter produced, customers are being asked to pay more than the marginal cost of water, and "too little" will be consumed. Conversely, if the price they pay is less than the cost of the last unit, customers will be paying "too little" and will consume "too much." Both situations are inefficient from an economist's point of view.

The computation of costs is, therefore, extremely important for evaluating alternative pricing policies, since efficient resource allocation requires that price must be equated to the relevant marginal or incremental cost of changes of consumption. The addition of a new customer or an increase in the consumption by an existing customer will impose additional or incremental costs upon the system, whereas reductions in consumption will save costs. It is these alterations in incremental costs, not historical costs, that should be reflected in prices.

If prices reflect incremental costs, they will reflect the value of resources used or saved by changes in consumption. Valuation of these resources requires a forward-looking estimate. After all, it is planning for the future that is the major concern, and it is future behavior that the utility is interested in modifying. The backward-looking estimates involve historical sunk costs used by accountants. The use of these costs creates the illusion that resources which can be used or saved are as cheap or as expensive as in the past. For this reason, these backward-looking estimates lead to either overinvestment or overuse, or underinvestment or underuse, depending on whether incremental costs are higher or lower than the historical average.

The demand for municipal water is characterized by large daily and seasonal variability (Linaweaver, Geyer, and Wolff 1966). This has important implications for the design, operation, and ultimately the computation of the marginal cost structure for water systems. The daily use cycle is accommodated by locating elevated storage-and-balancing reservoirs in distribution areas, with the design criteria for much of the required storage and associated distribution piping being determined by fire-flow requirements—a factor unrelated to other demand fluctuations. For this reason, it is asserted that little variation in marginal cost can be attributed to daily cycles of demand experienced by typical water utilities.

The second variation in demand, that of fluctuating seasonal demand, has important implications for marginal cost. The capacity of most major elements of a water system—transmission lines, treatment facilities, pumping stations, and certain types of supply works—must be designed to accommodate the maximum day demands which occur during the peak season. The capacity costs associated with these facilities reflect the demands realized during these peak periods, which almost always occur in the summer. Therefore, the marginal capacity cost of a water system is higher in the summer than in the winter.

This analysis suggests that marginal capital cost for water utilities should be computed on a seasonal basis. Furthermore, marginal operating and maintenance costs should be computed and added to marginal capital cost, yielding a different marginal cost for the off-peak and the peak demand seasons. It is this seasonality in marginal cost that should be reflected in rate structures. However, the marginal costs actually vary within seasons, and consequently, some losses in efficiency will occur if additional costs associated with metering and billing on a basis that would perfectly reflect continuous fluctuations in marginal cost would most likely outweigh the efficiency gains associated with such a practice.

Many people would agree that there are desirable effects associated with setting prices equal to the relevant marginal costs. The major problem with marginal cost pricing as a policy prescription is that many economists have been unwilling to apply it. They have been too willing to point to industry pricing practices as being inefficient, without at the same time demonstrating to the industry how to compute marginal costs that would improve that efficiency. Clearly, economists will have the right to criticize the industry for misinterpreting and misusing economic analysis only after they demonstrate that their own ideas can be applied.

Earlier this year, in an attempt to rectify this problem (Hanke 1976), a study was made of marginal cost in Adelaide, South Australia. The engineering and water supply department of Adelaide serves approximately 277,000 accounts and, like most utilities, experiences seasonal peaks in system demands; for example, 68 percent of the total demand occurs in the summer season (October–March), and the ratio of peak to average day demands is estimated to be 2.75:1. Hence, a seasonal representation of marginal cost is warranted. In the following paragraphs a necessarily technical description of how these seasonal marginal costs were computed is presented.

THE CALCULATION OF MARGINAL COST COMMODITY CHARGES: A CASE STUDY OF ADELAIDE, AUSTRALIA

To compute the marginal capacity cost, planned investments were divided into the following categories:

1. Capacity costs associated with those facilities designed to meet maximum day demands

2. Capacity costs associated with those facilities designed to meet average day demands

3. Capacity costs associated with those facilities that are largely related to customers growth or growth in the number of services in the metropolitan area.

For each of these categories of capital investment, intervals of five years were used to construct a forward-looking profile of planned investments in 1975 dollars; additions to demand requirements and number of connections for each of the five-year intervals were projected; and estimates of additions to the stock of capital required to meet the projected increments in growth were made. For example, five-year increments of planned investments that will be required to meet projected increases in maximum day demands—those facilities designed with a maximum day demand parameter—were itemized. This category contains those elements of the system between the headworks and the local reticulation system. It should be noted that local storage tanks were included in this category, along with trunk and feeder mains. This type of itemization was also conducted for anticipated increments to capital required to meet growth in average day requirements. Headworks (large pipelines and large reservoirs) were included in this category. Additions to capital required to meet growth in the number of services in the Adelaide service area were also itemized on a five-year basis. Local reticulation and metering investments compose the bulk of capital in this category.

Given these planned investments, an interest rate of ten percent, an anticipated economic life of each capital component,[1] and the capacity added by each component, one can annualize the capital cost and relate it to anticipated expansions in output.[2] The functional relationships between increases in output per year and annualized dollars per megaliter of capacity per year reflect the appropriate marginal cost of expanding the system.

Figure 1 shows the marginal cost associated with augmenting the components of the system designed to meet increases in maximum day requirements. The marginal cost "curve" is discontinuous because the marginal cost was computed on the basis of the incremental capital investments required to meet five-year increments in demand. Although the marginal cost of meeting increments in maximum day requirements increases, then decreases and increases again, the data appear to be satisfactory and reflect a roughly constant marginal cost. Given the elements of the system in this category, the incremental cost of meeting increases in maximum day demands is roughly $200/megaliter over the planning horizons.

Calculations of the marginal capacity cost to supply additions in average day demands were also made. These were accomplished by using the same method as that employed previously. Figure 2 represents the marginal cost associated with augmenting the components of the system de-

---

1. The following economic life assumptions were used to annualize capital investments: reservoirs, 60 years; storage tanks, 60 years; water mains, 60 years; house connections, 60 years; pumping station machinery, 20 years; buildings, 60 years; water treatment plant machinery, 20 years; and meters, 20 years.

2. The following formula was used to compute the relevant marginal cost for the various categories of capital considered

$$MC = \frac{\sum_{t=0}^{4} rI_t}{Q_5 - Q_0}, \text{ where}$$

MC = the relevant marginal cost for the relevant output range,

Q_t = output of water in year t,

I_t = investment required in year t, and

r = the capital recovery factor, which is equal to $\dfrac{Ii (1 + i)^n}{(1 + 6)^n - 1}$, where

I is the investment cost, i the appropriate interest rate, and n the useful life of the investment.

FIGURE 1
MARGINAL COST (MAX DAY)

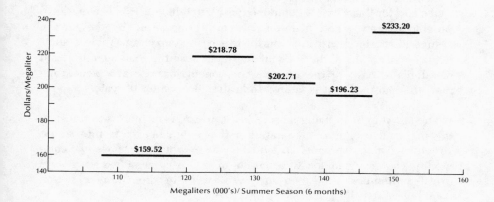

signed to meet increases in average day requirements. This "curve," like the one in figure 1, is discontinuous. However, it reflects decreasing returns to scale, rather than the roughly constant returns to scale for investments required to meet additions to maximum day demands. Decreasing returns can be expected in any headworks program, since the more productive resources are developed first, and then the more marginal ones are utilized.

FIGURE 2
MARGINAL COST (AVG DAY)

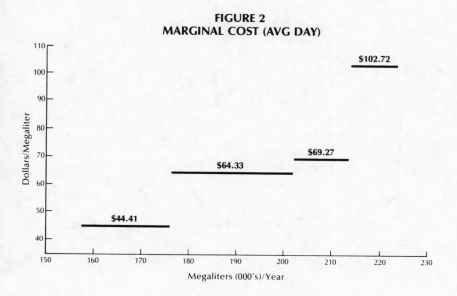

Another category of marginal cost involves those operating and maintenance costs that vary with changes in system output. Chemical and electric costs are included in this category. The total operating and maintenance cost for this variable component is plotted in figure 3. The marginal variable operating and maintenance cost is measured by the rate of change in the total cost function for this cost component. Table 1 summarizes the results of these calculations. Because the total operating and maintenance costs of the variable component increase at a decreasing rate, the marginal cost is falling, indicating economies of scale.

The last step in applying marginal cost pricing principles is to translate the marginal capital and operating and maintenance costs into a rate structure. The correct rate structure is one in which there are two commodity charges: one for water used in the Australian winter season (April–September), and one for water used in the summer season (October–March).

Under this seasonal structure, the consumer is charged on a per kiloliter basis for every kiloliter of water used in the winter, with the price/kiloliter being set equal to the marginal cost of providing additional water in the winter. This cost is calculated by adding the marginal variable

FIGURE 3
TOTAL UNIT COST versus PLANT SIZE

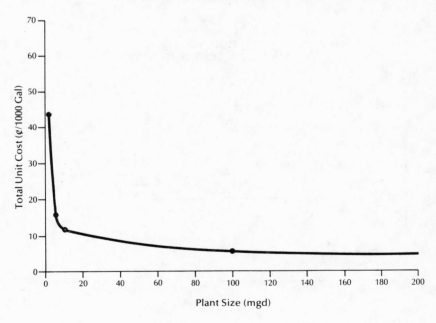

Table 1

VARIABLE OPERATING AND
MAINTENANCE COSTS
(MARGINAL COSTS)

Ml/Year	Marginal Cost/Ml
156–159	80.00
160–162	80.00
163–165	73.33
166–168	66.67
169–171	60.00
172–174	60.00
175–177	53.33
178–180	53.33
181–183	53.33
184–186	50.00
187–189	50.00
190–192	18.33
193–195	18.33
196–198	18.33
199–201	18.33
202–204	18.33
205–207	18.33
208–210	18.33
211–213	18.33
214–216	18.33
217–219	18.33
220–222	18.33

operating and maintenance cost (table 1) to the marginal capital cost required to meet average day requirements (figure 2), and is equal to 14¢/kiloliter. Since winter consumption does not press on the peaking capacity of the system, winter consumption is not required to pay for capital required to meet peak day demands.

The summer consumer is also charged on a per kiloliter basis for every kiloliter of water used in the summer, with the price/kiloliter being set equal to the marginal cost of providing additional water in the summer. Since the summer consumer presses on system capacity—the maximum day demands occur in the summer—he is required to pay for components of the system designed on the basis of maximum day demands. The marginal cost of adding to the system to meet maximum day demands is contained in figure 1. To these costs must be added marginal variable operating and maintenance costs (table 1) and the marginal capital cost required to meet average day requirements (figure 2), yielding a summer marginal cost of 30¢/kiloliter.

Economic efficiency will be realized in the Adelaide system with the rate structure and levels of commodity charges calculated. All consumers impose a marginal cost on the system of 14¢/kiloliter during the winter season. If price for all customers is equated to this marginal cost, all customers will use water up to the point where they receive 14¢/kiloliter of benefits from the last kiloliter of water that they consume. Consumers will not use water beyond this point, because the benefits per kiloliter would be less than 14¢/kiloliter. Alternatively, they will not stop using water before reaching this point, because incremental benefits per kiloliter would exceed 14¢/kiloliter; consequently, total net benefits could be increased by increasing consumption. The same logic can be used to argue that efficiency is reached in the summer by setting prices equal to 30¢/kiloliter.

OTHER RATE STRUCTURE ELEMENTS

With a rate structure such as the one just described, efficiency is achieved and no involuntary subsidies would occur between customers or classes of customers. All customers are required to pay the marginal cost of consuming another kiloliter of water. No customer is being "taxed" or "subsidized" by paying a price that exceeds or is lower than the cost he imposes on the system by consuming another kiloliter of water.

Income redistribution neutrality and efficiency could be altered, however, if the total revenue generated by the marginal cost commodity charges falls short of the water authority's revenue target, and the authority must eliminate the deficit. To maintain income redistribution neutrality and efficiency, other types of marginal costs within the system should be considered as additional elements to the rate structure. Since marginal costs are associated with reading meters and billing for water used, a fixed charge, equated to the marginal cost of these activities, should be levied. Also, marginal cost is associated with adding new customers to the system. These customers should pay the marginal cost of being added to the system. Clearly, the incremental cost of parts of the reticulation system must be computed in order to assess this charge.

If, after these marginal cost charges have been included in the rate structure, revenues still fall below the target, "taxes" must be levied. One common method is to increase the level of the commodity charges. The major disadvantage in this approach is that it generates efficiency losses, because consumers will be asked to pay more for additional kiloliters of water than the cost of those kiloliters, resulting in uneconomic water conservation. The result of this consumption "tax" is to force consumers to conserve water that has a higher value if it is used than if it is not used.

The consumption "tax" on water use also carries with it a perverse income redistribution effect. Since the consumption of water rises less than proportionally with increases in consumers' incomes (Howe and Linaweaver 1967), a consumption "tax" is regressive, that is, it takes relatively more from low income consumers than it does from those with higher incomes.

Another commonly used approach to eliminate revenue deficiencies is increasing the fixed charges or minimum bills. Because it offers revenue stability, this approach is popular. However, it acts as a regressive "tax." Since poor, as well as wealthy, customers pay the same absolute "tax," the "tax" is a larger portion of a poor customer's income. Efficiency would not be affected by such a "tax," since fixed charges, at observed levels, probably have no effect on either consumers' water use or their decision to remain in the system.

Ad valorem assessments, property taxes, and income taxes appear to have the characteristics that make them the best taxes for generating revenues when, after employing marginal cost elements, revenue deficiencies exist. These taxes are found to be less regressive than the other "taxes" discussed, and are often proportional or progressive in their incidence. No efficiency effects within the utility occur with these taxes, since the tax bases (property or income) are not directly connected to utility operations. However, distortions in the use of property and in the relationship between work and leisure could result from the application of property and income taxes, respectively. These distortions are likely to be very small, largely because the property and income tax rates required to correct for water utility budget deficits would be small.

Before concluding the discussion of rate structure elements, it is important to note that the marginal cost pricing approach has one drawback: it rates poorly when evaluated by the criterion of rate similarity. Perhaps the Washington Suburban Sanitary Commission (WSSC) is the only utility in the United States that employs a seasonal rate structure of the type described. However, it is not known whether the WSSC seasonal rates are set at levels equal to summer and winter marginal costs. As a result, any utility considering this approach must be prepared to explain why it wants to adopt a rate structure not widely accepted by the industry.

Marginal cost pricing and accompanying seasonal rates, although they might encourage reduced peak use when introduced, should not be viewed solely as a conservation measure; that is, they only encourage the proper amount of conservation, and do not encourage reductions beyond the point where the marginal benefits from conservation (the marginal costs from production saved) equal the marginal costs from conservation (the marginal benefits from consumption foregone). This is an extremely important point that is usually misunderstood. The economist views conservation as a worthy goal only insofar as the marginal benefits from conservation exceed conservation's marginal costs. The economist, therefore, wants to maximize the net benefits from conservation. This occurs where the price (marginal benefits) for water is equated to its marginal cost. Conservation as a goal is incorporated into the economic efficiency criterion. Conservation for conservation's sake does not fit into the economic frame of reference, and is not viewed by economists as a useful goal.

Given the desirable characteristics of marginal cost pricing and a seasonal rate structure, one can view them as a baseline from which to evaluate other rate structure policies. The remaining sections of this paper are concerned with an evaluation of various rate structures in light of the marginal cost principles outlined.

DECREASING-BLOCK STRUCTURE

At the present time, decreasing-block structure is the dominant rate structure in the industry. This type of rate structure can be efficient only under rather unusual conditions:

1. that all customers used water in the same last block in each season

2. that the level of the decreasing blocks was higher in the peak demand season than in the off-peak season

3. that the level of the last block where all consumers were located was equated to the marginal cost in each season.

Under these conditions, the result, in terms of efficiency, would be the same as that obtained with an unblocked, seasonal, marginal cost price;[3] all consumers would be paying the proper marginal cost for the last unit of water that they consumed, resulting in the efficient level of water use in each season.

The only difference between this rate structure and the unblocked, seasonal, marginal cost rate structure is that more revenue would be collected with the decreasing-block structures. The magnitude of the difference in revenues is determined by the width of the blocks—the narrower the blocks, the greater the revenue derived. Inframarginal consumption would be "taxed" with a decreasing-block rate structure. Even though this "tax" would not influence water consumption and efficiency, under the conditions outlined it would have a redistributive impact. Since

3. This assumes that the total revenues collected from water sales were a small portion of consumers' budgets and that no income effects existed.

the total "tax" would be the same for all consumers, it would take a larger portion of a poor customer's income than of a wealthy consumer's income; thus the "tax" would be regressive.

Let us move from this hypothetical case to the real world. Decreasing-block rate structures are not usually varied seasonally. Since consumption for most consumers is higher in the summer than the winter, they may face a lower marginal price in the peak demand season than in the off-peak season. This is inefficient, because too little water is used in the winter and too much is used in the summer.[4] To look at this feature of declining-block structures in another way: if the winter marginal block price is set at the winter marginal cost, then the proper quantity of water would be used in the winter. However, higher summer demands would result in a summer marginal block price that was lower than the marginal block price in the winter (unless the blocks were extremely wide). This means that marginal price would fall in the summer, while marginal cost in the summer increased, causing a waste of resources and excessive water consumption. The other extreme would be where the summer marginal block price was set equal to the summer marginal cost. In this case, winter marginal block prices would be higher than those in the summer; winter consumption would be inefficiently constrained, since winter marginal prices would be much higher than winter marginal cost.

Relaxing another assumption implied earlier, all consumers do not use the same quantity of water. This means that they might not all face the same marginal price for water, even within the same season. However, they are all members of the same system and place the same marginal cost on the system when they consume water during the same season. Varying prices in the face of a constant marginal cost constitutes price discrimination and results in a misallocation of resources. This means that small consumers might be forced to conserve water uneconomically if the marginal block price they face exceeds marginal cost, while some larger consumers might even be encouraged to waste water if the marginal block price is less than marginal cost. Since the inframarginal "taxes" are higher per unit of consumption for small users than for large users, small users tend to subsidize large users. Given that use tends to increase with growth in income, although less than proportionally, the implication is that poorer customers generally subsidize the wealthier customers.

Decreasing-block rate structures, as they are presently practiced, lead to an inefficient allocation of resources in water utilities, a cross-subsidy from small to large consumers, and are a regressive system of "taxes."[5]

4. This assumes that the level of the decreasing-block structure is such that the marginal block price is greater than the marginal cost in the winter and less than the marginal cost in the summer.

5. The only situation in which the last condition would not be met is where the level of the decreasing-block structure was always below the level of marginal cost.

INCREASING-BLOCK STRUCTURES

Increasing-block rate structures or inverted rates represent a recent development in rate-making policy. These rates are the mirror image of decreasing-block structures. The implications of inverted rate structures have not been fully evaluated by the industry. This is probably because it is claimed, largely by environmentalists, that these structures will encourage conservation. With pro-conservation attitudes, inverted rates are judged to be desirable. In economic analysis, however, conservation cannot be judged as a desirable goal per se. An economist must ask whether the marginal benefits from conservation are greater or less than the marginal cost from conservation. It will be shown that, contrary to popular opinion, inverted rates, like decreasing-block rates, generally lead to resource misallocation and cross-subsidies among consumers.

An efficient, increasing-block rate system would have the following characteristics:

1. The blocks would be set so that all consumers used water in the same block in each season; and

2. The level of these blocks would be set so that the relevant block prices in the winter equaled the winter marginal cost, and the relevant block prices in the summer equaled the summer marginal cost.

It is highly unlikely that these conditions would ever be met in the real world. Let us begin our evaluation with a simple increasing-block structure that appears to be equivalent to marginal cost seasonal pricing. The structure will be one with two very wide blocks. The first block will be set equal to the winter marginal cost, and the second block will be set equal to the summer marginal cost. If the first block is wide enough to encompass all winter use, efficiency will be achieved in the winter, and the result in this season will be identical in all respects to that obtained by marginal cost pricing. The problem arises in the summer, since some of the customers will not expand their consumption enough to reach the second block. These consumers will face a marginal price that is lower than the marginal cost of water supplied in the summer. They will be encouraged to waste water by applying it in uses that yield marginal benefits that are less than the marginal cost of supply. There will also be a redistributive aspect, since low-volume customers' use will be "subsidized." This might not offend most, if the small users generally had low incomes. However, one must ask whether water utilities should engage in redistributive policies through their rate structures.

To the extent that actual increasing-block structures contain more and narrower blocks than the two-block system described, they will generate even more inefficiencies and redistributive effects. Small users, to the extent that the marginal block prices they face are less than the relevant marginal cost, will be encouraged to waste water, while the large users, to the extent that they face marginal block prices that exceed the relevant marginal cost, will be forced into uneconomic conservation. Price discrimination will exist, since consumers will pay different marginal prices for water that has the same marginal cost to all consumers within each season. In addition to the perverse efficiency effects resulting from this discrimination, smaller users will be "subsidized" to the extent that the marginal block prices they face are less than the relevant marginal cost.

SEASONAL RATE STRUCTURES IN PRACTICE

As mentioned earlier, the Washington Suburban Sanitary Commission has recently adopted an unblocked seasonal rate structure. All winter consumption is billed at $1.60 per 1,000 gallons, and all summer consumption is billed at $1.92 per 1,000 gallons. This is the proper rate structure for a water utility's commodity charges. However, it is not known if the level of the structure is appropriate in the commission, since these rates are not based on an analysis of marginal cost but were introduced as a conservation measure. A crude analysis of the WSSC rate level suggests that it is too high, and is resulting in uneconomic water conservation. There are two reasons for this conclusion. First, all WSSC revenues are derived from the commodity charges that yield an amount of money equal to fully allocated costs. Since many fully allocated costs are not marginal to water consumption—for example, meter reading, billing, and fixed overhead expenses—the marginal cost is probably less than the fully allocated average cost. Second, in a large, fully developed system with some excess capacity in headworks, marginal cost will be less than fully allocated average costs.

Table 2

CUSTOMERS PAYING EXCESS USE CHARGE
FCWA 1975

Customer Class	Per Cent in Excess Use Category
Single Family	24.4
Town House	10.4
Apartment	24.6
Commercial and Industrial	29.1
Municipal and Institutional	31.3
Total	22.7

The second innovative seasonal rate structure reviewed is that of Fairfax County, Virginia. A surcharge of $2.00 per 1,000 gallons is placed on use in excess of 1.3 times the winter quarter use (provided such excess is at least 6,000 gallons). Again, this structure was adopted as a conservation measure, and was not based on an analysis of marginal cost. The major problem with this approach is that it creates a great deal of price discrimination. In the three nonwinter quarters, only a small fraction of the customers pay the surcharge, as shown in table 2 (Fairfax County Water Authority 1976). This means that the marginal price is higher for some customers than for others, while the marginal cost of water is the same for all. If the high marginal price happens to equal the marginal cost, the bulk of the consumers are being encouraged to waste water. At the other extreme, if the low marginal price is equal to the marginal cost, the minority of customers is being forced to conserve water uneconomically. In addition to inefficiencies caused by discrimination, large users are "subsidizing" small users, much the same as they would under an increasing-block rate structure.

CONCLUDING OBSERVATIONS

Historically, the design of water rate structures has not been based on economic analysis. The dominant rate structure in the industry is the decreasing-block rate structure. It is inefficient, discriminatory, and perverse in its income-redistributive properties. Although most environmentalists and those in the industry view increasing-block rates and blocked seasonal rates as an economist's dream come true, the economist views them as a great nightmare. These innovations that fly the banner of conservation encourage an uneconomic use of resources and create cross-subsidies among customers.

All of the blame for this new set of events, in which the industry has been taken in tow by the environmentalists, cannot be placed on the shoulders of the environmentalists who pursue the goal of conservation. Moreover, it cannot be placed on the shoulders of the industry, which accepts the environmentalist's faulty arguments. Economists are largely to blame. If economists want to stop experiencing nightmares, they must begin to apply their concepts, and they must communicate with those persons responsible for implementing water-rate policy.

REFERENCES

Baxter, S. S. 1960. "Principles of Rate Making for Publicly Owned Utilities." *Journal American Water Works Association*, October.

Boland, J. J. and Hanke, S. H. 1976. *Water and Wastewater Rate-Making Policy in the District of Columbia: A Report to the People's Council.* Baltimore, Maryland. September 27 (processed).

Boland, J. J.; Hanke, S. H.; Church, R. L.; and Carver, P. 1975. *An Examination of Alternative Rate-Making Policies for the Washington Suburban Sanitary Commission.* Baltimore, Maryland: Rivus, Inc.

Doran, J. J.; Hoppe, F. M.; Koger, R.; and Lindsay, W. W. 1973. "Electric Cost Allocation Manual." Washington, D.C.: National Association of Regulatory Utility Commissioners.

Fairfax County Water Authority 1976. *Staff Report Re: Excess Use Charge.* Fairfax, Virginia. April 21 (processed).

Faust, R. J. 1959. "The Needs of Water Utilities." *Journal American Water Works Association,* June.

Guarino, C. F. 1976. "Metering." *Journal American Water Works Association,* September.

Hanke, S. H. 1976. *An Examination of Alternative Tariff Policies for the Engineering and Water Supply Department.* Adelaide, South Australia: E.& W.S. Department, February 22.

————. 1975. "Water Rates: An Assessment of Current Issues." *Journal American Water Works Association,* May.

Helt, A. and Chambers, D. L. 1976. "An Updated Hartford Metropolitan District Water Rate Survey." *Journal American Water Works Association,* August.

Howe, C. F. and Linaweaver, F. P. 1967. "The Impact of Price on Residential Water Demand and Its Relation to System Design and Price Structure." *Water Resources Research,* First Quarter.

Howson, L. R. 1966. "Review of Ratemaking Theories." *Journal American Water Works Association,* July.

Linaweaver, F. P.; Geyer, J. C.; and Wolff, J. B. 1966. *Final and Summary Report of the Residential Water Use Research Project.* Baltimore, Maryland: The Johns Hopkins University, Department of Environmental Engineering Science, June.

Marshall, A. 1920. *Principles of Economics* (8th edition). London: Macmillan and Co., Ltd.

WATER PRICES IN NEW YORK CITY:
A CASE HISTORY

MARTIN LANG,
Commissioner of Parks and Recreation
New York City

The City of New York, which consumes 1,400 million gallons per day of high-quality potable water, provides an excellent illustration of the many factors entering into water supply pricing. These factors are not only economic in nature; they are also historical, philosophical, sociological, demographic, political, intergovernmental, intragovernmental, geographical, geological, and lastly, technological.

Engineers and economists, in their coolly objective, rational approach, devise logical and technically impeccable solutions to water supply source development, distribution, and pricing problems. In so doing they have a regrettable tendency to ignore aspects of these problems which pit state against state, rural areas against suburbs, suburbs against cities, industry against government, deprived inner city against affluent peripheral neighborhoods, tenants against landlords, and environmentalists against everybody. Therefore, it is useful to dissect the anatomy of the water supply situation in New York City and to examine some of the most important factors which influence water prices. Most of these factors are not economic in nature, but they have strong if not overwhelming influence upon major economic decisions.

THE PRESENT SYSTEM

New York City has a long history of farsighted planning for its water supply. The city department of water resources cherishes the well-preserved, bored logs, still dug up from time to time in downtown Manhattan, which Alexander Hamilton used about 1790 as the city's water mains. An extremely significant decision was made in the 1830s when New York City adopted a planning approach to its water supply system—an approach which has remained viable up to the present day. The approach was based on the acquisition of upstate property for stream impoundment and creation of reservoirs at a high enough altitude to ensure gravity flow to the city. After all, the virgin hinterlands were sparsely

240

populated, land was cheap, and without the proximity of man and his works the water was pure and needed no treatment other than sedimentation in the reservoirs. The first system constructed, the old Croton system, included land that was as much as 30 miles away from the present city line.

The decision to acquire unspoiled upstate land proved valid, and today the system extends 120 miles north of City Hall. The 8 million inhabitants and the 2 million daily transients in New York drink water that needs only chlorination and fluoridation.

Unfortunately this simple treatment will not long be adequate. The designers and builders of the original system did not anticipate the centrifugal social, economic, and transportation phenomena which threw a suburban belt around the original city. The urbanization of the suburbs and the suburbanization of the countryside have inevitably resulted in the deterioration in the quality of the raw water in the impacted areas. The city is now operating a pilot plant to help select the technology for coagulation and filtration of the reservoirs closest to the city. Furthermore, the system no longer supplies enough water to meet the inexorably rising demand, and supplemental sources must be found before the beginning of the next century.

FRONTAGE RATES

Nonetheless, the ability to deliver an ample supply of excellent water was to have a profound effect upon the growth of the city. The water pressure was sufficient to rise six stories, and the city's famous, or infamous, "Old Law" tenements also rose to that height. The tenants were scarcely aware that water cost anything, since they did not pay directly. But how did the landlord pay? The so-called "frontage rates" were established in 1849. Such rates were based primarily on the width of a building, with increments for additional stories. The rates were reduced in 1851, and they remained unchanged until 1934. They were again increased in 1966 and most recently in 1971.

By now, the "frontage rate" has grown rather complex. It is currently based on the frontage width of the building, number of buildings on the lot, number of stories, type of establishment, and number and type of fixtures. Indeed, there are 55 different categories of charges. Altogether there are 717,000 buildings with over 7 million chargeable items. Besides being unwieldy this system is certainly inequitable to the city, and may be so to the consumer.

There are other drawbacks to the frontage rate system. Foremost among them is that no compelling incentive exists for conservation or prompt repair of leaks. The landlord who meticulously maintains his plumbing pays the same as his negligent neighbor. Furthermore, the current system is fixture-oriented, not user-oriented. Clearly, people use water and fixtures do not, but maintaining an up-to-date user census would create an administrative nightmare.

METERING

Metering is often proposed as a reasonable alternative to the current rate structure. In fact, metering was started in New York City in 1876. At that time the rate was 15 cents per 100 cubic feet of water. The most recent increase, in 1970, was to 52.5 cents per 100 cubic feet, with a minimum annual charge of $21. All commercial establishments are mandated to meter. However, the owners of residential dwellings may choose to meter or to stay on a frontage rate.

Of the 840,000 accounts in the city's water system, only 200,000 (24 percent) are metered. The metered accounts consume about 30 percent of the water. All other accounts are on frontage rates.

Please note that metering on a building-by-building basis does not necessarily affect consumption very greatly. There are only 400,000 one- or two-family dwellings in the city. Approximately 80 percent of the population lives in multiple-family dwellings, probably the highest such ratio in the nation. If the city bills a landlord on the basis of a single meter for an entire apartment building, the landlord will simply divide the bill up and pass the charges along to the various occupants. Thus, the individual apartment dweller will have little incentive to reduce his own water usage.

In addition, 4,000 city properties are exempted from water charges. Many of these are substantial institutions such as schools, hospitals, nurseries, libraries, museums, religious establishments, community centers, and so forth. Metering would scarcely have an effect on them.

If we define "per capita" water consumption as the total of domestic and industrial use to the total resident (including some 2 million daily transient users), that consumption has grown from 114 gallons/capita/day in 1900 to 178 gallons in 1975. Both frontage and metered rates have been increased substantially during this period. Nonetheless, the fiscal impact of this increase has hardly impinged at all on the awareness of tenants of multiple-family dwellings, since increases in rents were attributable to many other factors which far outweighed the incremental growth in the cost of water.

RATE INCREASE

The New York State Constitution allows the city to establish water charges on the following bases:

1. Fair return on value of property
2. Costs of operation and maintenance
3. Necessary and proper reserve
4. Amount equivalent to taxes.

Thus, it would seem clear that the city is entitled to raise water rates to the extent necessary to ensure the continuation of the present high level of service. In theory, this is absolutely true. Unfortunately, for a number of reasons, things are not that simple.

A major problem is that there is no way to ensure that the additional monies from a rate increase would be used to maintain or expand the water system. All the revenues generated by the department of water resources go to the city's general fund, and, since 1975, so do sewer revenues. Water and sewer rates are, in turn, based on the deficit in the city's budget, and are raised accordingly. In plain truth there is no sequestered account for water revenues to be recycled to the system.

There are also social factors that cannot be ignored. The city's population has doubled in the twentieth century, and each successive wave of immigrants, whether from Europe, Puerto Rico, or the depressed agricultural areas of the South, properly regarded the acquisition of more domestic water-using facilities as an essential part of their continuing effort to participate in the mainstream of American life. Therefore, the city's ability to deliver cheap, pure water was certainly one factor which aided the slum dweller in his struggle for improved living, and it increased the city's capability to build better housing.

Therefore, we should avoid the converse condition in this decade of municipal stress, when so-called "ghetto" areas are blighting the inner cities. Landlords have literally abandoned square miles of multiple dwellings as unprofitable to maintain. Many more can be deemed only marginally viable, and the sudden imposition of higher rates could well give the coup de grace to some of these areas.

The redistribution of the population is another important factor to be considered in relation to water rates. After World War II New York City, like most of the country's mature metropolises, experienced an explosive development toward its peripheral boundaries. The first vital life support to accompany new development was, of course, the extension of the water supply network. This was an expensive undertaking, and if the cost had been spread over the entire population of the city by a concomitant increase in water rates, the inner city would have sagged still further in order to support the semisuburban style of those who have fled to the city's edge. Thus, there are cogent philosophical and sociological questions about the extent to which the escalating costs of water, and its distribution, should be imposed on the public at large.

SYSTEM EXPANSION

The problem of generating adequate revenues looms even larger when the discussion turns to the future expansion of the system. This is a vital issue. Even if we attribute all possible savings to leak control, metering, water conservation drives, and the possible restraining effects of higher water rates, still the city must look to expand its water supply for the needs of the twenty-first century, and the time to do so is now. The lead time between the conception and delivery of any new major source of supply is at least twenty years.

In addition, it must be recognized that system expansion is not only an economic question. For New York City it raises serious political issues and involves negotiations with relatively distant and generally hostile parts of the state. To counteract this hostility the city must do everything possible to enhance its credibility as a prudent purveyor of water—only a first step toward eventually increasing its reservoir system.

The issue has become emotionally surcharged by the obvious massive water waste on a few hot days each year by illegal hydrant openings in some ghetto areas. These episodes have taken place in other cities, albeit without the fanfare that accompanies every such incident in New York City. As much as 300 million gallons have been wasted on some exceptionally hot days. This is unbridled vandalism, since pressure drops throughout the city, posing a health and fire menace, and it is completely unrelated to "keeping cool." I saturated the city with spray caps for hydrants to provide a gentle cooling spray for children, but a 1,000 gpm stream from a 4" nozzle is a defiant antisocial act of anarchy. The episodes subside, the pressure is restored, but a virulent anti-city attitude is left in the upland areas of our reservoirs.

Even if we consider, as we now do, the great Hudson River as an adjunct source of water supply, our sister state, New Jersey, occupies the west bank at its mouth, and will have its own demands. Furthermore, the fresh water of the Hudson can only be tapped above its "salt line." This line is some sixty miles upstate, and thus involves the needs and rights of upstate communities. So again the city must take the posture of an impeccably conservative dispenser of upstate water if it is to have any hope of tapping even this relatively undesirable source.

The magnitude of the problem of expanding the system becomes clearer when we consider Long Island. The 4 million people of the boroughs of Brooklyn and Queens share Long Island with the adjacent counties of Nassau and Suffolk. The 2 million people of Nassau County rely entirely on groundwater for their supplies, and they read the handwriting on the wall as quality declines, replenishment of the aquifer dwindles, water levels drop, and saltwater lenses encroach along the Atlantic Ocean. Furthermore, in the Borough of Queens, 600,000 people are yet supplied by a private utility from wells tapping this same aquifer, a supply inexorably becoming increasingly saline. Thus, 2.6 million people, both within and adjacent to the city, are looking to upstate sources for relief and are as yet unaware of the true costs of the massive distribution system that will be required.

In short, the next generation will be confronted not only with the continuously rising costs of system maintenance but also with the heavy capital requirements of the modern treatment facilities for the Croton system and, very possibly, for the expansion of the supply and distribution systems to accommodate several million more people.

THE FUTURE

How, then, is the city going to improve the water rate structure, change the accepted practices of over a century, and at the same time not impose any acute fiscal trauma on the taxpayers and businesses of a city already under stress? Furthermore, how can this be done in a manner acceptable to elected officials acutely aware of the delicate equilibrium between the preservation of existing business, the need to enhance new industry, the thin viability margin of old housing, the temporary absence of the city from the bond market, and the need to restore the city's managerial credibility to reenter that market?

There is no instant solution. But there is an approach, now in draft form, that should solidify the financial position of the water system in New York City. The plan is no panacea, but it would, over a reasonable period of time, enhance revenue and by the end of the century have New York City substantially metered, with the built-in incentive for water conservation and prompt repair of leaks that follows from such metering.

Draft local legislation has been prepared which would mandate metering for all residential buildings constructed after the effective date of law. It would also mandate metering for any existing residential building which undergoes major alteration. The legislation has a number of objectives:

— It would apportion water costs more equitably.

— It would encourage reduction of unnecessary use of water.

— With a reasonable target of 10,000 buildings to be constructed or renovated annually, the present unmetered 70 percent of the consumption would be considerably reduced by the end of the century.

— It would put the city in a credible posture to seek new sources of supply.

— The change would be self-adjusting to the state of the city's economic growth.

— It would strike a balance between those who voice strident demands for instant universal metering and the equally vociferous proponents of no change at all.

— It would increase water revenues, conservatively, by 10 percent within a generation.

— Above all, it would sensitize 8 million people, and their supporting industry and services, to the true cost of water so that intelligent decisions and rational investments can be made in the next generation as we go through the transition from considering water as a limitless municipal service to husbanding water as a finite, precious resource.

PUBLIC RELATIONS AND PROFESSIONAL ATTITUDES

Many of the solutions that have been proposed for our water problems will require changes in attitudes. Arguments against new solutions have frequently been based on the contention that the public is unwilling to accept them. Another more subtle but perhaps more important aspect of this issue is the unwillingness of water system managers to adopt new points of view.

It is conventional political wisdom that public perception of the seriousness of a problem and public attitudes toward those who are responsible for finding a solution impose important constraints on the range of acceptable solutions. This is the age-old "communications problem." For water utilities, this problem has grown in scale because of the sheer size of their jurisdictions and the greater complexity of their management problems.

The influence of professional water management attitudes on the adoption of new solutions to problems has only recently come under study. Professional bias has, however, been shown to be an important force in determining the acceptability of a solution, particularly in areas where decisions are usually based on the advice of outside experts. Thus, professional bias can also impose constraints upon the range of acceptable solutions.

The following selections treat both problems. John Sims presents an intriguing analysis of the reasons for the existence of these biases and demonstrates the ways in which biases limit responses to a problem. Arthur Brigham presents an action-oriented program designed to improve the communication between a water utility and its customers so that new approaches to problems can be made acceptable to the public. He goes on to discuss the practical difficulties encountered by the Washington Suburban Sanitary Commission in attempting to implement a range of innovative management alternatives in our nation's capital.

THE SOCIOPSYCHOLOGY OF RESPONSE TO RESOURCE ISSUES

JOHN H. SIMS,
Professor of Psychology and Human Development
George Williams College

Professionals whose work concerns some aspect of the interaction between man and the physical environment are haunted by a ghost. This specter hovers over their heads and constantly exerts its influence on how they conceptualize a problem and how they go about solving it. It is the more powerful because it is unseen, unfelt, and unacknowledged.

In his classic work *Administrative Behavior*, Simon (1957), in his analysis of the models of man found in the sciences, identifies this mysterious shade:

> We have the economists, who attribute to man a preposterously omniscient rationality. Economic man has a complete and consistent system of preferences that allows him always to choose among the alternatives open to him; he is always completely aware of what these alternatives are; there are no limits on the complexity of the computations he can perform in order to determine which alternatives are best; probability calculations are neither frightening nor mysterious to him. Within the past decade, in its extension to competitive game situations, and to decision-making under uncertainty, this body of theory has reached a state of Thomistic refinement that possesses considerable normative interest, but little discernible relation to the actual or possible behavior of flesh-and-blood human beings (p. xxiii).

It is this conception of man as a wholly rational being that in greater or lesser degree continues to impair, mislead, and constrict the thinking of professionals whose work necessitates their awkward encounter with man.

This assumption of grandiose rationality is met everywhere:

— In the assumption that man learns from experience,

— In the assumption that education, or information, or knowledge will produce its avowed aim,

—In the assumption that, if warned of a problem, man will heed that warning.

249

Of course, such statements have merit; we all know of facts that demonstrate their relevance. But let us be honest: facts also contradict them. Those familiar with work in any environmental field can cite instances where prior experience *failed* to bring about learning, where education failed in its goals, and where information was ignored and warnings went unheeded.

Let me be clear: I am not advocating the total abandonment of a partially correct model; I am arguing for the abandonment of the *totalism* of such a model. Of course man is rational—but *partly* so, and *sometimes*. But he is also other things. The nonsocial sciences must stop being foolishly exclusive and include other aspects of his nature—emotions, values, attitudes, beliefs, fears, desires, traits of personality, any of which may lead to blatant disregard of reality and heroic illogicity. Indeed, what defense will man not mount to protect a cherished belief, to maintain self-esteem, or to avoid fear and anxiety? Only such a model of man contains the potential to explain the many phenomena that currently frustrate those professionals whose work involves man as well as natural resources.

Lest I be accused of setting up a straw man, let me say immediately that a growing number of environmental professionals hold increasingly sophisticated conceptions of man's cultural, social, and psychological determinants, both conscious and unconscious. But even here it is noteworthy that much of the work which has moved away from a simplistic conception of man's rationality has done so in a telling manner. Thus, it has focused upon only the *cognitive* limits of man's rationality. For example, it has stressed the *intellectual* difficulties he has in estimating probabilities rather than emphasized his sometimes unconscious refusal to do so even when he could because it would force him to acknowledge something that he wishes to deny.

Relatively speaking, work which acknowledges any limit to rationality is rare, and its implications are often ignored or denied. Once the idea has been applauded it is sent away, like a precocious child; its continued presence causes embarrassment.

Why do most professionals in the nonsocial sciences have such antipathy to the unavoidable implications of the psychological research of the past 50 years? For it is hardly news that man's behavior is determined not only by his reason. For example, Simon (1957) cites three famous studies: Bruner and Postman's demonstration that coins look larger to poor children than to rich; Asch's demonstration that group pressure can convince a man he sees spots that aren't there; and Bales's studies on group problem-solving that demonstrate the inevitable deployment of group roles according to personality. Since these studies were made, more than a quarter of a century has seen thousands of similar demonstrations reflecting a wide spectrum of social and psychological variables that influence behavior and which, under no stretch of the imagination, can be mirrored by the model of rational man.

The question, then, is why the resistance of professionals to the lessons of such research? Or, to put it ironically, why *their* irrationality? There are certainly a number of reasons; among them we suggest the following:

First, to acknowledge that an understanding of man's interaction with the physical environment necessitates viewing man in all his complexity, rational, irrational, and arational—and that the constraints on his reason come from innate cognitive limits, from culture, from society, and from individual psychodynamics—poses a professional dilemma. Most professionals who work with aspects of the physical environment are not trained in the behavioral sciences. They lack the conceptual sophistication and skill to deal competently with social and psychological variables. No one enjoys his own ignorance, and few enjoy relying on professionals outside their own discipline.

A second factor that may well be at work resisting the acceptance of a psychologically sophisticated model of man is discomfort at the implications for action such acceptance may hold. Thus it is ethically acceptable to *persuade* man, that is, to appeal to his reason. Education is congruent with the value of noninterference with man's freedom. It is a situation in which man willingly modifies his own behavior.

But when you acknowledge other qualities in man you open the door to other means of effecting behavior change. And that may be terrifying, for where does it stop? Thus, for example, no moral principle is violated when a warning system is improved by providing more reliable information more rapidly, thus improving man's *opportunity* to heed the message. But what about improving a warning system by having it delivered in such a manner as to raise anxiety, or by a person whose presence gives the message authority? Here one is employing strategies which are for the public's "own good" by using means of which the public is unaware, means which do not appeal to reason, but to arational and often unconscious factors. It is not education but manipulation.

A third and final reason for professionals' unwillingness to use a comprehensive model of man is perhaps the most profound of all: resistance to the implications that such a model has for the self. Long ago, Freud (1952) identified the fall from the particular grace of rationality:

> Humanity has in the course of time had to endure from the hands of science two great outrages upon its naive self-love. The first was when it realized that our earth was not the centre of the universe, but only a tiny speck in a world system of a magnitude hardly conceivable.... The second was when biological research robbed man of his peculiar privilege of having been specially

created, and relegated him to a descent from the animal world. . . . But man's craving for grandiosity is now suffering the third and most bitter blow from present-day psychological research which is endeavouring to prove to the "ego" of each one of us that he is not even master in his own house (p. 296).

It would seem then, that we are up against formidable odds: professional socialization and preparation are against a comprehensive psychological model of man, our ethics are against it, and our deepest needs for self-esteem are against it—and yet, there is no question that if we are to make progress in the field of man's interaction with the environment, we must put such nonrational factors aside and rationally conclude that we must employ a psychological model of man that has room in it for nonrational behavior.

For many reasons, then, there is tremendous resistance to adopting a sociopsychological perspective on resource issues, at least to admitting the relevance of sociopsychological forces *explicitly*, head-on, so to speak. What usually happens, rather, is that the more sophisticated give an acknowledging nod and mutter something to the effect of "Oh, yes, of course, we can't do anything without taking such things into consideration," or "Yes, these issues are indeed political dynamite," or "This will have to be handled carefully, because people are funny," and so forth. But I'm afraid this is like vaccination—you take in a little, in order to build up a defense against a lot.

Perhaps I can sensitize you to the inescapable psychological framework within which you work, and perhaps I can do this best by focusing on America's traditional attitude toward water—an increase in demand requires an increase in supply. That logic is "obvious," indeed, assumed. But let us pause over it for a moment to see in what system of values and beliefs that logic is rooted. What is the ethos from which the formula of greater need/greater supply takes root?

Surely such an ethos is significantly related to the value placed on growth. Growth, in the sense of quantitative increase, is generally seen as good. Growth equals progress, that is, change in a desirable direction. Growth should, therefore, be facilitated. And it is the function of social organizations, such as government, to mobilize resources to meet the demands of growth.

This valuing of growth per se has long been a part of the American ethos—a successful business is a growing one, a successful industry is an expanding one, a successful university is one with an increasing student body and a larger faculty, a successful religion is one with a growing membership.

Growth is not only seen as good by most Americans; it is also seen as being inevitable. One cannot stop the clock, one cannot resist the future.

It does not naturally and easily occur to us that there is a choice involved in accepting change, growth, or progress. Indeed, while our society is characterized by many and complex institutions to assure the persistence and acceleration of growth, it is only recently that social structures deliberately dedicated to resist growth have come into being.

These counter-forces are of increasing importance. But while we remain sensitive to such changes in the ideology of the American people, we must beware of giving too much weight to publicity. I think we risk less error if we continue to emphasize that growth, that is, increased demand, tends to be equated with goodness; and that this ethos resides comfortably in the back of the heads not only of the public but of professionals as well; and that it will, usually unwittingly, influence what we do or how we respond to what is proposed regarding a natural resource.

In discussing the projection of demand for water earlier parts of this book stress how traditionally important the assessment of economic expansion has been. And if there is any area where growth has been held sacred by Americans, it is that of economic growth. But there is another economic value we must identify if we are to understand American attitudes toward the use of natural resources such as water. That is the value of profit, seen as the great motivational engine of the economy: that which increases profit is good, that which decreases profit is bad, whether a technological process, a political party, a way of organizing men, or a philosophy of work. The history of the so-called human relations movement in industry is, to its proponents' embarrassment, a superb example of the ascendancy of the profit motive over other values. That is, the movement was embraced by business and industry when and only when it demonstrated that it would increase profits.

Yes, there are counter-trends of seemingly increasing importance here, too. There are advocates, for example, of organizing work in ways that increase worker satisfaction, *at the expense of keeping costs down.* But aside from the question of whether a business implementing such values could survive in a nonmonopolistic context, there remains the conviction that most Americans continue to find such a possibility as alien—it isn't a "natural," sensible way to organize economic activity. One arranges machinery in space in such a way as to be most efficient, to produce most at least cost—not in such a way as to make workers happier; unless, of course, one discovers that due to the perversity of man's nature, the "illogical" arrangement of machinery in space that makes them happier also makes them more productive. The desire for making money, whether a worker's desire for higher wages or a company's for greater profit, is something that Americans continue to understand, even when it makes them morally nervous or uncomfortable; it is felt as fundamental, as basic. This, then, is another element in the American ethos that most of us incorporate as being in the "natural" scheme of things, and it, too, will influence our approach or response to resource issues.

Others have identified four methods of balancing water demand and supply: (1) augmenting supply; (2) increasing efficiency; (3) reducing or controlling demand; and (4) wastewater reuse. Wastewater reuse has its own problems, and we'll discuss them later; but, curiously, it is not the use of wastewater that in my judgment runs most counter to the American psychology—it is, rather, the idea of reducing or controlling demand. For most of us, that is an anti-American idea. It constitutes interference, and governmental interference at that, with the free market. It means controlling and limiting what is perceived as natural, that is, spontaneous, unrestricted growth. And worst of all, reducing or controlling demand would require *planning*.

Americans are generally very wary (and indeed rightly so) of planning—there is fear of a fusion between the political and the economic, and a belief, perhaps naive, that social transformations should be allowed to occur in and of themselves. This suspicion that planning is equivalent to managing, to constraint, and to manipulation is a part of the American attitude, and any plan that involves controlling demand must deal with it.

These are but a few examples of values and attitudes that illustrate the traditional and enduring social–psychological context within which resource issues are placed by both the public and professional groups. We must acknowledge, too, that new elements have recently come into vogue, and that although they are almost surely less important than their publicity would have us believe, they are probably more than mere fashion. One such value may be termed ecological concerns—the protection (meaning usually noneconomic development) of natural environments and of wildlife because they are valued in and of themselves as gifts to the human spirit.

If one can take such attitudes seriously, then such values constitute a true revolution, for it would mean a displacement of the very values we've already touched upon—of growth as good, of economic profit, of free, unplanned change. Perhaps I am overly conservative, but I have yet to be fully convinced of the enduring power of these new values. They need to be tested in the crucible of economic need. Thus, the question: will these values remain when they are no longer the affordable luxury of a well-off citizenry but a value paid for by a sacrifice in the standard of living?

The preceding is an attempt to draw your attention to the obvious: that there is what Talcott Parsons calls a "dominant American value pattern," and that it is one realm of reality within which we work, in that we ourselves hold it and see the world in its terms, and in that those who respond to our work hold it. And yet only rarely, I think, are resource problems and solutions posed or conceptualized in value terms seen as either implementing or opposing an ideology. And this unawareness or denial of ideology often seriously impairs our work when considering resource problems and solutions.

However, although generalities about culturally dominant values and attitudes are useful, they are, of course, no substitute for research that is directed toward identifying public and professional attitudes regarding a specific resource issue. And indeed, as is always the case, we must beware that knowledge of ideological generalities does not mislead us. Let us illustrate the point through two examples of research designed to explore the psychological responses to renovated wastewater of the public and of two groups of relevant professionals: public health officials and consulting engineers.

First, the public. It is generally assumed, and especially by professional water managers, that the public will not accept renovated wastewater for potable use. When Duane Baumann and I (Sims and Baumann 1974) originally designed an instrument exploring response to water reuse, we too were convinced that public resistance to the use of renovated water would be formidable *and* enduring, that is, extremely resistant to any attempt at persuasion. After all, what is more ingrained than revulsion to body wastes?

To put it succinctly, it would appear that we were dead wrong. Our instrument attempted to measure six psychological dimensions we thought were relevant to the acceptance or rejection of wastewater:

1. Fear of or disgust at the incorporation of or contact with the impure

2. Faith in science and accompanying trust in expertise versus suspicion of technology and mistrust of scientific authority

3. Internal versus external locus of control; that is, the extent to which people feel in control of what happens to them

4. Innovative, progressive approaches to problem solving versus traditional, conservative "holding on" to established methods

5. A view of the world in which technology is seen as interfering with nature's or God's ordained system

6. Aesthetic commitment to the natural as opposed to what is perceived as being artificial.

Surprisingly our data indicated that none of these dimensions was related to attitudes toward renovated wastewater.

What we did find was that acceptance or rejection is related to John Q. Public's level of education and knowledge of water renovation. This had been found before, by Athanasion and Hanke (1970) and by Johnson (1971). In brief, what laymen think and feel about using recycled water appears to depend primarily upon what they know about it and their general educational level, rather than on unconscious fears of contamination or general belief and attitudinal systems concerning nature, technology, aesthetics, authority, progress, and destiny.

These findings immediately raise two questions. First, if variation in response to renovated water is related to variation in educational level, so that the higher the education, the more positive the response, we would like to know why. What is it about education that would lead to a greater acceptance of renovated wastewater? An answer is certainly not obvious, but perhaps it is reasonable to speculate that one result of more education is increased confidence in science and technology as appropriate and effective means of coping with environmental problems. The second major question raised by the findings of this study arises from the nagging suspicion left by the negative psychological findings. Can it really be that the public takes such a reasonable or at least such an intellectual approach to the intimate use of wastewater, to drinking what was once sewage? We worry that the preponderantly positive attitudes that we found might reflect in these days of environmental concerns a desire in our respondents to be ecologically responsible. Might not the sweet reason of the layman, when asked how he would respond if he were to use renovated water, collapse when he is confronted with the actuality of using it? The answer requires further research that puts the glass to his lips. We have, by the way, been unable to get money to explore this question.

I would now like to turn my discussion to a recent research project conducted by Duane Baumann and myself (Sims and Baumann 1976). Before I describe the purpose of the project, I think it would be instructive to ask you to take the simple test that was employed. Please study the accompanying picture (in figure 1), read the following instructions, and answer for yourself the questions at the end of the instructions.

> This a picture of a meeting in a mayor's office—a meeting called to discuss the possibility of coping with an impending local water shortage through the use of reclaimed wastewater. I would like you to use your imagination and tell me a story about it. Who do you think are the various persons attending the meeting? What is going on at the moment? What are the men thinking and feeling and saying? How do you think this situation will turn out?

The rationale for using such an unstructured, projective technique is the desire to avoid the power of suggestion inherent in more direct questioning. Such open-ended story telling reveals more truly who one thinks should participate in such a decision, what might go on at such a meeting, and what course of action would finally be outlined, than does a series of

FIGURE 1.

leading questions, such as would lawyers be present? would the press have been invited? would you anticipate conflict at such a meeting?

The picture test was used to determine the attitudes of public health officials and water engineers toward the use of renovated wastewater. You can compare your own response to those which characterize these two groups. The first question is who is seen as attending the meeting. What interests are represented, what professional groups have been invited—and, indeed, who has been left out?

In general, consulting engineers and state health officials agree as to who would be involved in a community decision about water reuse. Besides the mayor (whose presence is automatic), the most frequently named figure is another elected official—a city council member, identified by almost three-quarters of the total sample. Both professional groups define the situation as one dominated by the executive branch of the local government.

The next three highest-ranking categories of persons hover around the 50 percent mark for the sample as a whole, but some interprofessional differences appear. Each professional group sees its own members as being more frequently involved in the meeting than those of the other: 58

percent of consulting engineers identify a consulting engineer in atten-
dance as against only 42 percent who so name a health official. As for state
health officers, 83 percent are sure a health official is present, but only 28
percent identify a consulting engineer as being at hand. State health
officials are more generous than consulting engineers about the local water
talent—69 percent of them identify the waterworks superintendent as
attending the meeting, while only 49 percent of engineers do so.

The next series of categories are mentioned by roughly a quarter of the
total sample. Two of them, members of the mayor's staff and members of
the city's engineering staff, are merely lieutenants of persons already
identified; but the third, that of legal counsel, introduces a new area of
expertise. Thus, 23 percent of both groups of professionals perceive the
question of using renovated wastewater as probably involving legal problems.

Ending with the lawyers, it should be emphasized that the first 8 out of
12 categories are executive administrators or professional experts. Over-
whelmingly, the picture is one restricted to government officials and their
professional consultants. It is only then that the respondents relax somewhat the criteria of admission: 21 percent identify the presence of a
nongovernmental representative of the public (civic leader, head of community organization, and so forth); 17 percent identify a representative of
business and industry (chamber of commerce, industrialist); 6 percent
admit a member of the press (reporter, TV commentator, and so forth);
and finally, 5 percent bring in the services of a public relations man.

It is tempting to interpret this pattern of figures in the light of Sewell's
study (1971) on the attitudes of engineers and health officials toward the
solution of environmental problems. Essentially, he found them to possess a conviction that such questions should be left to them, as experts,
and to elected representatives of the people. The people themselves—
both the general public and organized public groups—were disdained and
feared. Our data would appear to fit such a psychology, yet some caution
must be exercised in this interpretation. The stories are these men's
projections of what they perceive to be the reality of such a decision-
making meeting. And it is in fact likely that such decisions would indeed
be restricted to government officials and their experts. At the same time,
there is nothing in the stories to suggest that the story tellers are not in
agreement with that conclusion.

Now that we know who was there, we can ask what they did. Both
professional groups are in complete agreement in their perceptions of
themselves, each other, and politicians. The consulting engineer is seen
as being the person most favorably disposed toward the recycling project
(54 percent), the public health official as most against it (58 percent), and
the mayor as most neutral, undecided, or equivocal (76 percent).

Further, not only is each of the principals in this office drama—the engineer, the health official, and the politician—seen as displaying a different attitude; all are seen as displaying a preponderant attitude. This contrasts sharply with the perception of "the public" which is seen as being more evenly distributed among positive, negative, and neutral attitudes. Thus, 25 percent of the sample see public representatives as being favorable toward the use of renovated water; 48 percent see them as against it; and 24 percent view them as neutral. Clearly, both engineers and health officials are far more certain of themselves and their professional brothers than of the unknown layman.

The majority of consulting engineers and health officials perceive themselves to be in opposition to one another. Indeed, 85 percent of the total sample tells stories of conflict rather than of cooperation. But these are general attitudes. What are the distinguishing concerns of each professional group?

It is interesting that the professional sample favorable to the idea of using reclaimed wastewater, the consulting engineers, is, at the same time, the group which finds it personally most repugnant: 46 percent of them admit to feelings of revulsion, and it is their primary concern. The next problems most frequently seen by engineers are three: public reaction (28 percent), health issues (22 percent), and technical feasibility (24 percent). This last figure is surprising; only a fourth of the engineers raise questions concerning their own area of expertise—the technical problems involved in recycling.

On the same level of logic, public health officials also respond somewhat unexpectedly—the health issues involved in the use of renovated wastewater are not their first concern, for that rank goes to their worried interest in what the public reaction will be (55 percent). And indeed, their anticipation that the public may "cause trouble" is shown again in their concern about such a program's possible political consequences, an idea expressed with equal frequency (46 percent) to that of their concern for health issues (46 percent).

In sum, the two professional groups contrast greatly in the issues discussed at the meeting in the mayor's office. Engineers have but a single primary concern: controlling their feelings of revulsion to the use of renovated wastewater. The problems of technical feasibility, public response, and health, while acknowledged, are not emphasized. Public health officials, on the other hand, are primarily concerned with three questions, of which health safeguards is but one; first and foremost is their anxiety over public response and political repercussions.

What results from the conflicts? How do the participants vote in regard to the proposed program of water reuse? The concluding attitudes are much like the initial ones: twice as many consulting engineers (39 percent) as health officials (18 percent) are in favor of the idea, while virtually twice as many health officials (68 percent) as engineers (38 percent) are against it. What has happened in the course of the meeting is a shift toward a negative view; originally 54 percent of the engineers were favorably disposed toward the water reuse proposal and only 58 percent of the health officials were opposed. This movement is probably best viewed in the light of professional conservatism—the well-known tendency of the invested professional to avoid the risks of change and to preserve the known and controlled status quo in his area of expertise.

Nevertheless, the interprofessional differences that appear here are considerable. More than two-thirds of the health officials (68 percent) are against the use of renovated water, while only 18 percent of them are for it, and then mostly for the "crisis time only." This contrasts sharply with the final attitudes of the consulting engineers—as many of them are for it (39 percent) as against it (38 percent). And indeed, a quarter of them are for it without qualification, a position taken by only 5 percent of the health officials.

These differences are surely best understood from the differing perspectives of the two professions' areas of concern. Consulting engineers are not directly involved with questions of public response or politics; their primary interest and responsibility is with the technical, its possibility and practicality. On the other hand, the public health official is, by definition, responsible to the public and for the public. He must be concerned about their response. And further, the potential consequences of his approval of a program to use renovated wastewater are far more threatening. The specter of a possible widespread disaster must loom large in strengthening the health official's resistance to an unfamiliar system. His risks are far greater than those of the engineer.

In summary, in telling stories about a hypothetical situation in which city authorities invite experts to consult with them on the possibility of a community program using renovated wastewater, consulting engineers and public health officials reveal orientations based on professional socialization in their initial attitudes toward such a proposal, in their perceptions of what problems might be encountered, in their personal concerns, and, finally, in their considered professional stance. At each point in the time sequence of the stories, health officials hold the more negative position—they begin by not liking the idea, then raise many and major objections to it, and, in the end, find their reflection has strengthened their antagonism. Consulting engineers, on the other hand, begin with a far more favorable attitude, raise fewer objections, and conclude with an even split between endorsement and rejection. To some extent, then, this use of a projective technique has illuminated the nature and strength of professional support and resistance to water reuse.

In doing so, it has made, I hope, two more general points. First, that in using professionals in the formulation and implementation of resource policies and practices, one often gets more than one has bargained for—not only their expertise but their biases as well.

Second, that the particular psychological constellation of attitudes and values and fears and preferences that defines a professional is but another illustration of how vital it is to see resource problems not only in terms of their physical, technical, and economic dimensions, but in terms of their social–psychological dimensions as well. In the final analysis, man is, after all, the measure of all things.

REFERENCES

Athanasion, R. and Hanke, S. 1970. "Social-Psychological Factors Related to Adoption of Reused Water as a Potable Water Supply." In *Urban Demands for Natural Resources*. Fort Collins, Colorado: Western Resource Conference.

Freud, S. 1952. *A General Introduction to Psychoanalysis*. New York: Washington Square Press.

Johnson, J. F. 1971. *Renovated Waste Water: An Alternative Supply of Municipal Water Supply in the United States*. Research paper 135, Department of Geography, University of Chicago.

Sewell, W. R. D. 1971. "Environmental Perception of Engineers and Public Health Officials." *Environment and Behavior*, March.

Simon, H. A. 1957. *Administrative Behavior*. New York: Macmillan.

Sims, J. and Baumann, D. 1974. "Renovated Waste Water: The Question of Public Acceptance." *Water Resources Research*, August.

———. 1976. "Professional Bias and Water Reuse." *Economic Geography*, January.

EFFECTIVE USE OF COMMUNICATIONS TOOLS TO MANAGE WATER DEMANDS AND WASTEWATER LOADS

ARTHUR P. BRIGHAM,
Public Affairs Officer
Washington Suburban Sanitary Commission
Hyattsville, Maryland

THE CHALLENGE

At the outset, I'll ask the critical question: "Is anyone listening?"

The major test faced by every communications program boils down to that one question. You will remember the old saw about the mule driver being upbraided by a do-gooder for hitting his long-eared livestock with a two-by-four. "Hell," the old mule driver said, "my mule will do anything I ask him to do; but, first, I have to get his attention!"

Many water utilities and municipal organizations involved as water suppliers have a large number of publics which need an attention-getting "love tap" with a figurative two-by-four. They include customers, political leaders at the local and state levels, employees, environmental activists, regulators, schoolteachers and students, developers, plumbers, equipment suppliers, consultant engineers, and investors, to name just a few.

Have you ever attended a board or council meeting of your organization and heard one of your leaders say: *"Our problem is we're not communicating"?* Have you ever met with a group of field employees and heard them say: *"You don't know our problems, because you never untie yourself from your desk and come out to talk to us (and see us) where the real work is being done"?* Have you ever had a phone call from a customer who said: *"How dare you raise rates for the third time in three years for the same lousy water I was getting ten years ago"?* In the latter example, the customer probably just finished putting a down payment on a $5,000 automobile that would have cost $3,000 five or six years ago, or on a $40,000 condominium that once was worth $20,000.

All these encounters are really avoidable accidents. It's true that organizations which provide public services probably never will be able to achieve Utopian communications, where all of their publics are paying positive attention, where everybody understands, where everybody agrees with what is being done, and where all the employees around the "water works" are one big, happy, unified family. There's a middle ground between what the late Ogden Nash described as "hotsy-totsy" —when there is total love between the communicator and the audience—and "coldsy-toldsy" —where there is a complete absence of rapport between the two.

Capturing and holding the middle ground—arriving at a position where there is a mutual understanding of the utility's needs and problems—should be the goal of a sound, *professionally* planned communications program. Unfortunately, many public service organizations move so rapidly from one crisis to the next that they frequently contend they "never have the time" to evaluate their communications problems and do some public relations program planning. After all, they say, "It's hard to concentrate on cleaning up the swamp when you're hip-deep in alligators!" As a result, many water utilities find themselves involved in defensive, seat-of-the-pants communications that often keep relationships with utility publics "coldsy-toldsy" and almost never "hotsy-totsy."

Today's challenge in effective communications is to take the time to plan public relations strategies, to give "relations" problems the same tender loving care and professional attention almost routinely given the utility's engineering problems, and to develop a program designed to acquaint all "publics" with the utility's needs and problems—and to get the publics involved in meeting those needs and solving those problems.

I have been deeply involved in the development of the water-saving and waste-reduction program at the Washington Suburban Sanitary Commission; and, in my mind, this has been the most rewarding and most positive public relations effort I have ever undertaken. It is a program I will discuss later on; first, however, it may be worthwhile to discuss some basic utility misconceptions and some modern, professional "PR" conceptions about communications.

THE CONVENTIONAL CONCEPT OF COMMUNICATIONS

Recently the American Water Works Association *Journal* contained a number of very useful and informative articles on a variety of management activities. I read them all, and I enjoyed them all—save one, entitled "An Effective Public Relations Program for the Water Utility." The piece made a few good points, but it was the kind of article that might have been written twenty years ago, before the philosophy of comprehensive public relations had matured and before the era of investigative reporting arrived to complicate the relationships between organizations in public view and the "watchdogs," the ladies and gentlemen from the media.

This AWWA article on "effective public relations" was definitely mistitled, because it dealt almost entirely with *press relations*. And, even in the area of press relations, it was out of touch with the times. For example, "Getting to the press is up to the man who is to deal with reporters." (TRUE) "Perhaps take them out to lunch." (FALSE) In today's climate, citizens, politicians, and newspaper editors clamor for a return to pristine levels of morality. Generally speaking, to their minds there is nothing more immoral than an official from a public service organization spending money to entertain a media representative, one-on-one, in an effort to "get to know"—and, thus "corrupt"—a vulnerable newsman. In fact, most media organizations—except for those in the "back country" where the "new morality" message hasn't arrived—have policies against their reporters and editors accepting meals or other gratuities from the organizations which are subject to their coverage; they properly surmise that a few cocktails and a tasty club steak might affect the reporter's taste for independent objectivity.

The article goes on to say that a utility should realize that being "open and even admitting something went wrong can neutralize the press' sting." (TRUE) "It is very difficult for a reporter to write a hostile article when he has been treated with honesty and cooperation." (FALSE) It is very easy for a reporter, on today's news beat, to write a hostile article about a utility or any other subject after he/she has been treated with honesty and cooperation by that utility.

The article also declares: "The public may not want to be informed about water treatment operations, but it never tires of hearing about attempts to conceal information from it." Well, I submit that the customer public does want to be informed about water treatment operations; the citizens, including the kids, do want to know about what water utilities are doing and how the important water supply task is being accomplished. What the author of the AWWA article really means is that the media, who have some considerable responsibility for keeping the citizenry informed, quite often do a lousy job of covering the positive side of water supply operations and services. In a complete transposition of the once popular song, they tend to "Accentuate the Negative and Eliminate (or at least, overlook) the Positive."

Finally, the AWWA article asserted that "A small community newspaper is often short of news. So it is quite possible that even small things in the utility operation could be of interest." Well, fortunately, weekly newspapers still do care about the small things, and that's usually why they carry items which are not attractive to the dailies or the broadcasting media. However, any of you who've been in contact with your local editors know that, in the present economic climate, many community newspapers are suffering from a shortage of advertising. When ads dwindle, available news space also decreases. When news space is reduced, it becomes more and more difficult to place stories telling the positive side of utility operations and management.

I have put some emphasis on problems related to dependence on the media because, more and more, public service organizations are realizing they cannot really depend on the newspapers and the broadcasters to reach their customers with the complete truth—the positive side of their story.

COMPREHENSIVE COMMUNICATIONS

The media are just one instrument of usefulness in a big chest full of communications tools. Other tools include all sorts of audiovisual materials: films, slides and display prints, training and orientation programs for employees related to customer service on the telephone and in correspondence, publications—which may be professionally designed and printed or developed in-house with imaginative use of mimeograph and multilith equipment—plant tours, contests, giveaway gadgets, public exhibits, speakers' bureaus, and special projects which may be based on ideas developed in communications programs by other utilities or based on original concepts developed within the organization.

MATTERS ON WHICH TO FOCUS

So, assuming that every water supply organization, large or small, rich or poor, has the tools available, the "big question" comes to the fore when management takes time to sit down and talk about "communications." Assuming that the utility desires to establish an effective communications program that will have the triple-threat impact of:

1. Building customer goodwill and understanding

2. Convincing employees and customers that the public service policies of the organization are sound

3. Accomplishing water demand reduction and better utilization of resources,

the first management question is, "Who will lead the communications program?"

Very few engineers and too few managers who have leadership responsibilities within a utility's table of organization have much natural public
relations sense. As I said earlier, effective communications require that
public relations problems be given the same "tender loving care and
professional attention routinely given to engineering problems." For the
large utility, professional assistance should be built into the organization
by the acquisition of a communications leader who operates with—and
not under—top management. The small organization, which perhaps
finds it cannot afford a communications manager, should appoint a bright
person within the organization to shoulder the communications task and
should make sure that person is interested enough to learn about communications tools and techniques, has the enthusiasm to put the tools to
work, and has the freedom (along with the responsibility) to develop,
implement, and manage the communications effort.

Once the communications leadership within the organization has been
established and has the unqualified support of management, the secondary question is, "What will be the focus of this marvelous new (or re-
juvenated) communications program?"

For most of us at the "water works," the answer to this question is much
more complex than it used to be. I would suggest that there are pressure
points in need of communications attention by every water utility:

1. Rates

2. Political and civic relationships

3. Customer service/education

4. Employee relationships

5. Special projects, which may support items one through four, but are
   designed to sustain positive public attitudes, show innovation, and
   adapt the utility's program to some current *popular notions* about
   what the utility should be doing.

Here's why I singled out this quintet of pressure points as the prime
targets of today's water utility communications effort:

1. *Rates*— For many decades water has been plentiful and cheap in
most of the United States. Historically, the management strategies of
many water supply organizations in this country have been to keep rates
low and, wherever possible, to keep charges as uncomplicated as possible. But times have changed. Today there are many more people to serve
than there were a decade or two ago, and some of the "babbling brooks"
(sources of water) have been abused. There are great national and local

demands for greater safety in the handling of the water product, for better water quality, for protection of the natural environment, and for improved systems maintenance and customer service. Further, more recently there has been double-digit inflation to contend with. Rates are going up everywhere, and the same customers who made the demands for improvements and have been living with inflation are doing a lot of bitching.

In fact, just about everyone thinks that the revenues from higher rates are being used to feather the nests of utility management. Well, it's up to the communications leader to make sure that evolving rates are explainable (have a well defined relationship to the actual cost of providing the service) and are thoroughly explained. For it is certain that, if the utility is moving in the direction of an innovative rate schedule (such as a scheme to promote water conservation and demand reduction), the customers need a lot of preparation.

Communication with and education of customers on escalating rates is the heaviest challenge facing most utilities. Direct mail in the form of bill-inserts, information sheets made available to all citizens, and the heavy use of utility managers as public speakers before community groups are the best ways to move out in front of the rate issue. I must admit, though, there are always many customers who don't get the message— customers who, like the old mule, don't start grousing until the two-by-four in the form of the water bill gets their attention.

I do discern an undesirable trend in this country toward more complex utility rates. In many cases, such rates are the product of confused thinking at the top level where the decision is made to camouflage the need for more revenues and a boost in basic rates with special service charges, minimum charges, surcharges, meter charges, and the like. Some of this has occurred in my own organization; and, frankly, as one of the people on the firing line who talks to a lot of thoughtful, sometimes irritated customers, I don't like the trend. I like to be able to say, "1,000 gallons of water costs everybody 65 cents (or whatever it might be). Your meter says you used 1,000 gallons. You have to pay for what you use, so you owe us 65 cents." Compare that simple explanation with "Well, you used 1,000 gallons of water and the basic charge is 65 cents for that amount of water, BUT there's the 20 percent summer surcharge for (various reasons) that amounts to ( ) cents, the service charge of $( ) to cover (various services), the environmental charge for (more grasping for straws), the special charge for (ad nauseam)."

The first consideration in communication of rate developments, even if the utility is considering an innovative schedule to foster conservation and demand reduction, is *simplicity*.

As I said before, rates must be *explainable* and *explained*, because they are a "pocketbook problem"—the toughest kinds of public relations challenges are those which rise from the customer's wallet and drift to the telephone and the mailbox.

2. *Political and Civic Relationships*— Those water supply organizations which must coordinate directly with various levels of elected government— and there are many of us—have our problems these days. Political leaders recently have "discovered" the water (and/or sewerage) system, and in many cases have decided it is a planning tool to be included under the broad umbrella of things which must be controlled and manipulated to assure "good planning" for the community. It's nice to receive this recognition of the system's importance, but the newfound fame frequently results in an overlay of controls which are basically uncomfortable for the people who have been used to going about their business of providing good water service to people who want it and need it.

Water resources management and environmental considerations also have become important concerns for the political people and for civic organizations, both of which used to take water service for granted and worried more about schools, zoning, traffic conditions, police protection, and other traditional community issues.

The "water works" simply has to recognize that it is an important ingredient of this new mix of political–civic concerns and it must produce the detailed information needed for presentation in easily understood written and spoken form. Again, I emphasize the importance of management-level leaders of the water supply organization—better informed themselves than any of their listeners—moving out front to explain clearly the positive functions and the *real* needs of the utility. As I said earlier, the organization's communicator has to operate with—not below— management; this is the only effective way to proceed with a political-civic "relations" effort.

3. *Customer Service/Education*— Time really doesn't permit me to cover this subject in great detail, but effective communications for a water utility must be based on a clear understanding by the consumer about the quality and extent of service being purchased from the "water works." In my mind, this means making sure that the utility is sustaining, or progressively moving toward, a level of service that measures up to the customer public's collective idea of satisfactory service. Every utility has the right—really the obligation—to brag about what its customers are receiving for their money.

In my own organization, I have developed close to 100 publications— some of them fairly extensive printed pamphlets, but most of them one-page, multilithed information sheets—to acquaint customers with activities, procedures, and services of the community's water and sewer agency. If someone wants to know what's in the water, there's a sheet presenting complete mineral/chemical analysis of tap water from both major water sources by monthly and annual average. There's a sheet on "How to Read Your Own Meter." There's another one on "People to Call," with names and phone numbers for various WSSC services. There's a packet on rate projections and analysis of actual operating costs related to cents on the water and sewer rates. There's something to help answer every major repetitive question about the WSSC; and, when a new and recurring question comes up, it doesn't take long to produce a new information sheet to cover it.

I think many utilities tend to get bogged down in the development of elaborate, sometimes expensive publications to educate customers, school kids, and other publics. Actually, the customer appreciates receiving a specific info-sheet-type of response to a specific question. The customer shouldn't have to wade through twenty-four pages of general information to find the answer to a question. Again, the secret of successful communication is simplicity and uniformity of response.

Later on, when I discuss our water-saving and waste-reduction program, I'll provide more specific examples of customer education tools and techniques which cover the broader spectrum of community relations activities. Needless to say, the total program involves seeking help from the media, working with teachers and students, keeping employees informed, and many other activities.

4. *Employee Relationships*— No doubt some of you have played on athletic teams. When I was playing high school football, my coach and team were delighted when a young man about 6-4 and weighing 240 pounds transferred to our school. No question: he was going to move quickly into the right guard position in place of the incumbent, who was no more than 5-9 and probably carried 160 pounds soaking wet. But no matter how long and hard we practiced with the new boy, the coach could never communicate with him on the difference between left and right. When the quarterback called for a left side sweep, our new boy invariably pulled out to the right, wiping out the right side of his own line. It only took a game or two for the coach to make the new man the biggest, tallest waterboy in our football league; and the little 5-9, 160-pounder was playing right guard again.

The purpose of this illustration is to point out the importance of having people in the front line of the utility—answering phones, writing letters, and providing service—who are able to understand the purposes and functions of the organization without lousing up the rest of the team.

Before they can be effectively used as reliable communicators, they must be trained and tested. They must be given the tools to operate, and they need a "playbook" from which to respond in a uniform way to customer inquiries and requests for service.

The employee who can't learn the plays should never be left to suffer along with the customers he/she is trying to serve. Additionally, the emergency field crew chief shouldn't be expected to respond to questions about rates, claims for damages from a water-main break, or restoration of a water-eroded street or driveway. Yet the crew chief should be armed with information on the proper persons at the utility to be called by the customer in search of answers on these subjects.

All of this requires internal training and education for personnel at all levels on subjects which will be helpful to them in dealing with predictable contacts with the people on the outside. The employee communications, or "relations," program should mix some morale-building activities into the schedule, too, in order to develop a "team spirit." Good mixers are employee dances, holiday parties, a night at the ballgame, an employees' picnic, and similar activities, which may be wholly underwritten by the "company" or partially "company-supported" to keep the employee cost down and encourage widespread participation.

The bottom-line purpose of *employee relations* in the area of comprehensive communications is the training of utility personnel to meet their predictable customer service responsibilities with a good attitude and with the right answers.

5. *Special Projects*— There are at least three or four dozen special projects I could talk about for an hour each. They are projects which have been helpful to one water utility or another in the pursuit of effective communications. However, I will discuss water conservation and demand reduction, a program in which I have been intimately involved, and that has effectively used virtually every known kind of communications tool.

OPPORTUNITY KNOCKS FOR POSITIVE
COMMUNICATIONS—WATER SAVING AND WASTE REDUCTION

The WSSC water-saving and waste-reduction program has been under way since 1970, when the first one-page flyers on conservation were developed for distribution to customers and school kids, and a series of news features was prepared for use by the Suburban Maryland Area (WSSC service area) media.

The early, low-budget efforts were so well received that a comprehensive water-saving and waste-reduction program was adopted by the commission in the fall of 1971 and has been on the move ever since. The apparent result has been the direct involvement of the commission's water and sewer customer population of almost 1.2 million in the bi-county Suburban Maryland Area adjacent to the nation's capital, with a conservation effort that helps clean up the environment by reducing the volume of sewage and helps people reduce the impact of rising water and sewer rates.

As an initial effort, the WSSC conducted a customer "Water-Saving Idea Contest" which yielded more than a thousand entries and produced conservation suggestions that ranged from the old "bathe with a friend" routine to a variety of thoughts on the "brick-in-the-toilet" approach to reducing the amount of per-flush water. In between, there were scores of excellent suggestions, which were organized into the WSSC Water-Saving and Waste-Reduction Handbook—"It's Up to You"—and distributed by direct mail to the commission's more than 225,000 customers. Later in the program, a similar handbook was designed for apartment developments and distributed to an additional 150,000 customer units through property managers.

The response to the handbooks was tremendous, with a 99 and 44/100ths percent "pure" positive feedback from customers who expressed an interest in being invited to become personally involved in the conservation program. Dads reported that they were cutting the shower time of their teenaged sons and daughters from twenty minutes to five minutes; housewives said they were building fires under their husbands to repair leaking faucets and toilets; and whole families announced they were brushing teeth with the water turned off.

While the handbook was making its rounds, in late 1971 and through 1972–73, the WSSC was pursuing other water-saving projects that constituted a comprehensive waste-reduction program. Activities included:

1. The organization of water-saving workshops for property managers in the WSSC service area. The meetings included the demonstration of water-saving fixtures and appliances, providing the managers with information on appliance installation, on leak detection and repair, and on water pressure reduction.

2. Development of a slide–speaker program on water saving for showing to civic and service organizations. This program, which presented information on leak detection, family water saving, and conservation appliances, was shown to more than 500 groups with a total audience of approximately 16,000 people. The slide–show has now been replaced by the WSSC's new "Drip" motion picture.

3. Assembly of product data on water-saving appliances, including flow controls, shower heads, pressure-reducing valves, aerators, toilet tank modifiers, and many other items, which were worked into a "WSSC Water-Saving Fixture List." This information sheet is constantly revised and updated as new water-related fixtures and appliances come to the commission's attention and are found to be appropriate for inclusion on the list. Thousands of copies of the list have been supplied to interested customers of the commission.

4. Preparation of a set of twelve television and radio public service spot announcements, which were released at the rate of four per quarter beginning in April 1973. The 30-second spots feature the WSSC's "I Save Water" theme and have been widely used, often in prime time, by the television and radio outlets in the national capital area. The spots relate the water-saving effort to saving money and reducing the loads on the community's sewage treatment facilities, thus reinforcing the message of the WSSC handbooks. The spots enjoyed a two-year run and probably will be reissued this year.

5. Maintenance of a continuing news–publicity program which has included the production of regular features, pictorial reports, fillers, and progress releases on the water-saving program in suburban Maryland.

6. The organization and implementation of a special test program which involved 2,400 customer units in the WSSC's Cabin John drainage basin service area and which checked out the performance of retrofitted water conservation appliances in existing household units. The six-month study, which was coordinated by the WSSC's public affairs office and Field Project Engineer Michael P. Bonk, generated detailed information on plumbing problems related to water waste, the customer service requirements involved in providing personal conservation advice and help to homeowners, and the cost—in time and money—pertaining to appliance purchase and installation. The project generally proved the water-saving effectiveness of shower flow controls, pressure-reducing valves, and toilet-insert devices, and gave the WSSC a platform for recommending the use of these conservation devices to its customers.

7. The adoption in 1972 of plumbing code changes to make water-saving fixtures mandatory for new development installations and for replacement required the use of a 3.5-gallon toilet (now on the market and a real "saver" over the conventional toilet models which may use 5 to 8 gallons a flush), shower flow of no more than 3.5 gallons a minute, and pressure-reducing on all units where outside water pressure exceeds 60 pounds per square inch. The code revisions also include the elimination of basement drains, a

move designed to eliminate what is considered to be a source of substantial surface water inflow to the sanitary sewerage system. It's worth noting that when the WSSC "led the way" with a code requirement for use of the 3.5-gallon-per-flush toilet, only one water closet with this capability was advertised on the market. As of early 1975, at least a dozen manufacturers were advertising a 3.5-gallon model. The WSSC plumbing code obviously was an effective "persuader" in the mobilization of water-saving toilet production.

8. Development of a range of community relations aids on water saving, including bumper stickers ("Reduce Waste—Use Water Wisely"); buttons and stickers for the young people who are anxious to spread the word on conservation; a special leak-reporting sticker for posting in apartments and public lavatory and laundry areas, which was made available free to property managers; balloons and postcards; and even "I Save Water" T-shirts for use by young people helping the WSSC with its conservation programs.

In early 1973, the WSSC public information office began its "think tank" process for the ongoing water-saving program, hoping to come up with a new customer oriented project that would sustain interest and continue the personal involvement of all suburban Marylanders in the conservation effort. The product of this creative pause was the WSSC "Bottle-Leak Detection Kit" program, which got under way in June and continued through the fall of 1973. It was a project which generated unusual challenges in terms of logistics and the organization of people.

The "bottle kit," conceived as a variation on the "brick-in-the-toilet" method of reducing flushing volume, was designed to include three plastic quart bottles for flush water displacement, two dye pills for making a leak check of household toilets, and an instruction booklet which told customers how to use the bottles and the dye pills and which provided some additional water-saving hints.

Aimed at covering the approximately 220,000 single-family homes in the WSSC service area, as well as another 100,000 or so apartment units, the program involved the ordering and staged delivery of about one million bottles, 600,000 dye pills, and a half-million pamphlets to a project-staging kit assembly area at the WSSC Headquarters parking lot in Hyattsville, Md.

Student (high school and college) workers were mobilized to form the distribution crews for assembly and door-to-door delivery of the kits. Eventually, 100 volunteer Scout units were recruited to help with the project.

On customer "feedback" forms, most waterusers praised the program and indicated their families had used the bottles for toilet water displacement, the dye check for toilet leaks, and had proceeded to repair the leaks.

In feedback comments from customers, just about everybody indicated a positive receptiveness to the "bottle kit," with encouraging comments such as "Thanks so much," "Keep up the good work," "Excellent idea," "Fine program," and "We appreciate your helping us save money, reduce waste, and reduce water pollution." 69.3 percent of the respondents indicated they tried the dye test for toilet leaks; 15.7 percent of these people said they found leaks, which were adjusted or repaired.

The "bottle kit" distribution program, which involved the expenditure of approximately fifty cents per WSSC customer and some 28,000 WSSC and Scout manhours, apparently paid dividends in terms of the commission's community relations, and it accomplished reduction of water use and resultant wastewater flows.

I analyzed comparative water consumption and customer growth data for the winter months (when outside water use is not a real factor) of December, January, February, and March for the 1969–70 through the 1973–74 period and came to the following conclusions with regard to program impact:

1. The first stages of the program, up to but not including the "bottle kit" project, had apparently dropped per capita water use for those months from 101.6 gallons a day (gpd) to 100.2 gpd, for a net minimum saving on the WSSC system of 1.7 million gpd.

2. Following the "bottle kit" project, per capita consumption dipped further to about 97.0 gpd, and the net minimum saving for the WSSC system was 5.4 million gpd. This change represented a 4.42 percent reduction from the minimum projected average daily consumption of 122.2 mgd that might have been expected to occur without the water-saving and waste-reduction program.

Perhaps more importantly, since the WSSC was interested in wastewater flow reduction, the sewage flows to the regional Blue Plains Pollution Control Plant from the WSSC service area dropped substantially in late 1973 and 1974 to below the volumes delivered to the plant during the same period of 1972–73. Although weather conditions and other WSSC programs diverting flows from Blue Plains to another plant and waging war on sewerage system infiltration by surface groundwater were also factors, the fact remains that the water-saving kit distribution and other WSSC conservation projects apparently have played an important role in the overall drop in sewage flows. Here are the figures (in mgd):

	1972	1973	% Increase (decrease)
September	128.5	120.6	(6.1)
October	124.6	116.8	(6.2)
November	136.7	109.9	(19.6)
December	148.4	123.0	(17.1)
	1973	1974	
January	142.0	131.8	(7.2)
February	149.8	124.1	(17.2)
March	148.2	123.9	(16.4)
April	163.2	133.9	(17.9)
May	150.6	126.4	(16.1)
June	146.7	122.8	(16.3)
July	130.7	115.2	(11.8)
August	122.4	114.4	(6.5)

Although the WSSC has a number of continuing projects in its water-saving and waste-reduction "bag," the question that naturally follows the completion of a gigantic effort like the "bottle kit" distribution is, "What do you do for an encore?"

Well, there has been an encore at the WSSC. In the spring of 1974, the commission approved a new "Summer of '74" Project involving the purchase of 400,000 shower control insert devices to reduce shower flow in households to three gallons a minute. The devices—developed at the Virginia Polytechnic Institute and now marketed by the Noland Company—feature nozzle-type design, are made of plastic, and can easily be inserted in most shower fixtures.

Rather than travel house-to-house with the devices, as was done with the "bottle kit," the WSSC offered the new kit through a special bill-insert pamphlet included in its water-sewer bills to customers during the 1974 June-through-August quarter. The offer has been repeated in subsequent billing cycles. Also, the devices have been distributed by special mailings to apartments and other property-managed units in suburban Maryland.

When requests for the devices are received, "shower control kits" —including the devices and an instruction booklet for installation—are mailed to the customer or property manager. The devices are supplied in the quantity needed to retrofit the individual home or building.

So far, more than 300,000 of the devices have been distributed, and the program is still going strong. It's too early to tell what additional impact this project may be having on waste reduction, but, with the implementation of this effort, the WSSC has made direct, helpful contact with its customers, targeting what are acknowledged to be the two largest factors in household water use (and waste)—the water closet and the shower.

In an attempt to sustain the gains achieved in the commission's conservation program, the WSSC continues to support new projects designed to improve its educational tools for public water conservation and waste reduction. Recent activities have included:

1. The sponsorship of a water-saving and waste-reduction poster contest, which offered more than $2,000 in U. S. savings bonds and yielded some 300 entries. The excellent art–idea material received from the little children, teenagers, and adults has been utilized in WSSC slide-shows, exhibits, and publications. A number of the drawings and paintings have been published as posters for distribution to schools and other public buildings in suburban Maryland.

2. The formation of a WSSC water conservation club designed to enroll young people in the waste-reduction effort and make them aware of the need for effective management of water resources. The club, launched just over a year ago, is picking up momentum and is a vehicle for distribution of current material on conservation through the young people to WSSC customer families. The club is replete with a membership certificate and card, both signed by the WSSC general manager; a special badge; and a "Water Conservation Pledge."

3. The production of a twenty-minute water-saving and waste-reduction film, "Drip," which has been jointly developed with Stuart Finley, Inc., one of the East Coast's top makers of water-resources motion pictures. The color film probably has replaced the WSSC slide-shows on water saving. It features an unlocalized format, so that the film should be useful to other water- and sewer-operating agencies, utilities, and municipalities throughout the nation. Organizations interested in seeing the film with a possible view toward purchase ($300 a copy) and use of it in their own conservation programs should contact the WSSC Public Affairs Office (ATTN: PAO Art Brigham), 4017 Hamilton Street, Hyattsville, MD, 20781.

4. The recent development of a new water-saving handbook on outside water use, entitled "Keeping the Garden Green." A logical sequel to the first WSSC handbook, which concentrated on in-house waste reduction, the new booklet provides information on water conservation applied to lawn

and garden care. Wilbur H. Youngman, recently retired garden editor of the *Washington Star* and the author of the Metropolitan Washington Area's "bible" for green thumbers, *The Star Garden Book*, wrote the text.

That is the story, in brief, of the WSSC program. However, I do want to emphasize that other organizations, notably the San Francisco area's East Bay Municipal Utility District (my counterpart there is Jim Lattie), have produced excellent water conservation projects and materials. East Bay MUD hired an educational consultant to create a student workbook and teacher's guide, which feature a colorful character named "Captain Hydro" and do an excellent job of presenting the water story to schools. The "Hydro" materials are very adaptable to other communities around the country and can be purchased from East Bay MUD at reasonable cost.

Denver also has developed an excellent water conservation and waste reduction program. Denver's short cartoon film "The Water Follies—A Soak Opera" is a gem and is now available for purchase from the American Water Works Association for use by the nation's water utilities. Denver, East Bay MUD, the WSSC, and other utilities around the country have exchanged ideas on water conservation and demand-reduction programming. I think all of us have been busier than we'd like to be answering inquiries from other American communities and from many foreign countries which seek to "pick our brains" on our conservation projects.

In a period when so many people are complaining about the extension of federal authority, it has been refreshing to see a national interest growing from what have been basically local efforts to promote the conservative use of a community resource. It has been pleasant for me to be one of the creators of this reverse osmosis, and I think my counterparts at East Bay MUD and Denver and I are a little bit proud of what we've done.

As I said earlier, the water-saving program is an example of a successful communications effort. *Success came with a lot of planning, creative thinking, innovation, and, most of all, hard work. Any communications program which contains these ingredients is bound to succeed.*

ENVIRONMENTAL CONSIDERATIONS IN WATER MANAGEMENT

There are approximately three million species of plants and animals on the earth today. Water is an absolutely critical factor in determining the numbers, distribution, and continued existence of all of them. Man is one of these species; human life without the others is literally unthinkable. Therefore, man must realize the necessity of *sharing* the earth's resources, including water, with the others.

This simple realization is the basis of the science of ecology. The ecologist attempts to take a holistic, integrative view of man within his environment, including all the complexities of man's interaction with both its living and nonliving components. Within this view, water is only a single component, although an extremely important one. And water resources management is only a single subsystem within a large complex of systems which man has devised to control his interaction with the environment.

Such a view implies a fundamental reevaluation of attitudes on the part of many of those who bear responsibility for the management of water resources. Understandably, this view may seem foreign to professionals in the field. It is probably fair to say that it is foreign to most Americans. Nonetheless, such a view of natural resource issues will necessarily become the basis of future management approaches. In its application to water resources, this view, although perhaps not yet clearly defined, underlies much recent federal legislation and regulation.

The selection by Beatrice Willard, an ecologist, attempts to place water resources in the context of responsible, long-term management of all resources. In doing so, she emphasizes first the need to add to the traditionally calculated cost of resource development the rapidly escalating costs now being incurred in attempts to rectify the damage done by development. She then goes on to describe the need to explore such topics as institutional arrangements, conservation, and recycling, which were the subject of previous chapters in this volume.

NATIONAL WATER POLICY AND THE ENVIRONMENT

BEATRICE E. WILLARD,
Council on Environmental Quality
Executive Office of the President

News reports of recent months have underscored both the critical importance of water to man, and man's failure to recognize this importance. We hear of severe droughts affecting cities and farms in California, the upper Midwest, and parts of the Southwest; of Kepone contamination in Chesapeake Bay, of Mirex in Lake Ontario; of land subsidence on the Texas coast; and of the breaking of the Lower Teton Dam in Idaho. Overseas, England has arrested, convicted, and fined a man for using too much water; and the Netherlands is actually contemplating dispatching a ship to Greenland in the hope of towing home an iceberg.

These are only some of the stories that were dramatic enough to hit the headlines. At the same time, we all know that water resources projects across the country are the object of an increasing number of lawsuits and organized protests—environmentalists against the TVA, railroads against the Corps of Engineers, states against the EPA, and everyone against the Interior Department. These conflicts represent more than the traditional give-and-take of American politics. In my opinion, they express much deeper disagreements over the setting of national priorities.

While human activity does not appear to be directly responsible for regional and global drought, we should, nonetheless, look in a mirror, rather than at the skies, to seek the causes of most of our water problems. Chief among these causes is, I think, our tardiness in balancing the claims of national economic development against the claims of environmental quality. These claims may appear to be in conflict in the short run, but in the long run they must be brought into equilibrium. The U. S. Water Resources Council—through a lengthy and admirably public process—has developed a policy statement regarding these issues. The document, entitled "Principles and Standards for Planning Water and Related Land Resources" and approved by the President in 1973, regards national economic development and environmental quality as two "coequal" objectives. One objective is not to be regarded as more important than the other.

No matter how clearly policies are stated, however, they are inevitably interpreted according to the shifting needs of the times. To paraphrase

George Orwell, though two policies may be created equal, one policy can become more equal than the other. In the context of our times, when the paramount needs seem to be for economic development, I'm afraid the value of environmental quality has frequently been underestimated in our decision-making processes. It is absolutely essential to realize that environmental quality contributes as much to human survival as does economic development. Indeed, a course of apparent economic expediency which also substantially degrades the environment may well prove to be economically expensive in the long run.

THE COSTS OF DEVELOPMENT

Those who work with water or study it in various contexts are surely aware of development projects in which substantial costs due to environmental damage have been added to the total bill. For example, irrigation projects along the Colorado River certainly greatly increased crop production in the United States; but at the same time these projects dispatched a soil-damaging flow of soluble salts down the river into Mexico. As a result, we have committed ourselves to build a large desalinization plant, at a cost of more than $155 million, to try to rectify this situation for our Mexican neighbors.

The Garrison Diversion, an irrigation project now under way in North Dakota, promises to have similar effects in Canada. It is more than ironic that agricultural research has shown that the soils to be irrigated by this project are most productive with *no* irrigation. Judging from conversations last year between the Council on Environmental Quality and Mme. Sauve, the Canadian Minister for Environment, the Canadians are acutely unhappy about the possibility of damage to their land. This is all the more understandable in the light of the project's negligible benefits to U. S. agriculture.

The history of flood control in this country provides us with another set of instances where environmental costs were not adequately considered. Severe flood damage near St. Louis in 1973 stemmed in part from levee construction and channel alterations designed to *prevent* flooding. The loss of 236 lives in the disastrous Rapid City, South Dakota, flood of June 1972 can largely be traced to the unwise human development of a floodplain—the natural right-of-way of every river. It has always been clear that we must restrict development in the rights-of-way of highways, power lines, and pipelines. We must learn to extend the same sort of treatment to our nation's waterways.

There are many other instances that might be mentioned to underscore the point that water can be a potent instrument for creating problems as well as progress. There is nothing new in that humble insight, of course; man has known it at least since Noah sailed off with a tiny chunk of the ecosystem aboard his ark, leaving the rest of it to a watery grave.

SOURCES OF CONCERN

There is, however, something new about man's relationship to his environment these days, something that involves the ability of the earth to continue supplying our demands for water as well as all other natural resources. This "something new" is our capacity for doing *rapid, massive* damage to our life-support systems.

This capacity, I would estimate, did not fully develop until about the end of World War II. Before then, man could not quickly do much lasting, extensive damage to the earth—for the earth has a prodigious capacity to absorb man's garbage, break it down into life-sustaining components, and recycle them back into the ecosystem. As long as the human population remained relatively small and slow to grow, as long as man's products remained few and relatively simple in composition, and as long as man's tools and works were small in size and impact, the earth could take all the punishment man could deal out, and come back smiling.

None of those conditions holds true any longer.

Fueling the damage man can now do on earth is *rapid, massive* population increase. There are now more than *four* billion of us. Within 35 years, at present growth rates, there will be *eight* billion of us. These numbers may have more significance to you if you realize that man's population did not reach *one* billion until A.D. 1830—and that was at least three million years after man first appeared on the planet. This rapid doubling is not a natural rate of increase; it is highly unnatural, resulting from the advance of our medicine, the widespread adoption of public health measures, and our newfound ability to control our immediate, built environment.

The second condition that formerly preserved the ecosystem's resilience is that man's organic wastes were relatively few, simple, and of similar composition to the wastes of other organisms. But man's products are now incredibly varied and strange. About two million chemical substances are known, and hundreds more are developed each year. We have created synthetic compounds that nature cannot break down, and we pour thousands of troublesome chemicals into our skies, our water, our soils. Last year—as you probably read—the EPA released a report on its study of chemical substances in the drinking water systems of 79 communities. All—repeat, all—showed measurable amounts of chemicals that are potentially carcinogenic.

There is a simple reason for our worries about these synthetic chemicals. Organic life on earth has evolved over hundreds of thousands of years to adapt in a variety of ways to the relatively few chemicals which occur in nature. The evolutionary processes are slow. That they are operating can be seen in the fact that malaria mosquitos are now immune to DDT. But normally these processes take time and many generations of offspring. Furthermore, adaptations are specific to each chemical. Today man is introducing hundreds of new chemicals into ecosystems each year, and consequently the *rapid, massive* changes in the chemical environment are escalating year by year.

The third force that is destroying nature's resilience is the new scale of human technology. Modern technology so multiplies the effort of one man that he can produce more goods—and do more damage—than a hundred or even a thousand men could do a century ago. For example, at the end of World War II, the largest oil tankers had a capacity of 18,000 deadweight tons; today, tankers of 250,000-ton capacity are commonplace, and several of 540,000-ton capacity are under construction. Through spills and normal refinery operations, we are pouring more than a million metric tons of petroleum into our oceans, rivers, and estuaries annually. Some of the costs—bird kills, disfigured beaches—are known to us because they are so obvious. We have good reason to suspect that there are other costs—for example, potentially irreversible damage to food webs that have sustained life in the seas since it first appeared on earth eons ago—but we cannot easily measure these costs.

These three factors—population growth, diversity of impact, and mass of impact—represent a great magnification of man's ability to injure the earth. Taken together, they not only add to each other's impact, but multiply it into unprecedented hammer blows at the earth's resilience. We must take very seriously the very real probability that we have exceeded the earth's capacity to clean up our garbage; for, as the ecologists tell us, damage to an ecosystem may not be obvious until it is irreversible.

WATER AS A RESOURCE

Alarmist as I may sound, I am cautiously optimistic about man's ability to restore the earth's capacity to heal its wounds. Only "cautiously" optimistic, however, because it is so hard to convince those people in policy-making positions that continuing environmental damage holds genuine potential for catastrophe. Unless they take that potential seriously, they will tend to minimize the importance of protecting environmental quality when it seems to conflict with economic development.

This tendency is harmful enough in the development of any natural resource, but it would be disastrous with water. For example, oil is a crucial element of our economy today, but it is not a crucial element of our ecosystem; we will, as a matter of fact, have to start learning to get along without it within the next generation. Water, on the other hand, is crucial to both our economy *and* our ecosystem—and, vast as the supply seems to be, there is a limit to the amount available for man to use.

As the National Water Commission noted in 1973, "The level of future demand for water is not inevitable, but derives in large part from policy decisions within the control of society"—that is to say that we are not *forced* to equate demand with need; nor must we regard the history of water development in our nation as a reliable guide to our future. To quote again from the 1973 report:

> The Commission recognizes that Federal programs for navigation, reclamation, flood control, and hydroelectric power, among others, have made an enormous contribution to national well-being. But demands on the Nation's water supply have accelerated so rapidly during the past century that national policies governing water conservation, development, and utilization have inevitably lagged far behind national growth. New policies reflecting today's needs and the needs of the 21st century are essential to assure efficiency in water use and to sustain a healthful, esthetically pleasing environment.

I have a few suggestions about how our view of water resources should be updated; but first let's look at some parallels between our country's use of water and of energy. In the energy field, exploration and discovery were followed by aggressive but often inefficient exploitation of the highest quality and most readily accessible reserves. As our economic system adapted to and became dependent upon readily available energy resources, we began to consolidate our processing and supply systems and reach out over longer distances for new sources, often with the assistance of government subsidies and tax breaks. The quality of the available resources began to decline; the prices went up; local shortages developed; and environmental problems emerged and grew in intensity. Recent history is more easily remembered—the energy crisis of 1973, long lines at the gas pumps, skyrocketing prices for Middle-Eastern oil, lowered thermostats, reduced speed limits, and other rapidly-adopted conservation measures, accompanied by new commitments to planning, research, and development of alternative sources.

The possibility of drawing a parallel with water development is intriguing and leads to some alarming conclusions. However, the extrapolation of present trends in water use and abuse is not inevitable, and much depends on the kind of policies we as a nation adopt for dealing with this critical resource. We are learning that water is not available in unlimited quantities. But will it take a regional or national "water crisis" to force changes in our water use patterns? Can we afford to continue providing each American household with 65 gallons of safe, drinkable water per day for every man, woman, and child? Can our industries continue to draw an average of 170 gallons per American per day from our surface and ground water? These two uses total 50 billion gallons of water per day. Can we meet these needs and also have water adequate in quantity and quality for agriculture, recreation, transportation, and energy development? Can we do this and still maintain a human environment which has beauty, diversity, and stability? We must face these questions, and the last one in particular, *before* we pour more concrete, not after.

In my home state of California, we have been damming and diverting rivers, and draining, irrigating, and developing land on an increasingly large scale since the turn of the century. We have indeed made the desert bloom—but at a price. We now worry about controlling salt accumulation in the soil, maintaining the water balance in the great Sacramento–San Joaquin delta, and obtaining sufficient energy to run the system. A recent issue of the journal *Cry California* contains a critical review of the California Water Plan in which authors Frank Stead and Walt Anderson conclude that, while we built one of the world's largest water systems,

> it is now a man-made system, a network of gigantic plumbing that cost a great deal to construct and will cost a great deal to maintain. Managing it involves a constant confrontation with ecological perils, and also a constant juggling of the needs of different geographic areas and the values of disparate interest groups.

This statement is equally true with regard to sewage collection and waste treatment systems.

Hindsight suggests that California should have given less emphasis to large-scale, energy-consuming water transfers and more emphasis to conserving, reclaiming, and recycling its existing resources. Water, unlike energy, is a highly renewable resource—but only if we plan and build with this fact in mind. As with soft drink bottles and automobiles, it is much cheaper, safer, and better for the environment to conserve water in the first place than to try to reconstitute it after it has been degraded.

MANAGEMENT POLICIES

I would make water conservation and recycling the keystone of our future water policy. I would pursue this goal even more vigorously than we are pursuing energy conservation, because until water is priced comparably to oil it is unlikely that we will be piping it from Alaska or buying it from the Arabs. Moreover, despite talk of fresh water from polar icebergs, that source seems a bit too speculative for the near term.

The federal government can and should promote water conservation where it has a direct role in building and funding water projects. We can encourage more efficient irrigation and wastewater treatment technologies, even combining the two where possible. I believe that additional study and attention should be given to implementing the reclamation and recycling objectives in Sections 105 and 201 of the Federal Water Pollution Control Act. We are now discouraging excessive design capacity and unwise location of water treatment plants and interceptor sewers, and should continue to do so. We should encourage water conservation through the "208" planning process. But the states and the municipalities—not the federal government—must act on their own authority to implement this policy effectively. Building codes, zoning ordinances, and land use plans should all reflect a commitment to water conservation, literally from the ground up.

And this brings me to a second feature which should be emphasized in regard to our future water policies, and which I am certain is obvious to many of you: water management and land-use planning must go hand in hand. Such activity is most effective when it takes place at the same level or on the same scale as the problems being faced, and water problems most often arise at the multicounty or river basin level. Again, the federal government can encourage such activity and has done so through Titles II and III of Public Law 89–80 and through other activities of the Water Resources Council and the river basin commissions. However, if the states do not wish the federal government to exercise further controls over water and related land resources within their borders, it behooves them to develop effective planning and regulatory programs of their own, with adequate staffing and funding to do the job.

As an illustration, we must break the cycle of uncontrolled floodplain development, followed by disastrous loss of life and property, followed by federal disaster relief funds for reconstruction, followed by appeals for federal structural measures such as dams or levees which serve to reward and reinforce the previous, unwise development patterns. The National Flood Insurance Program of HUD and Section 73 of Public Law 93–251 provide partial alternatives to this cycle, but effective state and local controls are still badly needed in many flood hazard areas.

Similarly, we must reverse the development trends which have already destroyed 40 percent of our nation's wetlands. The federal government has already intervened to do this. If this regulatory authority is restricted by Congress, as has been threatened in current legislation, we must ensure that effective state or regional controls on wetlands development will have been implemented to replace federal authority. An orderly delegation of this authority to the states may be appropriate where states have demonstrated that they have the capability and the will to exercise it—but it is important that wetland resources not be lost in the shuffle.

A third point I should like to make is that the first step in state, regional, or river basin planning should be to delineate important aquatic and terrestrial systems, sometimes called Critical Environmental Areas, which deserve special protection or other designation. These areas include wild, scenic, or recreational rivers, key fish and wildlife habitats, prime agricultural lands, and areas with special flood or erosion hazards. This is already being done in some states, but it should be standard operating procedure in all.

It is important to realize that ours is not the only country struggling with land and water management problems. In May of 1975, more than 100 specialists from 25 countries took part in a seminar on Long-Term Planning in Water Management. This seminar was held in preparation for the ECE contribution to the United Nations Water Conference in Marva del Plata, Argentina. Here are two extracts from an ECE summary of the seminar's findings and recommendations:

> The management of water resources calls for urgent improvement, so as to reduce the risk of serious shortages and ecological damage. . . .
>
> Long-term planning . . . is one of the most important tools of national water policy, and it should be used in decision-making at the regional and basin levels. Plans extending over 10 to 15 years should be supplemented by forecasts for periods of 30 to 50 years, in which alternative courses of action would make it possible to take into account changes in technology and in living patterns.
>
> The link between the long-term planning of water management and land-use planning deserves special consideration. Zoning to protect water resources, the compatability of new industrial and municipal areas with the quality and quantity of water available, and the preservation of agricultural lands and forests were among the measures suggested.

Sounds familiar, doesn't it? I note also that a careful reading of this summary reveals that the words "planning" and "management" each appear ten times in the two pages, while the word "development" appears only once, and there it is used in reference to providing training to water resources planners in developing countries.

This brings me to my final point. While the United States may still be in some ways a "developing country," we would do well to hasten our own transition from a water resource *development* perspective to one of water resources *management*. We can best achieve the dual planning objectives of economic development and environmental quality if we pursue this development within the context of a systems approach to environmental quality—and not the other way around. Where federally funded water resource projects are under consideration, cost–benefit calculations and cost-sharing formulas should reflect current economic realities, rather than past political customs. Frankly, it is our experience at the Council of Environmental Quality that those federal water resource projects with the least substantial economic justification are often among the most environmentally destructive. We believe that, in assigning project priorities, greater weight should be accorded to the willingness of project beneficiaries to make a substantial contribution to project construction and maintenance costs. We need, therefore, to devise equitable means of sharing both the expenses and the planning responsibilities for environmentally sound water resource management.

If this can be accomplished, a new and viable alliance might well emerge—an alliance between the advocates of environmental protection and those responsible for water resource management. This alliance is long overdue, and it will begin to answer in the water resources management field Aldo Leopold's famous query:

> When is man going to see land and its waters as a community to which he belongs, rather than a commodity he must exploit?

BIBLIOGRAPHY

Kormondy, E. J. 1976. *Concepts of Ecology*. Englewood Cliffs, N.J.: Prentice-Hall.

Odum, E. P. 1971. *Fundamentals of Ecology*. Third edition. Philadelphia: W.B. Sanders.

Willard, B. E. 1975. The natural ecological principles underlying water reuse. Second National Conference on Water Reuse, American Institute of Chemical Engineers, May.

———, 1974. Ecological criteria for balancing energy with environment and growth. Keynote, Second Arizona Governor's Conference, December.

———, 1974. Environmental analysis and earth science in the public service. Symposium for U.S. Geol. Survey, Reston, Va., July.

A LOOK TO THE FUTURE

THE CHALLENGE TO MANAGEMENT

DUANE D. BAUMANN,
Department of Geography
Southern Illinois University

DANIEL DWORKIN,
Department of Geography
Southern Illinois University

Planning for municipal water supply is a drastically different challenge today than in the past. Reliance on solely traditional approaches is no longer adequate.

The reasons for this difference are complex and border on the speculative. First, with urbanization and higher standards of living, the per capita demand for water has increased markedly (there is, however, some doubt as to whether this trend will continue). Second, new reservoir sites are scarce. Third, groundwater is usually available only as a supplemental source. Fourth, technological, economic, and political problems of inter-basin transfer of water have proliferated. Fifth, higher energy costs have been translated into higher production costs. Sixth, the current high cost of money increases the consequences of premature exploitation of or overinvestment in new supplies. Seventh, the Safe Drinking Water Act and the National Water Pollution Control Act have set the federal mandate for strict water-quality considerations for municipal water supplies. Local utility representatives are continually faced with problems and conflicts in meeting these standards; and the high costs of compliance indicate that water-quality criteria need to be based on extensive research into the benefits and costs of treating to remove or decrease residuals of various types of water contaminants.

It seems safe to speculate that in planning for future demand, complex questions concerning quality and quantity, as well as social, economic, and environmental costs, will dictate the choice of alternatives. Our understanding of these interactions is far from complete; for example, the increasing amounts of both natural and man-made substances in our waters may have potentially serious effects on human health. Consequently, water managers find themselves responsible for the solution of a totally new set of problems for which even experts find the risk–benefit ratios difficult to determine.

The social and political forces being brought to bear on resource issues are proliferating in number and complexity. The traditional approaches to water management are being questioned by more and more people. Policies regarding water management are the subject of much public interest and debate. Moreover, it is no longer a simple matter to justify

Table 1

ALTERNATIVES FOR BALANCING SUPPLY
AND DEMAND FOR MUNICIPAL WATER SUPPLY

Do Nothing	Modify Supply	Modify Demand
1) Accept Shortage Unplanned rationing	1) Increase Supply Divert new streams Provide increased storage Use groundwater	1) Restrictions
		2) Price Elasticity Peak pricing, i.e., peak summer pricing Marginal cost pricing
	2) Increase Efficiency Reduce reservoir evaporation Eliminate leaks Increase runoff Reduce evaporation	3) Meters
		4) Educational Campaign Emphasizing Water Use Conservation
	3) Renovated Wastewater Nonpotable uses Potable uses	5) Technological Innovations and Application, e.g., changes from water cooling to air cooling

huge expenditures on waterworks projects primarily on the basis of meeting an unbridled demand.

However, in response to the increase in demand, cities have traditionally chosen to increase the available water supply. Except under such emergency conditions as drought, alternatives that would lower demand have been ignored. For example, the most common response of 48 Massachusetts communities during the drought of the early 1960s, aside from the unenforced pleas for restrictions on water use, was to plan for increases in supply, new sources, improvements in present supply, emergency sources, and a cloud-seeding experiment (Russell, Arey, and Kates 1970). Those adjustments directed toward a reduction of demand were rarely considered or adopted.

Such a traditional reliance upon technology designed to modify the environment, instead of reliance on policies directed toward reducing demand, has been equally pronounced with another water resource problem. White (1973, p. 161) has succinctly noted that "For a long time it was out of the question for a planning officer to study any way of dealing with flood losses other than by constructing engineering works or by providing relief."

Table 1 is a summary review of some of the alternatives for balancing supply of and demand for municipal water supply. While past efforts have generally focused upon those alternatives that increase supply, future strategies may reap the benefits of evaluating the full range of choice by including those alternatives that modify demand.

METHODS FOR PROJECTING DEMAND

In discussing the management alternatives for municipal water systems, there is little disagreement on the need for demand projections that will more accurately estimate future use. While a few traditional and relatively simple demand-projection methods have been widely used, the newer analytical methods which involve investigating the contribution of the relevant components of municipal water demand hold the greatest promise for accurate water-demand forecasting. However, such analytical models require a more extensive data base than is presently available in many utilities. Furthermore, application of these new techniques presents some formidable problems.

PRICING TO MODIFY DEMAND

Pricing is considered to be a tool that automatically guides the consumer and the producer to appropriate levels of use and supply. However, marginal cost water pricing may not provide sufficient return, in that any fixed price capacity charge may serve to distort the elasticity of demand. In addition, the elasticity function itself, on which the theory relies, varies from month to month and year to year, depending on cumulative departure from mean rainfall. Nevertheless, while several problems are present, implementation of some pricing method which will reflect marginal costs should result in a more efficient use of municipal water supplies.

PUBLIC CONSERVATION MEASURES TO REDUCE DEMAND

Several water-saving devices and programs can be characterized as structural, operational, economic, and social. However, water conservation potential from such measures seems to be limited: water-saving devices may be more appropriate for periods of low supply than for extensive use in ongoing water utility operations. Limiting the amount of water use independent of costs and benefits should result in economic inefficiencies.

INCREASING SYSTEM EFFICIENCY

Similarly, the need to increase system efficiency by detecting and controlling leaks and unauthorized use, and by replacing inaccurate meters, constitutes a water management tool which should be employed when the costs of detection and control are less than the benefits realized from such a program. Unaccounted-for water still remains a challenge to management.

INCREASING WATER SUPPLY

In addition to reducing water demand and increasing system efficiency, an increasing water supply presents an obvious solution to satisfying urban water demands. In the past, the only alternative to balancing supply and demand was to increase the amount of groundwater or surface water available to the system. Today, however, this alternative is often constrained by physical unavailability and is frequently too expensive; the future indicates a continuation of this trend of increasing costs and decreasing availability. In part, the willingness of water utilities to consider the other alternatives is motivated by the recognition of this present and future situation regarding traditional sources of supply.

WASTEWATER REUSE

The conflicting attitudes toward the alternative of wastewater reuse are centered primarily on issues of health and safety. While concern about the potential health aspects of reuse is certainly justified, it is also true that to some extent the same problem exists for traditional sources of supply. Clearly, while extensive and costly epidemiological studies are required to accurately assess the health risks of potable reuse, unfounded speculation concerning possible adverse effects should not deter serious consideration of reuse as an alternative in municipal supply planning. What is required is an additional step—identification of the incremental risks. Once the risks have been identified, we need to focus our attention on the best methods of weighing the benefits against the associated risks.

NEW INSTITUTIONAL ARRANGEMENTS/REGIONALIZATION

The problem today is not a deficit of knowledge in the physical and technological aspects of water resource planning, but rather the need for new institutional, political, or jurisdictional arrangements for municipal water supply planning. These arrangements are generally characterized by a regional approach which assumes—not necessarily with complete justification—that regionalization automatically promotes efficiency in water management. The need has been stressed for regional planning and the use of simulation for investigating the dynamics of providing water for regions throughout the country. Providing that the data base exists for such an effort, such computer modeling activities would be appropriate if closely linked with the regional and local decision-making processes.

FOUR FUNDAMENTAL PROBLEMS

Underlying the techniques and alternatives in planning for municipal water supply previously outlined are several fundamental problems that transcend individual aspects of each component of the planning process. Four major problems deserve consideration. First, we need to reassess some of our basic assumptions and beliefs in water management. To improve efficiency in planning we need a more critical appraisal of our conventional or traditional wisdom. A few examples should suffice:

1. Water should be viewed as an economic good or service, not as a unique physical substance or as a fixed or limited resource. This latter

view is a major obstacle in communication between the economist, the engineer, and the hydrologist. An immediate outcome of bridging this conceptual gap should contribute to resolving the problem; that is, in the current planning process we find the application of sophisticated engineering models, but only crude and elementary economic and demographic analyses.

2. The belief that a protected source of supply is a major defense against waterborne health hazards needs to be reviewed. Our reading of the literature indicates that the evidence to support this assertion is lacking. The point is simply put: While such a policy may have been appropriate in 1890, it may be entirely inappropriate today.

3. The advantages of regionalization of water supply systems requires close scrutiny. Should we have one management unit for the entire nation, or for a river basin, or state, or economic region? Rather than assuming that regionalization is inherently good, we find that the available evidence is insufficient to determine the optimum management unit.

A second major problem concerns differing perceptions among groups of professionals. Research has shown that engineers view problems in physical rather than social terms, and opt for solutions which are primarily structural. Similarly, public health officials are more likely to rely on warnings followed by litigation as a resolution of problems. Each profession feels that it holds a monopoly on rationality in water management.

A third problem concerns our capability to change not only our own ideas but our institutions. For example, while new pricing schedules might be deemed desirable, consensus is pessimistic concerning actual political adoption and implementation. The experience of the past is a compelling force to maintain the status quo, but such a strategy may be too costly today. We have too few suggestions that would greatly contribute to overcoming this reluctance to innovate. Another manifestation of this problem is the fact that, while in many cases local resistance to federal standards is high, such federal involvement would not have occurred had local units been more responsive to our changing society.

Finally, a fourth basic problem concerns the need to develop a method or model of public investment in urban water planning. Simply stated, we need to evaluate the relative benefits of proposed alternatives, both structural and nonstructural, as well as to identify the optimal combination of alternatives for each urban area. Or, to state it another way—we cannot identify an ideal prototype-management water utility because we lack an analytical model to evaluate optimum system design, process, management, and impact.

We are now confronted with vast quantities of new information on pricing, health effects, conservation devices, regionalization, and political and public acceptance of new strategies. Even if the research needs for each alternative were complete, we would still be faced with the problem of identifying the optimum combination of these options at a particular place and time. Until we can formulate such a methodology, policy change will be haphazard, piecemeal, and unconvincing to many in the professional and public sectors.

In summary, we close not on a pessimistic note, but with an encouraging emphasis on the need to focus our attention on these broader problems so that municipal water supply management can capture the high potential dividends in our changing environmental and social setting.

REFERENCES

Russell, Clifford S.; Arey, David G.; and Kates, Robert W. 1970. *Drought and Urban Water Supply*. Baltimore: The Johns Hopkins Press.

White, Gilbert F. 1973. In *Environmental Quality and Water Development*, edited by C. Goldman, J. McEvoy III, P. Richardson. San Francisco: W. H. Freeman & Co.